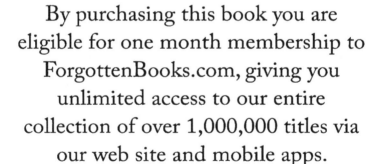

ISBN 978-0-260-03308-6
PIBN 10923588

BLISTER RUST

NEWS

JANUARY 1926.

Volume X   *Number 1.*

U.S. DEPARTMENT of AGRICULTURE

Office of Blister Rust Control.

CONTENTS - VOL. 10, NO. 1.

Page

Agents Work
A Blister Rust Conversation 10
A Story of the White Pine Blister Rust 6
Blister Rust Items from Oxford County, Maine 14
Conferences
Forestry Extension Conference 13
Control
Our Work Must Extend into New Territory During 1926 9
Yearly Progress in Maine Under the Cooperative Eight-Year Control
Program 3
Cooperation
Banker in Manistique, Michigan Interested in Blister Rust 20
Cooperation With the State Horticulturist 4
Non-Resident Cooperation via Telegram 12
Editorial
All Together and We Get There 8
On the Firing Line With Ribee Bill 28
Overlooking a Bet 16
Secretary Jardine and Dr. W.A. Taylor Send New Year's Greetings . . . 2
Educational Work
Contests Prove Valuable Aid to Follow-Up Work 17
Good Results in Individual Field Demonstrations 5
Lantern Slides of the Waterford Area 22
Liven Up Your Lantern Slides 15
Motion Pictures 23
New Type of Exhibit Material 13
The Pines Proved to be a Drawing Card 25
The Right Choice of Words 18
Forestry
Eliminating the Hemlock in the Northern Rockies to Favor Western
White Pine and Better Species . 21
Forest Planting in Finland 20
Glens Falls, New York, planting White Pine on a Large Scale 7
Pine Data for Maine 19
Office Comments 22
Personal 26
Publications 27
Quarantines
California Restricts Shipment of Blister Rust Host Plants from Oregon 17
The Oregon Situation 17
Technical Studies
Scientific Investigation of the White Pine Blister Rust 8
Mr. Kimball Atwood is Pruning his Infected Pine 14
State News
California 17
Connecticut 24
Maine 3,4,5,6,7,9,10-12,14,19,24,25
Michigan 20
New Hampshire 13,15,16
New York 7,17
Oregon 17
Western States 17,21,26,27

UNITED STATES DEPARTMENT OF AGRICULTURE
BUREAU OF PLANT INDUSTRY
WASHINGTON, D. C.

T H E   B L I S T E R   R U S T   N E W S.

Issued by the Office of Blister Rust Control
and the Cooperating States.

VOL. 10, NO. 1   MAINE NUMBER   JANUARY 15, 1926.

SECRETARY JARDINE AND DR. W. A. TAYLOR, CHIEF

OF THE BUREAU OF PLANT INDUSTRY, SEND NEW YEAR'S GREETINGS.

January 4, 1926.

Gentlemen:

The following letter has been received from the Secretary:

"December 31, 1925.

Dear Dr. Taylor:

There is nothing which has given me greater
satisfaction during the past year than the efficiency
and spirit with which the members of the Department
of Agriculture have carried forward the work of serving
the farming interests of the nation. I want you and
the members of your bureau to know that I thoroughly
appreciate what has been accomplished and that you have
my best wishes for a New Year full of prosperity,
satisfaction, and pride in the competence and usefulness
of your work.

Sincerely yours,

(Signed) W.M. Jardine."

Will you kindly see that the foregoing is called to the attention
of members of your staff?

I wish to add my very best wishes to you and your associates in
carrying forward the work with which we are charged for the coming year.

Sincerely,

Wm. A. Taylor
Chief, Bureau of Plant Industry.

YEARLY PROGRESS IN MAINE UNDER THE COOPERATIVE EIGHT YEAR CONTROL PROGRAM.

	1922	1923	1924	1925	Totals
Number cooperating towns	8	39	49	50	146
Town expenditures	$1,300.00	$6,899.99	$8,154.25	$7,199.63	$23,553.87
Number pine owners eradicating currant and goose-berry bushes	464	1148	1701	1595	4908
Amount spent by pine owners	$4,409.32	$8,760.34	$10,619.58	$9,337.30	$33,126.54
Number acres eradicated by pine owners and towns	20,363	35,354	49,610	40,452	145,779
Number acres eradicated by scouts	169,846	301,097	351,617	274,226	1,056,787
Total acreage all work	190,209	336,452	401,227	274,678	1,202,566
Number wild currant and gooseberry bushes destroyed by pine owners	439,311	1,191,418	1,632,341	1,691,287	5,154,357
Number cultivated currant and gooseberry bushes destroyed by owners	3,686	12,095	11,479	14,941	42,203
Number currant and goose-berry bushes destroyed by State and Federal scouts	9,976	13,862	14,738	18,828	57,404
Total number currant and gooseberry bushes destroyed	452,975	1,217,375	1,858,558	1,725,056	5,242,720
Per acre cost to town and private owners	.24	.44	.38	.40	Av. $0.37
Per acre cost scout work	.018	.013	.013	.02	Av. 0.016
Per acre cost all work	.042	.052	.06	.074	Av. 0.057

W. O. Frost,
State Leader of Maine.

COOPERATION WITH THE STATE HORTICULTURIST.

Augusta, Me. Nov. 10, 1925.

Mr. W. O. Frost,
State Leader Blister Rust Control,
Augusta, Maine

Dear Sir:-

Replying to your letter of recent date, will say that this spring while doing orchard inspection work in the town of Fayette for E. G. Palmer of that town we had occasion to cross the edge of a pine lot, and discovered blister rust on some of the pine trees. We immediately began to look for currant and gooseberry bushes, and found a few of them on the high land. They increased in numbers as we worked near a swamp that joins the lot on the south. There we found them in such quantities that Mr. Palmer got two of his neighbors to help in pulling them. We found the ground in ideal condition for the work, it being wet enough so we could pull the entire root with the plant by being careful. I think this one of the best pieces of eradication work that I have seen done. In early September I went over a part of the swamp and was not able to find any of either the currant or gooseberry bushes starting to grow. The fact is that all of the men who did the work were vitally interested in making a thorough job as they owned pine land in that section.

The time spent on this lot was 28 hours the first day, later Mr. Palmer and I put in 6 hours in cutting out all the pine that we found to show the slightest signs of the disease having attacked them.

I find that the farmers who own pine lots are very much interested in the work that you are doing and feel a debt of gratitude for the things that are being done for them by the Forestry Department.

We have two large nurseries that make a specialty of growing pine stock. These trees have been given our most careful attention, not only inspection at the nurseries, but special trips to them when we knew that shipments were to be made. This precaution was taken to make doubly sure that nothing got by the inspectors, because we realize the importance of keeping the disease out rather than eradication after it once gets started. I have given my inspectors orders to be on the watch at all times and to report to me anything that might even look suspicious of being the blister rust.

Very truly yours,

G. A. Yeaton

State Horticulturist.

GOOD RESULTS IN INDIVIDUAL FIELD DEMONSTRATIONS.

For the past two months I have been scouting for blister rust in towns that have not yet started eradication work. I find that nearly every pine owner has heard of blister rust from articles published in newspapers, etc. On the other hand not one man I called on knew what blister rust looked like, and their first statement was: "I am sure that my pines are free from this disease".

I called on an owner sometime ago and told him about the rust and asked him to look over his lot with me. For the first half hour I could not see any signs of blister rust, and as it was a cold day my good friend wanted to return to his fireside, feeling sure his pines were not in danger. I asked him if he knew of any wild currant or gooseberry bushes near his lot. He said about ten years ago there was a patch of skunk currants on a rock pile. "Could you find the place today?" I asked him. "Well, Boy, its up on the hill. I doubt if we could find them now."

I said that we ought to make sure while we were at it. We did find the skunk currants and only three feet away there was a pine a foot in diameter that had a trunk infection. That struck home."Lets look for more," he said. Before leaving we had found about sixty trees badly infected. When I left him he was fully convinced that his pine had blister rust. He also cut down two of the largest trees for me so I could use the cankers for an exhibit at the local post office.

This work will no doubt bring good results because this man told his friends about it. They all agreed that they did not want blister rust to ruin their pine growth.

A. J. Lambert, Me.

A STORY OF THE WHITE PINE BLISTER RUST:

WHAT TO DO TO SAVE THE PINES OF MAINE.

From the Lewiston Sun, Lewiston, Maine.

A farmer friend asked the Sun farmer to write an article for this page for him. Said he: "I'll give you my ideas and you fix 'em up so they will read well." These are his "ideas" as near as the typewriter can make them understandable.

"I suppose I am a good deal like other people in that I don't pay much attention to things that I read about or hear about until they touch me or my family or my affairs. Then I pay attention all right."

"A few years ago I had a piece of timbered land that I cut the timber off and later dug out most of the stumps and intended to clear the ground and plow it and lay it down to grass. But press of other work interfered and the birch bushes got the better of me and now there is a good stand of birch and maples ten or a dozen feet tall. I have looked at the piece from a distance and wished that it was laid down as I intended. As it is now it would cost more than the land is worth to fit it and plow it.

Within a month I made my way through the piece and much to my astonishment and gratification I found that the ground has come into small white pine almost as thick as they can stand all seeded from a clump of big ones left in one corner.

This good start of pine suited me first rate as it looks better than grass land. Then I thought what about this white pine blister that I have read and heard about. What's the use to cull out birches as I intended to do to give the pine a better chance to grow, if this blister now or a few years hence will kill the pine? That sort of put a "blister" on my scheme of growing white pine. I remembered then that there was a "county agent blister man" somewhere. I got hold of the chap, Guy H. Kimball in Auburn, and told him my story. "Let's go look at it" said he. This we did.

To be sure we found some blister and. again I was discouraged "What's the use" said I? "Why", said he, "you are lucky, you've taken it just in time. You don't need to lose any trees except these small ones that are already infested." "What'll I do," said I ? "Scout it" said he, "and get out all the gooseberry plants and skunk currants."

Then he told me the plan. "If your town contributes funds for this work as it did last year the town foreman and his men will come on here and cull out all these plants and if this is done once in five years you won't have any blister to speak of."

"All right," said I "and if there is no other way you come on here and show the men how to do it and I will gladly pay the bill."

Then Mr. Kimball, to encourage me, took me to a farm where the pine blister had got in its work. These trees were ten or a dozen years old and were badly infected. This was in the Lewiston limits and as the city council had cooperated in the control work this man's land was scouted and the bad bushes all taken out. The trees were of fairly good size and it was too bad to cut them but all that could be done was to cut them up for firewood. "If this man had taken his in time as you are doing with yours there would be very littl loss", said Kimball.

So next spring I will save my little pines from destruction. If anyone doubts this story they can visit the farm where the pine is growing and see just what is happening. This man had paid no attention to pine blister talk until it hit his pine.

People going by auto or electric between Lisbon Falls and Pejepscot have seen the handsome lot of young pines that were set out by the Pejepscot Paper Company a dozen years ago, or so. These were grown from seed right on the ground. Will they lose any of these because of blister? They will not, because they have eradicated the gooseberries and skunk currants. As a contrary illustration in the town of Livermore a Mr. Wing set out an extensive acreage of pine. He eradicated the gooseberries but not knowing about the skunk currants did not touch them. They got in their work and the spores from them attacked the small pine and killed a good many. He discovered this before it was too late and dug out the skunk currants so now his pine land is all free from blister.

Maine is the "Pine Tree State". Will it remain so? It depends on whether every pine owner looks after his land and that surrounding it.

- - - - - - -

GLENS FALLS, NEW YORK, PLANTING WHITE PINE ON LARGE SCALE.

According to American Nurserymen for December 1925, 1,000,000 two-year-old white pine seedlings have been ordered from New York State nurseries for planting in the municipal forest at Glens Falls, N. Y.

More than 10,000,000 trees (kind not stated) have been shipped from the State nurseries during the year closing with the 1925 fall season.

M. T.

SCIENTIFIC INVESTIGATION OF THE WHITE PINE

BLISTER RUST.

There appeared in the October 1925 number of Phytopathology, a series of three articles concerning the white pine blister rust, which should be read by every Agent.   The articles are as follows:

1. Conditions antecedent to the infection of white pines by Cronartium ribicola in the northeastern United States, by
Dr. Perley Spaulding and Annie Rathbun-Gravatt.

2. Inoculation of Pinus strobus trees with sporidia of Cronartium ribicola, by
Dr. Walter H. Snell and Annie Rathbun-Cravatt.

3. A partial explanation of the relative susceptibility of the white pines to the white pine blister rust (Cronartium ribicola, Fischer).
Dr. Perley Spaulding.

The above investigations were carried on by the Office of Forest Pathology.

ALL TOGETHER AND WE GET THERE.

> It ain't the individual nor the army as a whole,
> but the everlastin' team work of every bloomin' soul.

The above motto hangs on the wall of an Agricultural Extension Director in one of the corn belt states.   The meaning is clear to all who read, and is not only applicable to the extension workers, but to all of us engaged in blister rust control.   It is the pull together of good team work that counts.

Taken from article by P. H. Stewart, in Better Crops, Dec. 1925.

OUR WORK MUST EXTEND INTO NEW TERRITORY

DURING 1926.

Boothbay Golf Links

Boothbay Harbor, Maine

December 21, 1925.

Gentlemen:

Inclosed you will find samples of pines taken from our golf links. Would greatly appreciate your opinion in regards to same. I find a number of trees infected and suppose it is blister rust.

Yours,

(Signed) H.R. Teel

Note: These specimens were bad cases of blister rust. Such letters and specimens have convinced us of the necessity of going into new territory in 1926. We may not do much in the above town but intend working in three or four towns in Kennebec County, adding them to Kimball's territory.

W.O. Frost
State Leader in Maine.

- - - - - - -

Agent: "Now that your cultivated bushes are removed, will you please sign this card showing that the work is completed?"

Madam: "No Sir! I won't sign your old card, and what's more I've got some currant jelly down cellar, wonder if you wouldn't like to take that along with those bushes of mine?"

G.H. Kimball,
Sagadahoc & Androscoggin Counties.
Maine

A BLISTER RUST CONVERSATION.

Last week I had occasion to call on an elderly lumberman and wood
dealer whose active career is nearing its end because of his blindness. He
is a fatherly old man, and we had a long and friendly conversation. Once
or twice he asked me what my business was, and I evaded the question, knowing him to be much opposed to blister rust control. Finally the following
conversation took place.

Lumberman: Well, what do you do anyway?

Agent: Why, I am the blister rust control agent for York County.

Lumberman: (Beginning to wave arms) That is all a lot of poppycock! I
           don't believe - -

Agent: Well - -

Lumberman: It's a humbug! They go around and pull out a few cultivated
           bushes to make a show; while out in the woods - -

Agent: But - -

Lumberman: I'm not blaming you, my boy; they set you to it and you've got
           to make a living!

Agent: I'm used to that. It slides off me like water off a duck's back.

Lumberman: (Pounding table) They tell me that there are thousands of those
           bushes out in the pastures! What about them? It's all a humbug!

Agent: Why man, I guess you don't realize that we cover thousands of acres
        of woodland every summer and destroy hundreds of thousands of
        wild bushes.

Lumberman: Huh! They spend money like water, chasing gypsy moths, and
           brown tail moths, and tu-ber-cu-lossis, and what does it ever
           amount to? And now it's more poppycock. I'm not blaming

you, my boy.

Agent: You have got the wrong impression somewhere.

Lumberman: All poppycock! Next they will be passing a law to kill all
mosquitoes! Everybody will be out killing mosquitoes!

Agent: We were talking about blister rust; not mosquitoes.

Lumberman: Blister rust will thin out the young pine. Lots of them have
got to die anyway. I've followed the woods, boy and man, for
fifty years, and --

Agent: You talk as if the rust would stop thinning as soon as the right
number of pine had been killed. Is that your idea?

Lumberman: I'ts all poppycock! But say, my boy, my nephew has just come
in from up country to see me and I can't talk with you any
longer today. Come in and see me again, my boy. Glad to talk
with you. I'm not blaming you, you know.

Agent: I'd be glad to drop in sometime again. Good day!

Curtain.

The above actual conversation is only a sample of some of the
peculiar conversations which take place during a year. When two people get
to talking on a subject upon which their respective ideas have absolutely
nothing in common, one interview only gives each man a chance to present his
ideas. The New England public in general is noted for its hard-headedness,
and many of the people cling tenaciously to the idea that there is some sort
of graft or slight-of-hand, in work such as we are doing. It takes a long
time to convince them. Once convinced, it will take approximately as long
for them to lose their convictions. It will be a sad thing if the blister
rust control program ends about the time that the majority of people have

begun to accept it as a commonplace thing.

In ninety-nine cases out of one hundred, people who are bitter against the blister rust control program have formed their opinions long before coming in contact with a blister rust control worker. The reported conversation illustrates this fact. Consequently, when a worker calls on such an individual, the individual has both barrels loaded with false ideas which he proceeds to pop off with great gusto. The blister rust worker must not only batter down all these false ideas (very diplomatically), but he must then proceed to build up confidence in the work on the wreck of the individual's preconceived ideas. It is difficult work, and it takes time, but it can be done in the majority of cases when an approach is made in a tactful manner.

Errol E. Tarbox
Maine.

- - - - - - -

NON-RESIDENT COOPERATION VIA TELEGRAM.

Sometimes it requires two or three communications to obtain non-resident cooperation, - here's one that didn't.

Richmond Sta. Quebec, Aug. 24, 1925.

G.H. Kimball,
Box #162, Auburn, Me.

Your letter eighteenth. Have instructed Supervisor Hobson to furnish you with men on your request through Agent Chandler, Lewiston.

Signed: A.B. Mc'Naughton,

Supt. Grand Trunk, R.R.

Hdqs. Canada.

FORESTRY EXTENSION CONFERENCE.

There was held in Washington on January 11 to 13, a mighty fine conference on Forest Extension, at which most of the eastern states were represented by their Forestry Extension Specialists. Mr. Parker O. Anderson of Minnesota, Mr. Floyd M. Callward of Vermont and Mr. Myron E. Watson of Maine, former blister rust control men were present.

One noteworthy thing was that the Conference was not on subject-matter (forestry) but on methods of putting farm forestry extension across.

NEW TYPE OF EXHIBIT MATERIAL.

At the request of Mr. George Richardson, Agent in Hillsborough County, New Hampshire, several sets of enlarged photographs have been made up on photo mount-board. Each sheet is 22 x 28 inches. Mr. Richardson desired the photographs for placing in the town halls in his county. Contrary to the opinions of some who think that the town halls are used only once each year for town meeting, many people visit the town halls for regular town business, as well as for motion pictures and other local affairs.

Since there were twenty towns which had to be covered, it was decided to make five different sets of pictures. There will be four of each set, allowing the photographs to be interchanged. Each set consists of two sheets of mount-board. Such an exhibit as this is relatively inexpensive and easy to make.

If other agents desire similar exhibits they can be made up in the Washington Office by designating the pictures to be used, or by leaving it to the judgment of the Office.

R.G. Pierce.

NATIVE WHITE PINES
DAMAGED BY BLISTER RUST

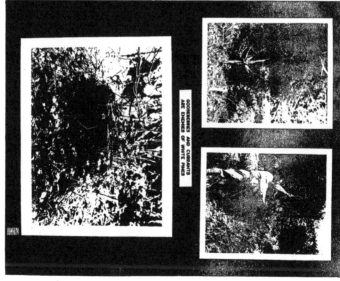

GOOSEBERRIES AND CURRANTS
ARE ENEMIES OF WHITE PINES

BLISTER RUST ITEMS FROM OXFORD COUNTY MAINE.

A series of lantern slides on blister rust and forestry will be shown in twenty-seven towns during January and February.

- - - - - - -

Mr. Kimball Atwood of Paris Hill and New York City had a crew of men cutting branches infected with blister rust, from his plantation located in Andover. The pines, numbering 15000, were planted in 1915 and blister rust attacked them in 1919 spreading from wild gooseberries growing in old stone walls and rock heaps. These bushes were pulled in 1924 and 1925.

- - - - - - -

Agent Booner of Carrol County, New Hampshire, and Agent Curtis of Oxford County, Maine, cooperated in exhibiting blister rust at fairs during the past season.

- - - - - - -

There were about 50,000 pine trees planted in Oxford County during the past season and interest is on the increase in planting waste land.

- - - - -

How the Blister Rust Scout is a Benefit to a Town in More Ways Than One -

In scouting for Ribes this last season the scout found Ribes on a lot of fifteen acres owned by a non-resident. In reporting this to the Selectmen, it was found they did not have any record of this lot on the tax books, and it had never been taxed.

- - - - - - -

What the Temporary Agents for Eradication Season Just Passed, are
Finding to Do This Winter.

Agent Lambert is scouting for a few weeks in some of the towns in the eastern part of the county, locating blister rust damage to pine, and interviewing pine owners.

Agent Rollins is on a cruising job for the Brown Company.

Agent Walker is attending to town affairs in Lovell.

Agent G. H. Curtis is back at Boston University.

- - - - - - -

Oxford County is not only noted for its pine trees and apples, but now has the honor of having Maine's champion old-time fiddler, Mr. Mellie Dunham of Norway, seventy-two years old.

LIVEN UP YOUR LANTERN SLIDES.

Mr. W.J. Cullen, Agent in Strafford and Belknap Counties, New Hampshire, recently made a suggestion which he believes will aid materially when lantern slides are shown. It is that word-slides be mixed in with picture slides to prevent monotony.

It is not necessary that the slides be on serious subjects, although there is a place for such educational slides. Just to start the ball rolling, I am making the following suggestions for different word-slides. Let's see if we can not get up a good collection of statements for word-slides! What do you think of this idea? Is it worth trying? - Let us hear from you!

1. What has Blister Rust given you?

   Nothing but trouble.

   Then why keep it?

   - - - - - - -

2. White Pine Pays Taxes When Protected
   From Blister Rust.
   - - - - - - -

3. Did you get your copy of Miscellaneous Circular #40,
   - the new blister rust colored leaflet.
   - - - - - - -

4. There's a blister rust control demonstration
   area in this town on the _____ road.
   Watch for the signs along the road.
   - - - - - - -

5. Last year we worked in _____ towns in the
   county. Did your town join in the cooperative
   work?

6. Teacher: "Johnny, what are current events?"

   Johnny: "Fusses like Dad makes about pullin' our

   currant bushes."

   - - - - - - -

7. Newlywed: "Must I buy only gooseberries to feed

   my geese,"

   Grocer: "No, Madam, even your geese would rather have

   pines than gooseberries, and they can't have both."

   - - - - - - -

OVERLOOKING A BET

Ye Editor of ye Blister Rust News has been watching certain farm
publications for a number of months and is compelled to say that the number
of blister rust or forestry articles in them is surprising by their absence.
Articles for these farm journals should be distinctly of local character,
that is, pertaining to the particular state putting out the farm paper.
Here is the opportunity that we are overlooking. Probably there is no
better medium for letting these people know what we are doing, than through
their own farm publication.

Don't preach, or use big words little understood, but give 'em
straight facts as to what you are accomplishing.

   - - - - - - -

Publicity is not always indispensable to success: Weeds don't get
their pictures into the seed catalogues. - Detroit News.

Edit: But currants, gooseberries, and barberries are weeds that
advertise.

CALIFORNIA RESTRICTS SHIPMENT OF BLISTER RUST

HOST PLANTS FROM OREGON.

As a result of the discovery of blister rust in Tillamook and Clatsop Counties, Oregon, Mr. G. H. Hecke, Director of the State Department of Agriculture deemed it necessary to place a restriction on the shipment of currants, gooseberries, and five-needled pines from Oregon.

From Weekly News Letter, California Dept. of Agriculture
Vol. 7, No. 22, p. 82.   Oct. 31, 1925.

- - - - - - - - - - - - - -

THE OREGON SITUATION

The Oregon State Board of Horticulture has prohibited shipment of all five-needle pines, currants and gooseberries out of Tillamook, Clatsop and Lincoln Counties, Oregon.

On January 8, 1926, a hearing was held by the Federal Horticultural Board to consider proposed Federal quarantine action against Oregon because of the discovery of blister rust in Tillamook and Clatsop Counties last fall.

- - - - - - - - - - -

CONTESTS PROVE VALUABLE AID TO FOLLOW-UP WORK.

W I N   A   P R I Z E

By Guessing the Number of
Leaves on the

1000 DOLLAR

GOOSEBERRY BUSH

At the Forestry Exhibit, Floral Hall

The above is a card which was used by Agent B.H. Nichols of Essex County, New York, at the Essex and Clinton County fairs last fall. There were three prizes given - First: $2.50; Second: $1.50; Third: $1.00. Such guessing contests as this staged by Mr. Nichols are very good, not only in getting the attention of a great number of people, but in getting the addresses of pine owners.

R.G.P.

THE RIGHT CHOICE OF WORDS.

One of the most fundamental rules of a writer or a speaker is that he shall "come down to" or not "go over the heads of his audience".

From very careful tests which have been made, it is estimated "that printed matter to be understood by the upper three fourths of the population must be intelligible to a child as young as eleven years."

An examination of the accompanying list of words will show what words can and cannot be understood by the eleven-year-old.

gown	southern	guitar
tap	lecture	mellow
scorch	dungeon	impolite
puddle	skill	plumbing
envelope	ramble	noticeable
rule	civil	muzzle
health	orange	quake
eye-lash	bonfire	reception
copper	straw	majesty
curse	roar	treasury
pork	haste	misuse
outward	afloat	crunch

_____ 11-Year Limit _____

insure	retroactive	avarice
nerve	ambergris	gelatinous
juggler	achromatic	drabble
regard	perfunctory	philanthropy
stave	casuistry	irony
brunette	piscatorial	embody
hysterics	sudorific	swaddle
Mars	parterre	exaltation
mosaic	shagreen	infuse
bewail	complot	selectman
priceless	forfeit	declivity
disproportionate	sportive	laity

Extracts from Psychology in Advertising, by Albert T. Poffenberger 1925.

Note: Isn't it advisable for those of us who write for the newspapers or who prepare material for the general public to take this limited capacity for understanding into consideration and be careful in choosing our words. Even in our talks with prospective co-operators we should be careful not to shoot over their heads.

R.G.P.

F O R E S T R Y

PINE DATA FOR MAINE.

1. Maine's forest area - - -(estimated) - - - - - - - - - - 15,000,000 acres

2. White Pine area - - - - -(estimated) - - - - - - - - - 3,000,000 acres

3. Percent of forest area in white pine - -(estimated)- - - - - - - 20

4. Percent of white pine area with white pine under
                        20 years of age - - (estimated) 50

5. Estimated value of white pine stumpage - - - - - - -$50,000,000

6. Lumber cut of white pine reported by Maine's mills, 1913-1923 incl.

    1913 - 239,303 M ft. B.M.   1918 - 237,466 M ft. B.M.

    1914 - 315,306 " " "   1919 - 223,843 " " "

    1915 - 270,581 " " "   1920 - 165,102 " " "

    1916 - 272,035 " " "   1921 - 150,610 " " "

    1917 - 256,014 " " "   1922 - 118,695 " " "

                                     1923 - 149,389 " " "

7. Maine's rank in production of white pine in 1922 and 1923, excluding
    western white pine - Third.
                        (only exceeded by Minnesota and New Hampshire)

Note: Most of this data appeared in the Blister Rust News, Vol. 7, No. 2,
    May 1923. - Authorities are cited there. The reported lumber cut
    has been brought up to date by addition of figures from Census
    bulletins.
                        - - - - - - -

    You can't catch fish unless you keep fishing and expecting.

FOREST PLANTING IN FINLAND

"There is no forest planting in Finland unless it be done experimentally, under the auspices of the National Experiment Stations which have actual charge of a number of National Forests. And yet the best and the most enlightened forest planting that I have seen in Finland – and indeed anywhere on the two hemispheres of this globe – is done by a retired state senator, Dr. Tigerstedt by name, on his Mustila estate near Borga. Tigerstedt is a planting genius. He knows instinctively or intuitively what factors are needed for success. There are no failures. At Mustila, by the way, the five-needled Pinus peuce is immune from blister rust in a magma of Pinus strobus succumbing to it."

> Extract from article by Dr. C.A. Schenck on Forestry in Finland.
> Journal of Forestry, Vol. 23, No. 12, p. 972-973. Dec. 1925.

Note: As for the susceptibility of the Balkan pine, Pinus peuce, Dr. Spaulding cites this pine as being found infected with Cronartium ribicola in Germany, in his Bul. 957 (U.S.D.A.)

- - - - - - -

BANKER IN MANISTIQUE, MICHIGAN INTERESTED IN BLISTER RUST.

A recent letter has been received from the Cashier of a large bank in Manistique, Michigan, requesting information and literature on the white pine blister rust and its control. The Cashier stated that he would like to have the latest data and literature available in order to be of service to their customers.

All of the facts at our command, as well as the available literature on the control of this disease, were of course given this progressive banker. A suggestion was also made to him that in a region such as the Upper Peninsula of Michigan where the blister rust had not yet appeared or been discovered, that it would be advisable to take preliminary steps to delay its spread over that region, by the destruction of the cultivated black currant.

R.G.P.

ELIMINATING THE HEMLOCK IN THE NORTHERN ROCKIES
TO FAVOR WESTERN WHITE PINE AND BETTER SPECIES.

Missoula, Mont.-- In the northern Rockies hemlock trees are passed up by the average lumberman. He takes the white pine, larch, and Douglas fir and leaves the hemlock and white fir standing. These survivors, says the Forest Service, United States Department of Agriculture, are aggressive competitors of the more valuable species. Their dense shade and their own prolific powers of reproduction discourage and choke out the white pine seedlings.

The Northern Rocky Mountain Forest Experiment Station has for some time been experimenting with ways of reducing hemlock in northern forests. Girdling the full grown trees before the white pine is logged is one method tried, but the results are generally unsatisfactory. The fire menace of fallen limbs, tops, and trunks of dead hemlocks on an area girdled six years ago was estimated on examination during the past year to far outweigh the gain in white pine reproduction. Girdling also is a rather expensive proces

In young forests of new growth 20 to 25 years old, where hemlock comprises possibly 85 per cent of the stand, the station is experimenting with what is termed a release thinning, cutting out considerable quantities of the hemlock and thereby freeing the white pine. It is hoped that it will be possible thus early in the life of the forest to accomplish less expensively what must otherwise be done at maturity at high cost.

- - - - - - -

Make it a point to learn five good blister rust selling points every day. Make note of objections you were unable to overcome successfully Necessity is the mother of invention.

The Office has a small number (say a dozen) of cloth-covered spring back binders 12 1/2" north and south, and 13" east and west. Requests for these should be made direct to our Property Clerk here in Washington.

- - - - - - -

State Leaders have a supply of special envelopes for Miscellaneous Circular 40. Agents should write to their state leaders for them, rather than to the Washington Office.

- - - - - - -

The Acme Motion Picture projector which belongs to the Office is in the keeping of Mr. E.C. Filler, 403 Appraisers Stores Building, 408 Atlantic Avenue, Boston, Massachusetts. Those desiring reservation of the projector should correspond direct with Mr. Filler.

- - - - - - -

LANTERN SLIDES OF THE WATERFORD AREA.

Five sets of **fifteen** slides each, all colored, on the Waterford, Vermont infection area, are ready for distribution. One set has already been sent Mr. W.J. Cullen, Agent in Strafford County, New Hampshire, and a second set with other slides has been loaned to the Botany Department of the University of Iowa. There still remain three sets available for distribution.

- - - - - - -

Nothing costs so little and goes so far as courtesy.

- - - - - - -

M O T I O N · P I C T U R E S

Blister Rust - A Menace to Western Timber.

Used by Mr. Detwiler, along with "The Pines" while on his recent appearance before the Canadian Phytopathological Society.

Used by Mr. Amadon of Albany, New York, during November and December.

Used by Mr. W.E. Bradder, of Vermont, along with "The Forest Ranger's Job". Mr. Bradder also showed "Trees of Tomorrow" and "Winter Logging in the White Mountains" during the first week of December.

Logging Eastern White Pine.

Shown at Eastern High School, Washington, D.C., during December.

Shown by Crompton and Knowles Manufacturing Company, Worcester, Massachusetts, during December.

Reserved by Mr. Horn of Laconia, N.H. for Jan. 11 to Feb. 28.

Used by the Rev. C.F. Rogers at Mountain Park Institute, North Carolina, during December.

NATURE'S CROP OF WHITE PINE

Used by Mr. Anderson of Rhode Island during December, together with "Undesirable Alien" and "Apples and the County Agent".

Reserved by the District Forester at Portland, Oregon for three months.

THE PINES

Reserved by Mr. Anderson for the month of January, along with "She's Wild" and "Trees of Tomorrow".

THE STORY OF WHITE PINE

Shown at Eastern High School, Washington, D.C., and at the Public School, West Branch, Michigan, during December.

Reserved by Mr. B.F. Wolfe, University of Oklahoma, Norman, Oklahoma, for use during January.

WHITE PINE-BEAUTIFUL AND USEFUL

Shown by Mr. P.F. Rolke, Farm Adviser at Mt. Carmel, Ill. during December.

Will be shown at Elwood School, Orange, New Jersey, during Jan.

WHITE PINE, THE WOOD OF WOODS

Shown by the Rev. E.J. Pluhm, Muskegon, Michigan, during Dec.

Shown by Mr. C.L. Miller, to employees of a Lumber Company with which Mr. Miller is connected, in Brocklyn, New York, during December.

- - - - - - -

AGENT CURTIS MAKES GOOD USE OF "THE PINES".

The following schedule was planned by Agent Curtis for showing "The Pines" in Oxford County, Maine.

Jan. 2 - At Mexico Theatre.

" 4 - Noon - Rotary Club - Rumford.

" " - Afternoon - School children - Rumford.

" " - Night - Theatre - Rumford

" 5 - Mexico Grange - installation night.

- - - - - - -

Mr. J.E. Riley, Jr. of Connecticut has planned a motion picture schedule for January and February and has already obtained six tentative dates and several open ones. He will use the federal pro- jector and the following films:

The Story of White Pine.

White Pine - A Paying Crop for Idle Lands.

Blister Rust - A Menace to Western Timber, and

Trails that Lure.

"THE PINES" PROVED TO BE A DRAWING CARD.

I had made arrangements for "The Pines" to be shown at North Turner on the first of December and thought it would be an excellent idea to do a bit of publicity work in the adjoining town which is only a little over two miles away, and in which there seems to be more or less opposition to blister rust work. I thought it might be possible to get some of the pine owners out to the "movies", so called on a few myself, and told the storekeeper (Selectman, by the way) and he promised to tell his customers and get as many as he could to go to see the picture.

A few days later I called to get the reels and asked if the attendance was good. — "Say, Kimball, they seemed to take quite an interest in that picture of yours. People came to the show that I haven't seen here for ages. One man, a mill man, heard about it and the second night of the show he was on deck to see it. I tell you they said 'It was fine'! Had a good crowd too, glad you brought those reels along, and anytime you have any more just bring them here, I'll show them for you."

G. H. Kimball

Sagadahoc & Androscoggin Counties,
Maine.

- - - - - - -

An ounce of loyalty is worth a pound of cleverness.

- - - - - - -

The man of endurance is the man who wins.

PERSONAL

Mr. W.J. Cullen, Agent in Strafford and Belknap Counties, N.H. spent the Christmas Holiday Season in Washington visiting his parents. The Office was favored by a brief visit from W.J. Come again.

- - -

The Washington Office is glad to report that two of the force, our artist-stenographer, Miss Alma Bishop, and file clerk, Mrs. Bessie B. Hart are out of the sick ward. When they are away we miss 'em.

- - -

Mr. A.B. Brooks of the West Virginia Game Commission, former member of this Office was one of a number of notable speakers at the joint session of the American Forestry Association and the Southern Forestry Congress, held at Richmond, Virginia, January 6 and 7.

- - -

Mr. Allison H. Hearn left blister rust control work on December 6.

- - -

Mr. Arthur J. Lambert was appointed Agent, effective Jan. 2, 1926. His headquarters are Augusta, Maine.

- -

Mr. Carl Epling was appointed Field Assistant, effective December 7, 1925 with headquarters at Berkeley, California.

- - -

Messrs. Jack W. Rodner and Harry F. Geil were appointed Agents, effective Jan. 2, 1926, with headquarters at Spokane, Washington.

- - -

Mr. Reuley E. Myers was appointed Agent, January 2, with headquarters at Spokane, Washington.

PUBLICATIONS

Blister Rust

Anon.   Blister Rust Control.
American Nurseryman Vol. 42, No. 5, p. 122. Nov. 1925.
A short paragraph noting the issue of Misc. Circ. 40,
the 4-page colored leaflet.

Blister Rust in Oregon.
American Nursery Trade Bulletin, Vol. 19, No. 6. p. 79

Hearing on Pine Disease in Oregon.
The Official Record, U.S. Dept. of Agric.
Vol. 4, No.50, p.3. Dec. 16, 1925.

Paragraph concerning wall charts by Maude A. Thompson on
Requirements in transporting nursery stock.   Quarantines
against movement of nursery stock.
American Nurseryman Vol. 42, No. 6, p. 137. Dec. 1925.

Manning, Geo. H. - "Hindenburg Line" May be Changed - Affecting
Nursery Stock Shipments West of the Mississippi.
White Pine Blister Rust Now in Oregon.
Samuel B. Detwiler Just Back from Inspection Tour.
American Nursery Trade Bulletin, Vol. 19, No. 5, p.59.
Nov. 1925.

Middle West Inspection.
American Nurseryman, Vol. 42, No. 6, p. 136. Dec. 1925.

Montana Quarantines.
American Nurseryman, Vol. 42, No. 6, p. 136. Dec. 1925.
The Montana quarantine declares the cultivated black
currant a nuisance and orders its destruction; it also
prohibits its shipment into or within the state.

Spaulding, Perley, and Annie Rathbun-Gravatt - Longevity of the
Teliospores and Accompanying Uredospores of Cronartium
Ribicola Fischer in 1923.
Reprint from Journal of Agricultural Research Vol. 30,
No. 10, Nov. 15, 1925.

More of pruning pines for blisters! Note Agent Curtis' remarks from Oxford County, Maine. I'll bet a lot of pine owners have done it 'th-out sayin' anything about it.

- - - - - - -

As Lambert says — 'seems like everybody has heard of blister rust from the papers, but durned few have seen it!. Seein' is believin', Agent, in Maine as well as in Missouri.

- - - - - - -

If that there banker in upper Michigan wanted to know about the pine blister for his customers, ain't there more reason for the bankers in the Northeast bein' primed with the latest on what we're doin'? It 'ud be for his good, as well as our'n.

56-26

BLISTER RUST

NEWS

FEBRUARY 1926.

Volume X   *Number 2.*

U.S. DEPARTMENT of AGRICULTURE

Office of Blister Rust Control.

C O N T E N T S - V O L. 10, N O. 2.

Agents Work   Page

Agents Work
    A Long Day's Work Brings Results Even On A Short Winter's Day 36
    Checking Ribes Eradication Keeps Work Up To Standard 41
Editorial
    Hello Agent! 30
Educational
    An Analysis of Our Educational and Service Activities for 1925 31
    New Blister Rust Poster 33
    Forestry Train in Michigan Affords an Opportunity for Education
                                            in Blister Rust 35
    Instructing the Young People Who Will be Pine Owners in a Few Years . 43
    Massachusetts Puts Out Manual in Attractive Form for Field Men . . . 43
    Give the Pine Owners the Facts 45
    Circular Letters to Pine Owners 47
    Lantern Slides 51
    Western Film Shown to More Than 34,000 in 1925 56
    Blister Rust Talk Over the Radio. 57
Forestry
    White Pine Feature of New York Farmers' Week at Cornell 51
    A Note on the Importance of the Sugar Pine and Western White Pine . . 54
    Volume Tables for Forest Trees 52
    How Many White Pines Should Be Standing on an Acre if Fully Stocked? . 55
Personal 57
Publications 50
    Stung By A Rye-Bee. 40
Quarantine
    Auto Tourists Carry Thieves and Plant Pests 42
Technical Studies
    Additional Notes on Pruning Pines for the Blister Rust 34
    Are We Doing Our Full Duty? 37
    Eradication Costs as Influenced by Abundance of Ribes 44
Western States 50
    Volume Tables For Forest Trees. 52
    A Note on the Importance of the Sugar Pine and Western White Pine . . 54
State News
    California 50,51
    Connecticut 40
    Maine 34.35,41,47-49
    Massachusetts 36,37-40,43,44,45,57
    Michigan 35
    Montana 50
    New Hampshire 43,45,46
    New York 51,57
    Oregon 50,57
    Wisconsin 42,43

UNITED STATES DEPARTMENT OF AGRICULTURE
BUREAU OF PLANT INDUSTRY
WASHINGTON, D.C.

T H E   B L I S T E R   R U S T   N E W S.

Issued by the Office of Blister Rust Control
and the Cooperating States.

VOL. 10, NO. 2   FEBRUARY 1926

Hello Agent:

    There's some good stuff in this number and you ought not have to hunt very far for it, either. If some of you can't find anything of interest here, write the Editor and tell him what you want, Get into the game, Agent, this News Letter is your'n, not mine. Don't let the other feller do all the thinkin'.

    How long since you have sent in a good article which you thought would help your neighbor in the next county or in the next state? Bill Endersbee has hit the bull's eye, so has Curtis, and so has Brockway - just to name a few.

    Now about "Brook"; maybe you didn't see how he scored at all - but look again at the long winter day he tells about. That day must have had a mighty good plan back of it, but besides the plan there was determination which enabled him to carry it through to success.

    Come on Agent, let's hear from you, not only when your State number of the Blister Rust News is comin' out, but at other times.

Yours,

Riley Bill

AN ANALYSIS OF OUR

EDUCATIONAL AND SERVICE ACTIVITIES FOR 1925

A Well Planned Outline for 1926 Desirable For

Best Results.

The success of the control program depends to a great extent on
the volume and effectiveness of the educational and service activities.
During 1925, the <u>monthly</u> average of educational features per permanent agent
was as follows: 1.4 meetings, 0.5 field demonstration meetings, 1.3 exhibits,
157.1 publications and 3.0 news items, and 15.1 posters. A study of each
agent's work gives even a more intimate insight into the educational project.
In one state two of the agents did not have any exhibits during 1925 and one
of the men did not speak at any meetings during the first ten months of the
year. In another state, two of the agents gave no blister rust talks.
During at least six months of the year, most of the agent's time is given to
educational and service work, while during the other months, only about one-
half of his time is spent on these two projects. (A large part of the agent'
office work can fairly be classed under these headings.)

The educational work needs to be better organized and given its
proper place in a well balanced control program. The educational activities
will not take care of themselves as one agent has mentioned in his annual
report. Systematic advertising, or education, is a part of every sales
campaign. As expressed by Mr. Graham - "It greases the skids for personal
contact." Effective service work cannot be carried on without well planned
and adequate educational activities. It is a case of every phase of the
control program being properly balanced. In planning the educational
activities, more thought should be given to the particular need, time and
place.

The results of the educational work in several states during 1925
showed the average field meeting did not justify the time and expense involved. Small impromptu group demonstrations proved to be much more effecti
and efficient. News items continued to be the best educational feature in
creating attention, interest and desire. Permanent blister rust exhibits at
the headquarters of several of the agents were of special value in arousing
local interest. The best results at meetings were obtained when a local
society was used to sponsor the affair. Dr. Martin's federal blister rust
circular and Dr. York's poster have amply met the need for new material of
this kind. The signs and tags produced by the Office of Blister Rust Contro
especially for roadside demonstrations and exhibits, were of great value.
However, the promiscuous use of such material fastened to trees along the
highway where there is no infection should be discouraged.

On the whole more thought, originality and care are needed to produce
better and more suitable exhibits. The following ideas, based on careful
observations are listed as an aid in preparing exhibits:

1. If possible, select a place where the crowd
   must pass.

2. Make the design simple, use original ideas if
   possible.

3. Have main objective stand out clearly, eliminate
   details which are not essential.

4. Motion and color attract most attention.

5. Label exhibit with large suitable signs.

6. Have all signs neatly lettered - vary size of
   letters to emphasize certain words - colors help.

7. Talking helps to attract the crowd.

8. Fresh specimens of infected pine and Ribes are
   always best. Yellow tags show up well on such
   material. The large cankers attract special
   attention.

9. Have suitable and sufficient literature within
   easy reach.

10. In suitable place, have book and pencil, so prospects'
    names can be listed for free inspection of their pine.

11. The securing of prospects depends largely on the one
    attending the exhibit. He must be a go-getter.

12. If charts are used, they should be very simple.

During 1925 the daily (working day) average of service work per
permanent agent was as follows: 1.1 initial interviews, .6 follow up
calls, .5 persons instructed in the disease, and .3 individuals shown
control measures. About 65% of the agents' interviews were to secure
moral support. Apparently less effort should be spent on such interviews
and more time given to securing cooperation in eradicating Ribes.

Service work is the backbone of the control program. It takes
backbone to do it. The arms and feet will never be used in eradicating
Ribes unless the "backbone" has produced cooperation. Every effort should
be made to increase the volume and effectiveness of this service work.

Better planning and organizing of the agents' work will allow more
time for this project. Concentration of interviews, as far as practicable,
will save time in travel and prevent hit-and-miss efforts. A greater use

of small group demonstrations rather than all individual work may be
possible under favorable conditions. In some states, scouting can be decreased and the time saved applied to service work, especially in district
where pine, Ribes and infection conditions are generally known. More inte
view work is needed, especially during the winter months. The sections fc
this work can be limited to accessible places.

E C. Filler

January 26, 1926.

- - - - - - - - - - - - - - - -

NEW BLISTER RUST POSTER.

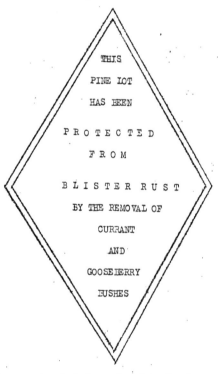

THIS

PINE LOT

HAS BEEN

P R O T E C T E D

F R O M

B L I S T E R R U S T

BY THE REMOVAL OF

CURRANT

AND

GOOSEBERRY

BUSHES

The above poster is being printed by the Government Printing Of

ADDITIONAL NOTES ON PRUNING PINES FOR THE BLISTER RUST.

In the January issue of the Blister Rust News there was included a short item on the pruning of infected branches in a plantation at Andover, Maine. At the request of the Washington Office I have secured additional data which I think will be interesting to the Agents in other states for it shows that on small trees the pruning can be done at a very reasonable cost.

Mr. Kimball Atwood planted 15000 white pines at Andover, Maine in 1916, partly in old fields and partly in pasture land. Thousands of wild gooseberry bushes were growing in rock piles and in a nearby swamp, but unfortunately destruction of these bushes did not begin till 1924 - 8 years after the pines were planted. The removal of the Ribes was completed in 1925.

By 1924 it was estimated that only 10,000 of the pines were living, the other 5000 having died from various causes which were not stated. Of the 10,000 remaining trees, nearly 25% were infected with blister rust; 10% or about 1000 trees having trunk infections and 15% or 1500 having only branch infections which the owner, Mr. Atwood, thought worth trying to save.

The pruning work began in 1924, but in that year only a few were pruned, and the work was not done thoroughly. This work cost $10.00. In October 1925 Mr. Atwood had a man inspect every tree by rows marking each row as he worked so that none were missed. The infected limbs were cut off carefully with a small axe while the pines with trunk infections were cut down. The 1925 work cost $20.00 (40 man hours at 50 cts. per hour).

It seems reasonable to suppose that some of the 5000 trees that had disappeared by 1924 had been killed by the blister rust. Pruning probably saved 15% of the trees living in 1924. Since the 1925 work included removal of 1000 trees as well as the pruning of 1500, the total cost of $20.00 should not be charged entirely against pruning, though probably $15.00 would be fair to charge against removal of infected branches. This sum added to $10.00, the 1924 costs, would make the pruning of 1500 trees cost not over $25.00 or 1.6 cents per tree. If no additional pruning need be done this cost of saving trees which have been planted for 10 years must be considered very reasonable. The average height of the pines at the end of 1925 was approximately 8 feet.

D. S. Curtis, Agent
Maine.

- - - - - - - - - - - -

FORESTRY TRAIN IN MICHIGAN AFFORDS AN OPPORTUNITY
FOR EDUCATION IN BLISTER RUST.

A special train including two forestry cars, is being run during February, under the auspices of the Northeast Michigan Development Bureau, Bay City, Michigan. During March and April this train will be running in the upper peninsula under the auspices of the Upper Peninsula Development Bureau whose headquarters are at Marquette, Michigan.

At the request of the Forest Service our Office prepared a three page leaflet on the White Pine Blister Rust Situation in Michigan, especially emphasizing the advisability of planting white pine in Michigan. This manuscript was approved by the United States Forest Service, and by Mr. E. C. Mandberg of the Michigan Department of Agriculture. Eight thousand copies were mimeographed at Washington and sent to Bay City for distribution on the train.

Attention is called to the possibility of wide-spread education by the use of mimeographed articles such as were used in this case.

R. G. P.

A Long Day's Work Brings Results Even On A

Short Winter's Day.

The following report of an Agent's average day's work in early February has been received from Massachusetts:

"Left Brockton 7:15 A.M. Returned to Brockton 7:30 P.M.

Arranged for window exhibit in Maurice Greaney's store, Whitman, Feb. 15 - 20.

Arranged for one at Baker's tobacco store next to post-office, Abington, Feb. 25-30.

Arranged for one at Bemis and Cooper's Drug store first week in March, at North Abington, and at their store in Rockland, the second week in March.

Moved a window display from Cohasset to Scituate.

Interviewed A.C. Morrison, Principal of Cohasset High School, and talked to Botany Class.

Placed news articles in Rockland Standard, Rockland Independent, Brockton Times, and Brockton Enterprise.

Interviewed selectmen of Cohasset, and copied names of non-resident pine owners.

Interviewed selectmen of Hingham for same purpose.

Interview with Tree Warden of Hingham as to location of pine areas, cooperation, etc.

That is all — Rather a busy day, don't you think?

I had a window exhibit in Cohasset and the pupils in the High School were requested by the principal to write an essay on the disease. They were really very good, so that exhibit did help a whole lot, as they all do."

E. M. Brockway, Agent.

ARE WE DOING OUR FULL DUTY?

As co-workers in this business of saving the pines from blister rust
are we agents going to miss the opportunity for greater coordination toward
the solution of several of the more important phases of our problem? For a
long time most of us have clamored for information on subjects of particular
interest to us but how many of us have turned a hand toward acquiring that
information, or having acquired it, have loaned it to his neighbor? We did
not get the information for the very cogent reason that those from whom we
sought it, did not have it, nor were they in a position to secure it. The
essential point that we overlooked was that we agents ourselves were and are
in the best position of anyone to solve most of these problems.

We are still confronted with several problems of tremendous importance to us and there is yet time and opportunity for us to seek a soluti
by our own united efforts provided those efforts are properly focused on a
central directing unit. A review of the situation to date, accompanied by a
outline of procedure is suggested for consideration.

The course of development in eradication methods has brought a constant improvement until now the standards for average efficiency are high.
first working of an area successfully removes, so far as we know, 90% of the
Ribes and unquestionably more of the leaf surface. On areas where the Ribes
have all been destroyed the pines have been fully protected against further
infection, at least until such time as new bushes may come in. On other are
where a percentage of the original bushes are left the pines are immediately
protected only in proportion to the infecting power of those remaining Ribes

In terms of pine protection the permanent effect of any high grade
initial Ribes eradication work depends chiefly upon the subsequent reappear-
ance and growth of Ribes on the area. Our present program initiates blister
rust control management on over a million acres of land annually. These con
ponent parts of this blister rust control program are: (1)Initial eradicatic
of Ribes on all pine areas where the pine value is worth protection. (2)Time
reinspection of eradicated areas followed by reeradication when necessary. 1
emergency existing throughout this program is adequate protection of presen
and future pine crops against blister rust. Obviously, it would be futile
apply initial eradication without proper regard for the subsequent reeradica
tion work needed to materialize the worthy aims of our program. Therefore,
initial eradication work on any particular tract should always anticipate
follow-up activities and provide the most competent assistance for the latt

In view of these facts we must ask ourselves concerning each eradication job (property or block) the following questions: How thoroughly have
the pines on this area been protected and how long will this protection las
These questions may be answered in light of competent knowledge of the foll
ing site factors:

1. Based on infecting power, how many Ribes of different sorts is it safe to leave per acre?

2. How many seedlings and sprouts return per acre after eradication and how soon do they come in? i.e. What is the relation between the abundance of bushes before eradication and the reproduction of new bushes after the ground has been cleared of Ribes?

3. How many Ribes are left to the acre after eradication of any tract?

4. How soon after the first working must any area be reeradicated, if at all?

At the present time we are handicapped in the solution of these problems because of a lack of complete facts and consequent standardized principles. The demand for the solution of the problems stated above calls for united effort by all the forces of blister rust control in order to obtain results in the shortest time possible, throughout the entire pine region and with the smallest costs. To do this it will be necessary for each individual to contribute a share from his particular field. Organization might well be the first step. The guiding head of the concern might be the Pathologist in charge of investigation in Washington. State Leaders could constitute an advisory committee and each one be responsible for carrying out that part of the program undertaken in his state. The agent could secure the data to be obtained in his district. By this or similar effort we establish uniform methods and we get united action, the power of which is tremendous. Not long ago a request for canker measurements from each agent produced remarkable results in a short time. Similar action on these other problems should give equally good results.

Let us consider the four site factors mentioned with a view to determining what data we have, what we need and how we shall use it.

Infecting power of Ribes.

Based on the infecting power of Ribes, how many bushes of any given sort is it safe to leave per acre? There is some data at hand which has considerable bearing on this subject but fails in certain respects to answer the question. In the first place the available data can only be applied locally because there is not enough of it to enable one to establish any broad principle for its application. Some of it, probably most of it, is incomplete so far as it relates to this problem. It follows then that we need data in quantity from the entire field. If two plots were established this year in each district and the agent secured the necessary data showing the relation between a specified number of Ribes and a given amount of pine infection, the combined data would immediately enable us to arrive at some conclusions on this problem. The time required for any one agent to do this work would not be more than a week, while he would gain by securing two plots to demonstrate the disease and figures for use as educational material.

Return of Seedlings and Sprouts.

The question of how many seedlings and sprouts return on an average after eradication and how soon they return may require a longer time to stu Most of this work will need to be done on areas which have been eradicated from one to several years. The machinery for doing this work has already sufficiently tried and perfected to warrant a beginning. There are also areas that have been eradicated five years and longer. Each agent working three days with two of his foremen should be able to cover five acres for this data. The total thus obtained throughout the entire region would reac about 250 acres which is a worthwhile working basis. There is no apparent reason why the time spent could not be increased to six days since by the o operation other needed data could also be obtained. Such records over 500 acres would be a power in determining this question.

Number of Ribes left by crews.

Adequate check records will give the needed information on the numbe of Ribes left by crews. The remaining Ribes have a direct bearing on the problem of the return of seedlings and sprouts and also on the amount of in fection spread to pine after eradication. These records are essential for correct application of results obtained from studies of the other phases of the problem. Each state is now checking its work as completely as conditio permit but it does not appear that complete and adequate records are being kept in all cases. Our checks in the past and to a large extent at the pres time have aimed to bolster up crew efficiency and neglected the more importa scope of our work, that of protection to the pine. Today we know that a wel trained crew under right supervision will do high grade work on areas wher they work. Let us then direct our efforts to placing well trained crews in the field and concentrate on supervising by checking to see that they work a areas that should be worked.

The term percentage of efficiency as previously used in connection with eradication has led us far afield in judging the real quality of the wo The method of grading unquestionably has had a place in the work since it served as a moral prod to get better results out of a crew. Further than th it has given us nothing of value. 50% efficiency where there were two Ribes per acre is ten times better protection than 90% efficiency where there were 100 Ribes. A sounder basis for grading work would seem to be the number of Ribes by height classes and amount of Ribes leaf surface left per acre.

Reeradication.

A solution of the points just previously mentioned will give a basis for determining when and where to reeradicate. The number and kind of Ribes on any area may be considered to constitute its normal stocking. Once these bushes are removed and so long as conditions there do not materially change, the probability is that the area will in time return to that same degree of original stocking. Once an area is eradicated, however, our focus should be the degree of Ribes stocking that is dangerous to the growth of pine. When

we have determined the degree of restocking under varying conditions and
the danger point to pine we will have materially simplified our re-eradication
problem. The solution of the three preceding points will automatically give
us the information needed for planning our reeradication projects.

It is not evident that there is any possibility of receiving aid from
sources outside our own organization, in solving any of our problems. It
seems equally evident that we do not need outside aid. We have the organization with time and ability to do the necessary work. Why not take advantage
of these assets to get what we want? There is an obligation on each and all
of us to do this job well. Are we doing our full duty when we fail to solve
problems that lie within our power?

W.J. Endersbee,
Agent, Berkshire County, Mass.

February 8, 1926.

- - - - - - - - - - - -

"STUNG BY A RYE-BEE"

An interesting article of two column length under the above title,
appeared in the Litchfield Enquirer (Litchfield, Conn.) of January 14, and is
signed by Peter Pine Planter, Mohawk Woods, Connecticut.

This is in the form of a short story and tells of a visit made by a
Blister Rust Agent to the home of Mr. John Smith and his small grandson. A
survey of the pine land, which had been given to the boy by his grandfather,
was made by the three. The Agent found the elderly man and the boy very enthusiastic followers and, after showing them several very good samples of
blister rust on the pines and Ribes, succeeded in gaining their full cooperation in the destruction of the bushes.

This shory story "gets over" nicely because of the simple, humorous way
in which it is told. The boy and his grandfather had heard of Ribes but had
the idea that they were some kind of bees which stung the pine trees.

After pulling a number of large bushes and securing a handful of thorns,
the grandfather said "I think the feller that named them 'Rye-bees' knew what he
was talking about". The Agent decided that the joke was on him because he had
not explained the meaning of "Ribes". This emphasizes the necessity for remem-
tering / that all of our friends are not as well acquainted with such scientific
names as those of us who have been associated with this work for some time.

" S

CHECKING RIBES ERADICATION KEEPS WORK

UP TO STANDARD   A

As the actual eradication work in Maine is performed by the owners'
labor, always inexperienced, the degree of efficiency varies from very high
to not so good, although on the whole satisfactory work is done. When poor
work is found the owners are advised of the fact and re-eradication is
demanded. The majority of such owners promise to go over their lands again.

Owing to the unusually wet season and early defoliation of Ribes,
all of the 1595 eradication jobs were not checked this year. However, a
large percentage of the work was checked and found good.

During the season

3 checks on work not supervised showed

96% efficiency

781 checks on supervised work showed

96% efficiency.

One agent reports, "Every lot worked was checked by
the town foreman and owners' crew before leaving the job, and this
showed the owners and the foremen the quality of their work. Each lot
was later checked by the agents. 267 such checks were made showing an
average efficiency of 95%." Another agent reports 308 checks taken in a
similar manner showing an efficiency of 94.5%. 257 crew checks on 163
acres show an average of 98% efficiency.

W. O. Frost
State Leader - Maine.

Extract from Maine Annual Report for 1925.

AUTO TOURISTS CARRY THIEVES AND PLANT PESTS.

Offer Facilities for Spread of Forest Diseases -

"Lifts" Often Given to Robbers.

The accommodating auto tourist is too free about giving strangers a lift when he knows nothing about their character. Sometimes he finds this out to his own cost, when his invited traveling companion turns on him and robs him; sometimes he is merely carrying a "bad egg" from one "job" to another.

How the army of auto tourists have increased the danger from robbers of another sort by offering facilities for the spread of plant diseases and insect pests of the most serious nature was told by Dr. S.B. Fracker, State entomologist of Wisconsin.

When the tourist hosts began to stream through Wisconsin a few years ago, carrying home young trees and bushes to plant, Dr. Fracker stated, it was realized at once that such forest diseases and pests as white pine blister rust, the jackpine tussock moth, the spruce budworm and several others might easily greatly increase their range and therefore the amount of damage they could do. Rules forbidding the transportation of plants in this manner were passed, but could not be effectively enforced, until a very simple educational scheme was hit upon. Huge signboards were erected with the inscription in six-inch letters:

> "Transporting trees and plants prohibited by law. Inspection required to prevent the spread of insect pests and plant diseases. Address State Department of Agriculture, Madison, Wisconsin."

- 43 -

These notices attracted instant attention and discussion, and the work of the conservation wardens in stopping and searching cars for diseased plants has been reduced practically to nothing.

The Star, Washington, D.C. - Jan. 17, 1926.

- - - - - - - -

INSTRUCTING THE YOUNG PEOPLE WHO WILL BE PINE OWNERS IN A FEW YEARS.

I have just returned from a very interesting meeting with the Junior High School here in Lebanon. They asked me to speak on Forestry and Blister Rust. Well, I went over and took the pictures and other things for a small exhibit and believe me it was as interesting a meeting as I have had for some time. Was there for more than an hour, but spoke only forty minutes; then answered questions for a while. After this I had a little conference with the teachers.

George F. Richardson, Jr.
Southern Grafton County, N.H.

- - - - - - - - - -

MASSACHUSETTS PUTS OUT MANUAL IN ATTRACTIVE FORM FOR FIELD MEN.

Mr. C.C.Perry, State Leader in Massachusetts, is preparing a very compact hand book entitled "Manual for Field Men". The new manual will contain practically the same material as was put out by Mr. Perry in former years but it will be in much more usable form. Covers will be of stiff leather-board and approximately 4 x 7 ". The former manual was 8 x 11" and because of its size could not be easily carried around in the pockets of the field men. For that reason it was not referred to by the men as much as it should have been. It is believed that the new manual will be of much more value. The mimeographing is being done in Washington.

BLISTER RUST KILLS
WHITE PINE

CURRANT AND GOOSEBERRY
ERADICATION PROTECTS PINE

— 44 —

ERADICATION COSTS AS INFLUENCED BY ABUNDANCE OF RIBES.

An analysis of the per acre costs for the 53 eradication jobs completed in this district in 1925, shows a direct connection with the number of Ribes destroyed. These jobs varied in size from one acre to 500 acres and the cost range was from 2 cents on 400 acres to 84 cents on a 10 acre job.

The table below has been compiled by grouping the jobs according to the number of Ribes destroyed per acre, except that in the last group four jobs having from 20 to 68 bushes per acre have been bunched in order to close wide gaps with inadequate data.

Table Showing Relationship Between the Per-Acre Cost of Eradication and Number of Ribes Per Acre on 6,478 Acres in Berkshire County, Mass. in 1925.

No. of Ribes per Acre.	1 to 2	2.1 to 4	4.1 to 6	6.1 to 8	8.1 to 10	Over 20
No. Acres Exam.	3055	1037	1032	220	375	759
Total cost	$160.82	$92.60	$127.50	$24.82	$49.30	$217.70
Cost per acre	5¢	9¢	12¢	11¢	13¢	28¢

The table shows a steady increase in eradication cost with the increase in the number of Ribes per acre. Analyzing further there appears to be slight difference in cost except for each increase of approximately five Ribes. The average cost for the first five bushes is about six cents per acre but when the bushes number from six to ten per acre the cost increases to about twelve cents. The same ratio seems to be maintained when the bushes number 20 per acre since the cost then increases to 28 cents. It would therefore appear that for each increase of five bushes there is a constant increase in cost of six cents per acre.

The real value of this or a similar table would seem to be in its appl cation to re-eradication work. For such application, however, there is need for adequate check records to show the Ribes factor remaining after the initial working. By knowing the number of Ribes per acre on any area the co could be determined by multiplying the total acreage by the unit cost per acre for the given Ribes content. This, or a similar basis for reckoning costs, would be of inestimable value to state leaders and others at the present time. Unfortunately all the factors for computing these costs are not now available. One missing essential is the Ribes content after eradica tion. This can and should be obtained by an adequate checking system.

During 1926 an effort will be made in this district to secure additio al data along this line. Meanwhile I would welcome any suggestions or suppl mentary data from other agents. The district agent seems to be the only s from which material of this nature is available. He is likewise the only source from which new records may be obtained in the future. Is there any Agent who cannot contribute worthwhile data in 1926 toward a better solutio of this problem? Let us hear from you.

W.J. Endersbee,
Berkshire County, Mass.

- - - - - - - - -

GIVE THE PINE OWNERS THE FACTS.

This is evidently the sentiment in New Hampshire which inspired the accompanying mimeographed "Letter to the Pine Owners of Danbury, N.H."

Every pine owner will be interested in seeing a map on which he can pick out the approximate location of his farm and timber holdings, and may, because of the value of the map, retain the sheet for some time.

T O T H E P I N E O W N E R S O F D A N B U R Y, N. H.

The triangles plotted on this map indicate the location of pines found to be infected with that serious disease, The White Pine Blister Rust. It is likely that much more infection exists.

It is certain that the rust will increase so long as currant and gooseberry bushes are allowed to remain in and around pine growth.

174 towns and cities, and nearly 500 individuals have cooperated with the State Forestry Department in this important work.

The Farm Bureau, The Grange and many other organizations are behind Blister Rust Control.

Every owner of white pine growth, and all persons who have at heart the welfare of their town will support control measures.

An appropriation at the coming town meeting will make possible the application of control mea-- sures. Currants and gooseberry bushes and white pines cannot live together,- without serious results to the pines.

Blister Rust
  CANNOT
  SPREAD
if currant or gooseberry bushes are removed in and around white pine growth.

For further information regarding this matter, address Forestry Dept. Concord, N. H. or Blister Rust

CIRCULAR LETTERS TO PINE OWNERS.

State of Maine
FOREST SERVICE

Augusta.

Feb. 23, 1926.

Mr. John F. Jones
Jonesburg, Maine,

Dear Sir:

I am writing you in regard to the menace to the commercial
production of white pine created by the presence throughout the
southern part of the State of the white pine blister rust. Measures
for controlling this destructive disease are well known and it has been
demonstrated that under adequate supervision these measures can be put
into effect by private owners, who are, in nearly every case, willing to
do their part to protect their own and their neighbor's pine. The disease is less spectacular than fire, but none the less effective in its
ultimate destructiveness. If left unchecked it will in time make impossible the growing of white pine on areas within 300 yards of currant
or gooseberry bushes. The sooner these are removed, the less will be the
damage done.

It is unnecessary to emphasize the importance of white pine. Its
preservation is of the utmost importance from every standpoint. It is the
mainstay of many individual farms and rural communities, and either directly
or thru its products furnishes in large part the taxes necessary for the
maintenance of town activities. A definite campaign for the control of the
disease has been undertaken by the State in cooperation with the Federal
Government. Under this program the State will handle the necessary educational, scouting, and supervisory work, thereby aiding pine owners in
locating areas needing eradication, teaching them blister rust control in
all its phases, and aiding them in their eradication work. In other words,
we are working on a cooperative program in which each of the interested
parties will do its share.

It is extremely important that the towns should cooperate in
this work, as blister rust is spreading rapidly wherever currant and
gooseberry bushes are found. Every town in southern Maine has pine infection, some lots running as high as 50, 60 and 80% infected pine. The
best authorities in the country say that in time either the white pine
or currant and gooseberry bushes must go. They cannot for long occupy the
same ground. Since 1922 145 Maine towns have made appropriations for
blister rust control work and over 1,000,000 acres of pine bearing lands,
owned by nearly 5,000 individuals, have been given blister rust control

measures. In every case the town's appropriation, not a large sum, usually averaging $200 to $300, is used for the hire of a local man, who is trained by the State in control methods, and who is used solely to assist the owner in the eradication work. Such a man is absolutely necessary, as it has been definitely proved that the ordinary pine owner is not familiar with the disease, or the many varieties of the wild currant and gooseberry bushes responsible for its spread.

The state is now on the second half of an eight year control program, and as delay is costly, it is earnestly hoped that your town will cooperate with us to the extent of a few hundred dollars, thereby obtaining your share of State and Federal aid, and to complete the work in your town before the present program is ended. The sooner control work is started, the greater the result in the saving of thousands of young pines - each year's delay means a steadily increasing circle of pine infection.

The accompanying map will show the progress made in controlling this disease and how your town stands among others in the county. For the good of all concerned, I hope very much that an item covering the appropriation of blister rust funds may be included in the warrant for your next town meeting, and that the subject may receive your thorough and favorable consideration. May we not look for your support? If you wish more information on the subject, please advise us, and we will send our local representative who will cooperate in any way possible.

Very truly yours,

Forest Commissioner.

Edit: The above letter is being sent out to 2000 or more citizens in the pine-growing districts of southwestern Maine. Each letter is accompanied by a mimeographed map similar to the following one, for the county in which the citizen is residing.

The idea of using the mimeograph for something else than for ordinary letters and announcements is a good one and has been used very effectively in some states. If your state does not have facilities for such work, the Washington Office can assist you in getting it out.

* × × * × × × ×

No person was ever honored for what he received. Honor has been the reward for what he gave.
Calvin Coolidge.

Extract from Forbes Magazine - January 15, 1926.

C U M B E R L A N D C O U N T Y, M A I N E.

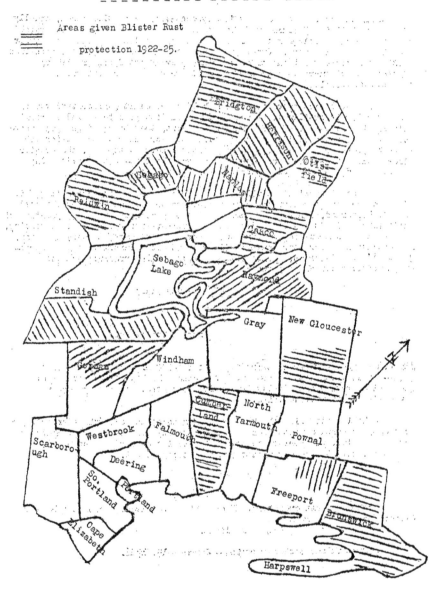

Areas given Blister Rust

protection 1922-25.

REPORT OF WORK IN WESTERN STATES DURING JANUARY.

Montana: Mr. C.H. Johnson spent most of his time during January assembling white pine data for Lincoln County, from county and Forest Service records.

Oregon: Mr. L.N. Goodding reports an educational trip through the sugar pine region of southern Oregon. The Blister Rust film was used and talks made to science classes in high schools. Visits were also made to Fire Wardens, Forest Service officials, County Agents and County Fruit Inspectors. Cuttings of several species of Ribes were collected for the investigative work in British Columbia.

During January, Mr. P.E. Melis completed some mapping work, prepared and placed a blister rust exhibit in the Forestry Building at Oregon Agricultural College, and conferred with Mr. C.C. Strong over possible standardization of eradication types.

California: Of much importance to the Blister Rust Control Program was the meeting of the Pacific section of the Society of American Foresters, held in San Francisco a short time ago. This meeting was devoted entirely to blister rust activities. It was held primarily to inform the lumbermen about this forest tree disease and future plans for its control in this state. These men expressed a keen interest in the work of the state and federal government and will undoubtedly approve whatever plans are promulgated to protect sugar pine.

County officials, including Horticultural Commissioners, were interviewed in El Dorado, Amador, Calaveras, and Tuolumne Counties, preparatory to black currant eradication to be conducted in these counties the coming season. From a preliminary survey conducted by several of the commissioners, previous to this time, some plantings of black currants have been found. As these counties contain valuable sugar pine sta. the importance of eradication in this region is plainly manifest.

- - - - - - - -

WHITE PINE FEATURE OF NEW YORK FARMERS' WEEK
AT CORNELL.

To show the important part white pine plays in the forest resources, the State Forestry Department will feature it in both talks and exhibits during Farmers' Week, February 8 to 13, at the State College of Agriculture, at Ithaca, bringing out every phase of its life history, its many uses, its astounding growth, and the way to fight its enemies.

Dr. H.E. York, head of the blister eradication branch of the state conservation commission, will tell how to control the rust which is threatening large areas of white pine. He will bring with him from Albany a complete exhibit that shows the stages in the rust attack.

From The National Nurseryman, Jan. 1926. p. 9.

LANTERN SLIDES

The Washington Office has just made up a small set of lantern slides on the uses of white pine, which are available for the Agents to use in connec tion with their blister rust lantern slide talks. These slides include views of white pine used for boxes, the making of buckets, screen doors, and clear lumber for pattern stock; the last being one of the most exacting uses requir of this wood. There is a view of the famous Ropes fence, Salem, Massachusett built in 1719, and the ornamental doorway of the Apthorp house at Portsmouth, New Hampshire. This set was made up at the special request of Mr. George Richardson, Agent in Southern Grafton County, New Hampshire.

R.G.P.

VOLUME TABLES FOR FOREST TREES.

The Forest Service has recently issued in three small booklets of pocket-notebook size, a series of volume tables covering fifty-four important timber species of the United States. On account of the small number of these booklets published, only sufficient numbers were secured to supply the state and district leaders in this Office. The booklets are as follows:

              Part I — Western Species

              Part II — Eastern Conifers

              Part III- Eastern Hardwoods

For the benefit of the agents, however, it is well to state that tables for individual species have been printed on single sheets and can be obtained separately by persons interested in one or only a few species, on application to the Forest Service, Washington, D.C. In writing designate the tables by number and part.

The log rules and volume tables found in Part I, which may be of particular use to our men in the West, are:

    Table 1. The International Log Rule.
       2. Scribner Decimal C Rule.
       3. Solid Cubic Contents of Logs.
       4. Area of Circles in square feet.
       5. Comparison of Log Rules.
      33. Sugar pine, Calif. Site 1, Dunning, 1925.
            Volume in board feet.
      34. Sugar pine, Calif. Site 2, Dunning, 1925.
            Volume in board feet.
      36. Western white pine. Kaniksu Nat'l.Forest,Ida.Millar,1908.
            Gives vol. in bd. ft. according to number of 16-ft. logs.
      37. Same as Table 36, but gives volume in bd. ft. according
            to total height of tree.
      38. Same as Table 36, but gives volume in bd. ft. according
            to merchantable length of tree.

Table 39 Western white pine
     Kaniksu National Forest, Millar, 1908
     Volume in cubic feet.
   50 Limber pine. Humboldt National Forest, Nevada.
     Rustay 1922.
     Volume in board feet
  107 Second growth sugar pine. Eldorado, Shasta,
     and Tahoe Nat'l. Forests, Calif. Dunning 1923.
     Volume in board feet.
  108 Same as Table 107.
     Volume in cubic feet.
  122 Second growth western white pine. Kaniksu and
     Kootenai National Forests, Idaho.
     Rockwell and McCarthy 1910 to 1920.
     Peeled volume — cubic feet.

The log rules and volume tables found in Part II, which may be of particular use to our men in the East are:

Tables 1 to 5 which are the same in Part II as in Part I.

6 & 11 White pine. Beltrami, Cass and Itasca Counties,
     Minn. Frothingham 1913, Barrows 1913.
     Volume in board feet.
7 & 9 White pine. Southern Appalachians.
     Mulford and Barrows 1912, 1916.
     Volume in board feet.
8 & 10 Second-growth white pine. Southern Appalachians.
     Barrows, Graves 1913.
     Volume in board feet.
12 White pine, Northern Minn. E.S. Bruce, 1912.
     Volume in board feet.
13 & 14 Second-growth white pine. Southern N.H.,
     Margolin 1906.
     Volume in board feet.
15 Same as 13 & 14.
     Total volume in cubic feet.
16 White pine, Massachusetts. Cook 1921
     Volume in cords.

* * * * * * * * * *

Character, to grow, must have roots.

Extract from Forbes Magazine - January 15, 1926.

A NOTE ON THE IMPORTANCE OF THE SUGAR PINE AND WESTERN
WHITE PINE.

In 1923, approximately 8,000 persons were employed in the cutting and manufacture of sugar pine and western white pine lumber. These persons were paid $13,000,000 in wages and salaries, and the products were valued at approximately $30,000,000.

Sugar pine comprises 10 per cent of the lumber cut of California, and western white pine represents 35 per cent of the lumber industry of Idaho.

The present stand of sugar pine in California and Oregon is approximately 35 billion board feet, of which two-fifths is on the National Forests. The stand of western white pine in Idaho, Montana, Washington, Oregon, and California is about 22 billion feet, of which one-third is on the National Forests.

The protection of the white and sugar pine regions against blister rust is even more important from the standpoint of future timber production than from the standpoint of the present supply of mature timber. The wood of these species is of especially high intrinsic value, the growth is rapid, and potential yields are comparatively large. It is probably conservative to estimate that under forest management it will be possible to continue indefinitely approximately the present output of western white pine, while the cut of sugar pine can be increased considerably. This will be possible, however, only as a result of effective fire protection and the adoption of proper silvicultural measures, and provided that destruction by natural enemies, such as insects and disease, can be reduced to a minimum.

The above was submitted by W.N. Sparhawk, Forest Economist, U.S. Forest Service, Washington, D.C. at the public hearing on the Oregon blister rust quarantine held by the Federal Horticultural Board, January 8, 1926.

When the stand is	White Pine		
	On good site	:	On an inferior site
20 yrs. old.	1600	:	2000
40 " "	700	:	1200
60 " "	300	:	600
80 " "	200	:	350
100 " "	175	:	250
120 " "	150	:	200

The late Professor Filibert Roth in his "First Book of Forestry" used the above table to show what a fully stocked stand should be. He writes — "The forester usually leaves the (pine) thicket to itself until it is about twenty years old when he thins it out, removing the dead, dying and inferior trees.

To get a better idea as to how much ought to be cut it may be said that for pine on good pine land there ought not to be left more than ten trees on one square rod at the age of twenty, four at forty, two at sixty, and one at a hundred years, as tabulated above.

By dividing the figures in the above table by 160 (the number of square rods in an acre) we can readily find how many trees we may leave on one square rod.

Many foresters are guided by the crowns and thin just enough to keep the crowns from crowding.

That injured and crippled trees and also those with unduly spreading crowns should be taken out is self-evident. After a thinning our woods should be evenly and well stocked with as perfect trees as can be produced.

*The United States Forest Service states that considerable variation from these figures is permissible.

M O T I O N   P I C T U R E S

Western film shown to more than 34,000 in 1925.

Messrs. S.N. Wyckoff and L.N. Goodding have recently submitted their annual report showing the use of the two reel film "Blister Rust a Menace To Western Timber" in the western states during the past year. In California the film was shown at 24 different places with an attendance in these cities varying from 50 to 5000. The total attendance in California was estimated at 15,466.

In Oregon the film was run at motion picture houses in 17 different places. At Medford 1000 people witnessed the showing. While figures for the total showing are not available, it is known that there were about 2,050 present at 4 of the towns.

In Idaho the film was used at 9 different places with an attendance varying from 100 to 2,795. The total attendance was given at 5,458.

In Montana it was estimated that in the 5 towns where shown, 11,400 persons saw our western film.

The record attendance at any city was achieved at Great Falls, Montana and Sacramento, California, with an attendance of 5000. Billings, Montana followed next with 4000.

- - - - - - - - -

"The Pines" in Maine.

This film was shown during January to about 8000 adults and 600 children, in the towns of Rumford, Mexico, and Dicksfield, according to Agent Arthur J. Lambert. In between his motion picture shows Mr. Lambert found time to scout for the blister rust in the locality. He stated that the blister rust was everywhere.

PERSONAL

Mr. C.C. Strong appeared before the Forestry and Logging Congress which was held at the Oregon Agricultural College at Corvallis, on January 23, and delivered a paper on Blister Rust Control and Its Relation to Forest management.

* * * * * *

Mr. N.H. Harpp, Agent in southeastern New York, was on the air Wednesday, January 27, when he broadcasted from Kingston, New York, Station W D B Z – Another blister-ruster has joined the family of radio talkers.

* * * * * *

Mr. W.J. Endersbee, (otherwise known as Bill) Agent in Berkshire County, Massachusetts, was called to Washington for a short assignment during the latter part of January. He was engaged in summarizing and putting into final form the field studies carried on by him during the past several years. The Office was sorry to let him go so soon, but the Berkshires were calling him.

* * * * * *

Mr. A.E. Fivaz, Specialist, arrived in Washington, February 3, for a short spell. "Al" will summarize for publication the data secured in the past 4 years on the North Hudson (N.Y.) experimental control area.

* * * * * *

Mrs. Florence LaCovey, Clerk in the Washington Office, has been on the sick list for a number of days. We are hoping for her prompt recovery.

* * * * * *

Mr. Allison H. Hearn, former Agent in New Jersey, writes under date of January 18, "I am now employed by the Long-Bell Lumber Company in the creosoting work at De Ridder, Louisiana. Mail will reach me at Box 519 De Ridder, Louisiana'.

BLISTER RUST TALK OVER THE RADIO.

Dr. H.H. York, Forest Pathologist, prepared a paper on the white

pine blister rust which was broadcast from W.E.A.Z. on the evening of

Monday, December 21, 1925.

Dr. York was also one of the speakers at an enthusiastic dinner

and meeting of the Greene County (N.Y.) Fish and Game Club at Catskill,

on the evening of December 17.

From the Observer, N.Y. Conservation Commission, Jan. 1, 1926.

P U B L I C A T I O N S

Blister Rust

Anon.   May Quarantine Oregon Because of Pine Disease.

Montana Bans Black Currant.

Survey Shows Blister Rust Has Not Spread in Pennsylvania,

White Pine Feature of New York's Farmers' Week at Cornell.
The National Nurseryman, Vol. 34, No. 1. Jan. 1926, p. 9.

Darrow,   G.M. and S.B. Detwiler. - Currants and Gooseberries
Spread Rust.
Better Fruit XIX, 11, p. 9, 20,21.   1925.
Extract in The Review of Applied Mycology, Vol. IV,
Pt. 10, Oct. 1925, p. 619.

Douglas, Benjamin Wallace - Gooseberries and the Rust.
The Country Gentleman - Jan. 1926. p. 92.

Neglected Fruits.
The Country Gentleman.   Jan. 1926, p. 92.

Jardine., Hon. W.M. - White Pine Blister Rust Control.
Forest Leaves Vol. 20, No. 7, Feb. 1926, p. 111,112.
This is a quotation from the Report of the Secretary
of Agriculture to the President.

Milton Nursery Company, Oregon. - Comments by Oregon Nurserymen.
The National Nurseryman. Vol. 34, No. 1, Jan. 1926, p. 9.

Violette, Neil L. - White Pine Blister Rust.
In 15th Biennial Report of the Forest Commissioner
of Maine. 1923-24. p. 51-55.

BLISTER RUST

NEWS

MARCH 1926.

Volume X   *Number 3.*

U.S. DEPARTMENT of AGRICULTURE
Office of Blister Rust Control.

C O N T E N T S - V O L. 10, N O. 3

Blister Rust Situation   Page
   Progress of Eradication Work in Vermont 77
Blister Rust Write-Ups
   Making Progress in Fighting Pine Rust 62
   Western Men in Role of Authors 63
   An Alien That Should Have Been Deported 67
   Blister Rust Agents Have Good Write-Ups in Leading Newspapers 76
   Blister Rust Papers Presented at Meeting of Society of Amer. Foresters 78
Cooperation
   Nurserymen Make Good Cooperators 81
Editorial
   Hello Agent ! 60
   Thoroughness 79
Education
   A Mimeographed Postcard Gives Wide-spread Publicity 64
   Healthy Young Pines on Old Infection Area 65
   A Series of Form Letters Used Successfully in Securing Cooperation
     With Non-Resident Pine Owners 69
   Holes in the Stocking 80
   Farmers' Week Exhibit at Ithaca, New York 81
   Special Program for Blister Rust Control Agents 82
   Working With Future Pine Owners 83
Eradication
   A Misdirected Effort in Ribes Eradication 61
   Chemical Eradication of Currants and Gooseberries 74
Forestry
   Its Trees Boom New Hampshire 68
   New York State and Japan Exchange Seeds 78
   President Proclaims American Forest Week 84
   Statistics on Production of Sugar Pine Lumber, Lath and Shingles
     as Reported by Mills 85
   Long-Bell Lumber Company to Plant White Pine and Other Trees in
     Washington 85
   Actual Vs. "Paper" White Pine Reforestation 86
   A 29 Year Old Planting Contains 22,240 Feet Round-edge Lumber . . . 87
Office Comments
   Instructions Concerning Shipment of Infected Blister Rust Specimens. . 89
Personal 90
   There are Only a Few of Us Left 87
Publications
   Western Men in Role of Authors 63
Quarantine
   Black Currants Banned by the Minnesota Horticultural Society 77
   Kansas Has Established New Blister Rust Quarantine Affecting
     Shipments from Oregon 88
State News
   California 61,63,85   New Hampshire. . . .64,67,68,76,83,87
   Idaho 74,86   New York 78,81,82
   Kansas. 88   Oregon 85,88
   Maine 66,76,87   Vermont 77
   Massachusetts 62,69,80   Washington 85
   Minnesota 77   Western States 61,63,74,85,86

UNITED STATES DEPARTMENT OF AGRICULTURE
BUREAU OF PLANT INDUSTRY
WASHINGTON, D.C.

T H E   B L I S T E R   R U S T   N E W S

Issued by the Office of Blister Rust Control
and the Cooperating States.

VOL. 10, NO. 3   MARCH 1926

Hello Agent!

"It's not much use to be on your way if you don't know where you're
going." Such was the theme of an address given by Prof. C.W. Gay of Ohio State
University to the members of Block and Bridle Club at the University of Minnesota a few weeks ago.

"Lack of a definite target", Dr. Gay declared, in the Gopher Countryman for February 1926, "is responsible for a large percentage of failures, whether
it is among students or in the various businesses and professions. The expert
riflemen cannot demonstrate his superiority over the mediocre marksman if they
are both blazing away at the blue sky."

In the East we have a definite cooperative control program, and in the
West we have another one; both being good targets to aim at. Both, however cover
a period of a few years and are long-range targets.

In the control work in the East perhaps we need to sorter lower our
sights a bit and shoot at a closer target - the year's work. Here's jest where
we may be lackin' in not erectin' a target fer the year, somethin' we can hit,
yet sorter hard to get a bull's-eye. The bigger the acreage we're aimin'
to cover, the harder its goin' to be to score. But then who wants an easy mark
to shoot at?

Yours for straight shootin',

Ribee Bill

A MISDIRECTED EFFORT IN RIBES ERADICATION

When a Bush is Once Pulled See That it Stays Pulled

A scout for the elusive cultivated black currant thinks some of the old-time mining sections of California reveal many things of interest. Many of the mining towns were settled by Cornishmen, perhaps because British capital opened and sustained many of the mines, or again because these people are considered among the best miners of the world. They brought from their mother-country the proverbial English black currant. Some of the bushes recently eradicated had been planted for over thirty years. The tops did not reveal their extreme age, for the branches may have died or the pruning knife taken its toll from time to time, but the crown and roots told the tale.

While sitting one evening in the lobby of one of the old hotels in the mining town of Downieville, now a mere shell of its former self, the subject of black currants naturally came up, for what "Ribes hound" has yet to enter a small town or village and not be approached with the time-worn question, "Well, young man, what be your business here?" Feeling in good spirits, we unloaded our troubles. We found that at a certain abandoned ranch (it would be a farm in the East), four miles up a rocky gulch, the owner some years previous had pulled up several black currant bushes and thrown them on a dump with the intent of destroying them. The gentleman who informed us regarding this had a faint recollection of bushes still being on the place. We followed up the clue and found a clump of black currants fifteen feet in diameter and about seven feet high. The owner failed to realize that a small mountain stream, a rich dark soil and ample shade were the best possible agents for Ribes growth of this species. He had thrown them over a fence under such conditions as just mentioned. Needless to say, the bushes simply reveled in their new habitat and furnished an excellent example of reverting to wild type.

After several hours of strenuous labor we were successful in digging up

the roots and disentangling the branches from the barbed wire fence. Little
did the owner realize that a second attack would be made upon his bushes,
involving three hours of hard work on one of the hottest days of the past
summer.

The motto of this simple story is "Watch where you throw your bushes".

Sacramento, Calif.   *George A. Root*

MAKING PROGRESS IN FIGHTING PINE RUST

The control of the white pine blister rust in Berkshire County has progressed steadily since last July when an agent was assigned to this work in the
county. A total of 16,862 acres have been examined for currants and gooseberries
and 57,656 of these wild bushes have been destroyed. The center of this work
has been in the towns of Great Barrington and Egremont, where a few scattered
pine lots had previously been protected.

The disease has been found on pine in every lot examined this past season.
In most cases it is as yet only threatening, but the fact that it is present
means that it will increase if the currants and gooseberries are not destroyed.
It is only through these bushes that blister rust spreads and it cannot be trans-
mitted directly from one pine to another. A few pine lots have been found where
the disease has taken heavy toll. Sample plots studied in these lots have shown
as high as 90 per cent of the pines infected and over 50 per cent already dead
from the rust. These conditions prevail where the disease got an early start
and the currants and gooseberries were not destroyed for several years. In these
and other stands where the bushes have been pulled there is no evidence of
further damage since their eradication.

During the coming season the areas completed in 1925 will be extended to
include all of the towns of Great Barrington, Egremont, Alford, New Marlboro,
Sheffield and Mount Washington. It is the aim of the State Department of Agriculture to carry the work along systematically by urging all contiguous pine
owners to destroy their bushes. The disease can be destroyed much more
effectively and permanently when all owners cooperate in the work than when
only a few scattered owners destroy their bushes.

From The Eagle, Pittsfield, Mass. Jan. 13, 1926.

Note: I like this article of Mr. W.J. Endersbee's for several reasons:
1 - His name didn't appear in it. 2. - It gives timely facts which all citizens
want to know, as to the progress of the control work. 3 - It states where work
will be carried on this coming season, and 4 - It puts it up to the owner
to cooperate whole-heartedly in a worth-while enterprise.

Edit.

WESTERN MEN IN ROLE OF AUTHORS

The Office at Washington is grateful to Mr. George A. Root for a copy of The California Countryman. This issue (December 1925) was of special inter to members of this Office because it contains articles by several blister rust control men.

An article, "Save the Forest" by Mr. Amihud Grasovsky, is the winner of first prize in the Charles L. Pack essay contest. In it a plea is made for th care and protection of the Country's enormous stands of high grade timber.

"The Plague of the White Pine" by Lester V. Harper, who was also a "blister ruster" emphasizes the fact that although white pine blister rust, which is one of the most virulent of forest diseases, is within a few miles of California's sugar pine forests, it has not as yet crossed the State Line. Mr Harper has recently been elected President of the University of California Forestry Club.

Another worthwhile article in this number is "Why a Forestry Education?" by Mr. Kenneth McLeod, Jr., who is one of our blister rust men working in the state of Washington.

In this issue of the California Countryman there were only eight major articles of which three were contributed by blister rust men. Fine work!

Edit: Messrs. Grasovsky, Harper and McLeod are to be congratulated on the above articles, especially Grasovsky, for his prize winning essay. The influence of the written word is as great, if not greater, than that of the spoken word. The audience is much greater, and the written word continues to bear fruit.

For the good of forestry as a whole, as well as for the good of our own particularly work, more of us should follow the examples of our western brethren and publish worthwhile articles.

A MIMEOGRAPHED POSTCARD GIVES WIDE-SPREAD PUBLICITY

> ### D O   Y O U   K N O W   T H A T
>
> A destructive bark disease has been found upon pines in your town; it is fatal to all white pine growth.
>
> It attacks and kills old as well as young white pines.
>
> Blister Rust cannot spread direct from infected to healthy pines, but must first live for a time on the leaves of currant or gooseberry bushes.
>
> Blister Rust can be controlled by the destruction of all currant and gooseberry bushes, in and around white pine growth.
>
> Eight years of control work have proved that the destruction of these bushes prevents further spread of this serious disease among white pines.
>
> The proper time to protect your pines is before they become infected; not after.
>
> 174 towns and cities have cooperated with the State Forestry Department since 1913. The State increases town appropriations 25 percent, and furnishes free supervision of the work.
>
> Further information may be secured by addressing Blister Rust Control Agent, 11 Shaw Street, Lebanon, N.H.
>
> - - -
>
> White Pine Is No Longer "Just A Tree"
> It is a valuable local asset.
> Act Now Before It Is Too Late!

Mr. G. F. Richardson, Agent in South Grafton County, New Hampshire, is responsible for putting out the above card. On a hurry call from "Rich" two thousand copies of this card were mimeographed at the Washington Office and forwarded to New Hampshire for his use. Let the Washington Office know when it can do similar work for you.

R.G.P.

HEALTHY YOUNG PINES ON OLD INFECTION AREA
MAKE CONVINCING DEMONSTRATION.

Ten years have elapsed since the beginning of blister rust experimental control work through Ribes eradication. There are now control areas in the different states eradicated 6 to 10 years ago, which must now bear a crop of pine seedlings. Granting that most of the work was well done in our early days of experimental work, there seems to be an opportunity for utilizing such areas as "silent workers", as Agent Lambert has indicated.

These old eradicated areas, full of healthy young pine, are a living proof and demonstration that Ribes eradication within a short distance of the pine has given practical control of the blister rust. Have you not, as Agent, one of these old eradicated areas in your district which you can make use of by posting with a well prepared sign? It is not entirely necessary that the area be along the public highway, although of course if this were the case it would be highly desirable. Let me cite a hypothetical case:

At Blanktown, Maine, there was a twenty acre lot of pines, where in the experimental days of 1916 the gooseberries and currants were destroyed. Records show that there were an average of 20 wild gooseberries and 30 skunk currants per acre, at that time. A check made after the close of the work the same year showed that 90% of the bushes were removed in the first working. At this time 25% of the young pines under 15 feet in height were diseased. In 1921, at the request of the owner, the blister rust control Agent examined this pine lot and found but 7 currants and gooseberries per acre. These were not evenly scattered about the area, but were found along stone walls and in low moist places. Around these scattered bushes there were a few young pines with blister rust cankers on trunk and branches. The currants and gooseberries found at this time were destroyed.

Five years later, that is in 1926, the owner of the pines who was
extremely interested in this protective work went through his pine area himself
and found on an average, but a single bush per acre, and these were quite small.

The owner was especially interested in noting that the holes in the
forest which had been made by the blister rust killing the pines up to 1916
had been completely filled by young pine ranging in age from 1 to 10 years.

Given such a pine lot with the facts as indicated, the agent made a neat
sign on a white painted board which the owner suggested be placed at the
entrance to the lot. This sign was as follows:

LOOK AT THE HEALTHY YOUNG PINES

They Replace Blister Rust Infected Trees
When Currant and Gooseberry Bushes
Have Been Removed

Year	No. Bushes Removed per A.	No. Healthy trees.
1916	50	300
1921	7	400
1926	1	500

What do you think of this suggestion, is it worth trying?

R.G. Pierce.

- - - - - - - - - - - -

HEAVILY INFECTED PINE FOUND AT CANTON, MAINE

A thirty year old pine with 224 cankers, ranging from 1 to 8
years of age, was recently found by Agent A.J. Lambert, at Canton, Maine.
The height of this tree is 40 feet and it has a diameter of 10 inches.

AN ALIEN THAT SHOULD HAVE BEEN DEPORTED.

By

L.E. Newman, Agent in Charge, Blister Rust Control,
New Hampshire.

Although the recent gymnastics of the weather make it difficult to
realize the nearness of Spring, a glance at the calendar proclaims that winter
has already commenced its northern retreat and promises that the warble of the
blue-bird and the piping of the frogs will be heard before long. The calendar
reminds us also that Town Meeting is not far off - - another sign that we are
on the threshold of Spring.

Several years ago a very undesirable immigrant from Europe stepped
ashore in New York. Had he been observed coming off the steamer, it is doubtful if he would have been permitted to land. However, a hiding place among
vast quantities of white pine planting stock had been found by the stowaway and
he was not discovered until he had been in our midst for some years. In
common with many of the immigrants who enter the United States, this stowaway
has a jaw-breaking name. It is Cronartium Ribicola Fischer. Similar to the
practice which many Europeans adopt upon arriving in our country, this alien's
name was translated and today he is better known as Blister Rust.

The United States has been termed the "melting pot" of the races of the
world. Ultimately, they emerge from out the caldron and assume the customs,
manners and speech of their new home. If they are discovered to possess traits
or characteristics objectionable to this country, they are deported. As many
pine owners in New England will agree, it is most unfortunate that C.R. Fischer
was not among those sent back. Upon his arrival, this "undesirable" immediately
settled down to work. Moreover, he has not been content with working "union"
hours but has been plying his destructive trade day and night ever since.
Although his presence in this country, and especially here in New Hampshire,
has been given much publicity, there are still many owners of white pine who
doubt his existence and ability to do them harm. It may not be generally known,
and it may even seem strange, but currants and gooseberries, with the aid of
the wind, are this "destructive alien's" chief assistants. It is due to their
combined activities that owners of white pine today face one of the most
serious forest problems.

Is there an effective and inexpensive method by which he and his forces
may be put to rout?

In answer to the first query let it be again repeated that currant
and gooseberry bushes, both wild and cultivated, constitute the only means
which permit blister rust to spread from diseased to healthy pines. Destroying
them throughout pine growth and for a distance of 900 feet around will put
this alien under control. The most economical manner in which this can be
brought about is through cooperation between the towns and the state. The State
Forestry Department has been working with 174 towns and cities and nearly 500
individual pine owners in the destruction of currant and gooseberry bushes since
1918. Town appropriations have been increased 25 per cent by the state, or for
every $400 voted, $100 has been added by the state. As a result, 1,587,158

acres have been examined and 19,537,775 currant and gooseberry bushes located
and destroyed. Success in this important work, though not completely achieved,
is in sight. In 35 New Hampshire towns and cities, pine areas have already
been completely examined the first time over. Is your town among this number?
What one community has accomplished can be duplicated by another.

From New Hampshire Forestry Department News Letter, Feb. 1926.

ITS TREES BOOM NEW HAMPSHIRE

Trees are the basic reason why New Hampshire has something to boom
through its newly formed publicity commission, states E.D. Fletcher, extension forester at the State University.

"Nobody goes to a treeless country for a vacation," he points out,
"and about 70 percent of our state is in some form of tree growth. If this
growth were not attractively broken by farmlands, lakes and mountains, however, it would not have so much scenic value. The farm woodlot, for this
reason, is no less important from a tourist standpoint then our state and
national forests.

"We can hardly expect the owners of these woodlots to maintain them
except on a commercial basis, and many trees which have pleasing form have
little timber value. In other words, there is a distinction between roadside
trees and the trees of the woodlot itself. Many gnarled trees or bushes
with beautiful foliage should be kept for this reason alongside the roads,
whereas the same trees if in the midst of the woodlot would be discarded."

The Rockingham County Farmer, February 1926.

A SERIES OF FORM LETTERS USED SUCCESSFULLY IN

SECURING COOPERATION WITH NON-RESIDENT PINE OWNERS.

The following series of letters to non-resident owners, drafted by
State Leader Perry and myself have been quite successful in securing cooperation.

Selectmen, of course, are first interviewed and a list of non-residents
and addresses secured. When possible an initial contact is made. This is
always better for all concerned than a telephone call or a letter. Ask
any business man if you don't believe it. But many letters have to be sent
out. The one marked #1 with #1 card is sent out. Last season I got 65% of
the cards back - Then I sent out (always typewritten) the one marked #2. The
first paragraph is always the same and the rest of the letter is adapted to
conditions.

The one marked #3 with #3 slip is sent to boards of selectmen and tree
wardens and to people where no control work has had to be done on their land
but they have sent back the cards so we feel it our duty to send this letter
as they have shown an interest in their pine and our work by returning the
card. By the way the name of the town is always filled in before sending to
the owner. Where control work was done we send practically the same letter and
slip only we leave out the word town and then it reads control work done on
your land, etc.

Earle M. Brockway - Mass.

#1

United States Department of Agriculture
Bureau of Plant Industry
in cooperation with
Massachusetts Department of Agriculture

Blister Rust Control

Headquarters:
Plymouth County Extension Service,
106 Main St., Brockton, Mass.

To White Pine Owners in Plymouth County:

We desire your cooperation in saving the WHITE PINE in PLYMOUTH COUNTY from serious damage by the WHITE PINE BLISTER RUST. Your young pines may never reach merchantable size, unless they are protected from this disease by the destruction of currant and gooseberry bushes within 900 feet of the pine.

YOU CAN HELP! Simply fill in the blanks on the enclosed franked postal card. One of our specialists will get in touch with you and examine your land and pines at no expense to you, and will advise you relative to blister rust conditions. If you do not own white pine, indicate by the use of ciphers. After signing, mail the card. No postage is required.

Very truly yours,

(Signed) E.M.Brockway,

Agent, Blister Rust Control.

Plymouth County Extension Service,

106 Main Street,

Brockton, Mass.

March 8, 1926.

Mr. John R.P. Smith,

Hingham, Mass.

Dear Sir:

    I wish to thank you for the prompt return of the postal card regarding the protection of your white pine from the white pine blister rust. Your promptness convinces me that you are interested in your pine and the problem that confronts us. Your hearty cooperation and moral support are earnestly solicited, in helping to control this disease in your neighborhood. This, as you know, is accomplished by the destruction of the currant and gooseberry, both wild and cultivated.

    An examination of Mr. O.O. Jones' property was made last fall and it was estimated by myself and Mr. T.H. Murphy, Tree Warden of Hingham, that approximately one-third of his 300 acres was infected with the above named disease. Mr. Jones has four men in mind that he is going to hire about April 15, and eradicate the wild currant and gooseberry bushes from his land.

    Your land borders Mr. Jones' land and after April 15 an inspector will examine your land at no expense to you. If we find that there is further work to be done to protect your pines we hope to have your cooperation and we will at the same time do all we can to assist you.

    Trusting this meets with your approval and that we may have your hearty support, I am

                Very truly yours,

                E.M. Brockway,

                Agent in Charge.

#3

United States Department of Agriculture
Bureau of Plant Industry
Massachusetts Department of Agriculture
136 State House, Boston, Mass.

Memorandum to Plymouth County Pine Owners re Blister Rust Control

We are pleased to send you at this time, a record of the blister
rust control work which was performed last season in the town in which
your land is located.

We suggest that from year to year you search your land for
currant and gooseberry bushes which may possibly have been overlooked
or that may have come up from seed since the land was first examined.
Our experience has shown that spring is a favorable time to locate these
bushes, since the foliage appears on them in advance of nearly all other
vegetation. If you will consider these bushes as pests and endeavor
to eradicate them from your land, in the same way that you would keep
the weeds out of your garden, you may be assured that your white pines
will be permanently protected from the blister rust.

If the department can be of any service, please feel free to
call us at any time.

Headquarters for Plymouth County (Signed)
Plymouth County Extension Service,   E. M. Brockway,
105 Main St. Brockton, Mass.   Blister Rust Control Agent.
p-100

- 73 -

Card
1

. . . . .Mass.

. . . . .192 .

Agent, Blister Rust Control:

    I own . . . . . . acres of Pine and a total of
. . . . acres of land in the town of . . . .
Mass. I would be glad to have you make an examination of
my lands and advise me relative to blister rust conditions.
My present post-office address is:

. . . .

. . . .

My telephone number is . . . .

             (Signed). . . . .

Slip
3

RECORD OF COOPERATIVE BLISTER RUST CONTROL WORK
SEASON OF 1925

      Town of . . . ., Massachusetts

Total area of land examined in control work . . . . acres

Number of wild currant and gooseberry bushes removed . . . .

Number of cultivated currant and gooseberry bushes removed . . . .

Date . . . .

             . . . .
              E.M. Brockway, Agent.

CHEMICAL ERADICATION OF CURRANTS AND GOOSEBERRIES.

It has been known for some time that the spread of white pine blister rust, a fungous disease which may attack any five needle pines, could be locally controlled by the removal of all currants and gooseberries from within and adjacent to white pine areas. The principal method of destruction of these currants and gooseberries (Ribes) has been that of hand-pulling, but when the blister rust project was formulated several years ago it was agreed that in many places Ribes grew in such profusion and under such conditions as to render hand-pulling very costly. Attention was directed to the possibility of chemical destruction of Ribes. An experimental project was undertaken by the Office of Blister Rust Control, Bureau of Plant Industry, to determine the feasibility of such a method.

This problem calls for a chemical that is reasonably cheap, one that can be applied without danger to man or stock, and of sufficiently toxic nature to kill Ribes in one application. A suitable chemical should be capable of ready transportation and not constitute a fire menace, since it would be applied in large quantities in the forests during warm, dry weather.

Experiments were commenced at Hobart, N.Y., in 1917 and extended over a period of years from 1917-21. During 1924 experiments were undertaken in northern Idaho and California.

On the basis of material gathered together from these previous experiments, work for the field season 1925 was begun on a slightly larger scale. Work was performed over two areas, namely three one-acre plots at Wallace, Idaho, and five one-acre plots at Santa, Idaho. Spraying, and crown and soil applications of the following chemicals, used in many different concentrations, were made with varying degrees of success: NaCl, NaBr, NaP, NaOH, $Na_2B_4O_1$,

NH_4Cl, NH_4F, $(NH_4)_2 Cr_2 O_1$, NH_4NO_3, KF, $CaCl_2$, NH_4Br, $CaCl(OCl)$, $BaCl_2$

Atlas N.P. Weed Killer, Kerosene, Acid Sludge, $HgCl_2$. Of the above chemi-

cals NH_4Cl, NaF and Atlas N.P. gave definite kills on small bushes when applied

in the form of a saturated solution around the base of the plant, and $NH_4 Cl$,

NH_4F, KF and Atlas N.P. killed a considerable portion of the live stem when

applied in the form of a spray.

We can safely say that absorption of the spray by the plant is taking

place, to some degree at least, and it is only a question of working out

some specific phases of the problem to increase this absorption to the point

where it will kill the plant. It might be noted that during the summer 1925,

the above mentioned chemicals were applied to some 8707 Ribes, representing

a total of 165,521 feet of live stem.

It is planned to carry on extensive laboratory work during the winter

months and to apply those results in a practical manner during the next field

season. There is every reason to hope that the eradication of currants and

gooseberries by chemical means will soon be playing an important role in the

fight against white pine blister rust.

                              H.R. Offord,
                              Field Assistant.

November 2, 1925
Spokane, Washington.

BLISTER RUST AGENTS HAVE GOOD WRITE-UPS IN

LEADING NEWSPAPERS.

The Washington Office is in receipt of a copy of The Union, of Manchester, N.H., for March 2. Valuable articles on the subject of Blister Rust, written by two of our Agents, appear in this newspaper and are given almost an entire page.

"Twenty Million Currant and Gooseberry Bushes Killed to Stop Blister Rust" is the title of an article by Mr. L.E. Newman, of Concord, New Hampshire. In this write-up Mr. Newman has used a "catchy" way of introducing blister rust under the name of Cronartium Ribicola Fischer, as an immigrant who came to this country from Europe. He also gives facts and history concerning the disease and uses photographs to illustrate.

Mr. Thomas J. King, also from Concord, New Hampshire, has an article under the title of "219 of 235 Towns in State Infected by Blister Rust", which is equall valuable, and numerates the many reasons why it is advisable and profitable to plant and protect white pine.

Another good article, written by Mr. Kenneth F. Lee, from material suppli... by Mr. W.O. Frost, of Maine, appeared in the Portland Sunday Telegram and Sunday Press Herald, January 31, 1926. This article was accompanied by a number of photographs showing different species of Ribes leaves, cankers, and damage to pine trees.

Edit: These articles call attention of pine owners to blister rust control and we are glad to see them given so much space in newspapers having wide circulation. The authors are to be congratulated upon these articles and also for securing the cooperation of the newspapers and getting the information before the public. The above articles are well illustrated, and non-technical. Another good feature is that they are timely.

N.S.

BLACK CURRANT BANNED BY THE MINNESOTA
HORTICULTURAL SOCIETY.

The Minnesota State Horticultural Society has dropped the Black Naples currant (one of the varieties of R. nigrum) from their Fruit List. A recent report of the Committee on Fruit List, of which Professor W.G. Brierley of the University of Minnesota is Chairman, recommended the following changes in the Fruit List:

"That the Black Naples currant be dropt from the list and that the statement be made to read - Black (Currants) - None on account of their susceptibility to white pine blister rust."

The Minnesota Horticulturist, Vol. 54, No. 1, January 1926. p. 10.

Note: Professor W.G. Brierley in a letter of February 9, stated that the report of the Committee mentioned above was adopted.

PROGRESS OF ERADICATION WORK.
IN VERMONT.

Yrs.	Acres.	Total Cost.	Cooperators Cost	Ribes Eradicated Wild	Cult.
1920	4501	$ 3224.45	$ 515.61	29,458	74
1921	6317	3471.26	3235.50	60,147	131
1922	13512	6100.70	5502.22	201,270	782
1923	25190	8498.43	7247.34	278,570	1234
1924	25688	9280.02	7392.74	182,154	585
1925	26622	9058.12	8221.87	317,337	640
Totals	101,830	39,632.98	32,115.28	1,069,436	3446

BLISTER RUST PAPERS PRESENTED AT MEETING OF

SOCIETY OF AMERICAN FORESTERS

At the New York Section of the Society of American Foresters, which was held February 23, at the Waldorf-Astoria Hotel, New York City, two papers on the blister rust and its control were read.

"The Blister Rust Situation" written by Mr. S.B. Detwiler was read by Mr. A.E. Fivaz, in the absence of Mr. Detwiler.

"Certain Results in Blister Rust Control in New York State" was prepared and delivered by Dr. L.H. Pennington.

NEW YORK STATE AND JAPAN EXCHANGE SEEDS

New York Will Try Out Korean White Pine (P. Koraiensis)

M. Tozawa, Director of the Forest Experiment Station at Keijyo-Chosen, (Japan), has forwarded two pounds "Pinus Koraiensis" seed to this Commission and we have sent to the Japanese Forest Experiment Station some of our native white pine seed. The seed received from Japan is that of the native white pine trees of that country, and will be sown in our Saratoga Nursery next spring.

Extract from The Observer, New York Conservation Commission, for Jan. 1, 1926.

Note: Pinus koraiensis is one of the white or five needled pines and belongs to the Cembrae group of white pines (after Shaw in The Genus Pinus). Other members of this Cembrae group include Pinus cembra, the Swiss Stone Pine, and P. albicaulis the white-bark pine.

Cronartium ribicola has been found on this species of Korean pine, according to Spaulding, but it is relatively little susceptible to the blister rust as compared with the eastern white pine. It will be interesting to watch the development of these Asiatic white pines.

T H O R O U G H N E S S

Jeff McDermid, genial editor of Better Crops, has a little essay
on thoroughness, in the February issue of his magazine, which is worthwhile
reading. He quotes Edw. W. Bok of the Curtis Publishing Company, the latter
claiming that America, especially young America, needs an education in
thoroughness. He cites the Dutch boy as an example of thoroughness.

Far be it from Jeff to back Bok up in his tirade on the lack of
thoroughness of our boys. Rather does Jeff take pride that we arrive at the
end, get the goal that we have set, by cutting out many of the thorough steps
which Bok says are necessary. To us in blister rust control this ideal of
achieving the end as J. McDermid has it, will appeal. And what is the end
for which we are striving? Not eradication of currants, surely; that is only
the means of reaching it, but protection of the white pines from the blister
rust. And we might add - - "the quicker the sooner", for the rust is increasing locally and spreading nationally.

Let Jeff close the editorial -

"Americans are the most thorough people on the earth. They go through
They get results. They slash right and left through encumbering debris - and
get to the goal.

Results count.

When a Dutch boy sees some apples in a tree and wants them, does he
make a ladder of teakwood, put together with hand trimmed dowels of ash, neat
Valspar the affair and then lean it carefully and thoroughly against the trun
of the apple-tree?

I believe he does. That is Dutch thoroughness. And that is why the
Dutch boy often gets no apples!

For about the time he gets around to the final job of climbing thoroughly up in the tree on his thorough ladder, he finds to his dismay and chargin that some unprincipled, untutored, rough-neck American kid, unversed in Dutch thoroughness, has seized the nearest club and knocked all the apples down! He has filled his pockets and is going down the road yelling that 'methods aren't much - results count!'

The American has learned when to short-cut to results, and when to be thorough. He is as thorough as any other nationality when he sees that thoroughness will bring more results than quick action. But he saves time, cuts corners and cans the frills when they are not necessary.

'American lack of thoroughness, 'Doesn't it beat the Dutch!"

- - - - - - - -

R.G.P.

HOLES IN THE STOCKING

The stocking of a pine stand is

The number of trees per acre.

Holes are made in the stocking

By White Pine Blister Rust.

This disease is spread by means of

Currants and Gooseberries.

You can prevent holes occurring

By destroying these bushes.

You may darn the holes

By planting more pine.

We are in the stocking business

Come in and ask us about it.

Note: W.J. Endersbee wrote the above, adapting it from a Clip Sheet, and used it in front of a store selling shoes and stockings.

NURSERYMEN MAKE GOOD COOPERATORS.

The Washington Office recently received a letter from a Nurseryman in Naperville, Illinois, which states that he intends securing 1000 copies of Miscellaneous Circular 40 to distribute to the landscape architects in the United States, who, he says, "should know all the blister rust control possible".

Edit: This man is an example of good citizenship. He is cooperating fully in the work of blister rust control and makes it his business to secure the interest of others in a problem which means much to the nation.

FARMERS' WEEK EXHIBIT IN ITHACA, N.Y.

The Conservation Commission had a Blister Rust exhibit in cooperation with the College of Forestry at Cornell University, the week of February 8 - Farmers' Week. The exhibit was arranged by Dr. York, Mr. Littlefield and Mr. Stevens. The entire forestry exhibit featured King White Pine, White Pine Blister Rust, White Pine Weevil and their control.

The interest shown in the exhibit was unusually good. Many inquiries were received relative to reforestation and the control of White Pine Blister Rust and White Pine Weevil.

Strange as it may seem, there were farmers at the exhibit who did not know there are State nurseries and that seedling trees can be purchased so cheaply.

A special series of talks on the growth and management of White Pine were given by the staff of the Forestry College for the benefit of the New York Blister Rust Control Agents.

The New York Observer - March 1, 1926.

SPECIAL PROGRAM FOR BLISTER RUST CONTROL AGENTS

Farmers' Week - February 9-11, 1926

Ithaca, N. Y.

Tuesday, February 9th

9:00 A.M.   Bringing Up White Pine (Illustrated)
                S. N. Spring.

10:00 A.M. Measuring the White Pine Crop
                J. Bentley, Jr.

2:00 P.M; A National Agricultural Policy
                R. W. Thatcher, Director of
                Experiment Station.

3:00 P.M. The Wood of a Thousand Uses.
                A. B. Recknagel.

Wednesday, February 10th

10:00 A.M. Hand Planted White Pine (Illustrated)
                J. A. Cope.

12:00 M.   Taxation Problems of Interest to Farmers
                M. S. Kendrick

2:00 P.M. A New York State Program for Agriculture
                Berne A. Pyrke

3:00 P.M. Demonstration in Filing Timber and Circular Saws.
                L. M. Roehl.

4:00 P.M. White Pine, Its Growth and Management in New York State.
                C. M. Guise.

Thursday, February 11th.

9:00 A.M. What White Pine Has Meant to New York State
                R. S. Hosmer.
10:00 A.M. Protecting the White Pine Crop
                Dr. H. H. York
11:00 A.M. The Life History of White Pine (Illustrated)
                J. H. Spaeth.
12:00 M.   Round Table Conference on Extension Methods.
                Dr. E. C. Ladd; C. A. Taylor

2:00 P.M. Taxation Problems. E. R. A. Seligman, (Columbia Univ.)

3:30 P.M. Round Table Discussion on Forestry Problems.
                Faculty of Forestry Department.

WORKING WITH FUTURE PINE-OWNERS.

Forestry is the major project of the Boys' Clubs in Carroll County. This fact makes it possible for me to meet and talk to them about forestry and blister rust. When conditions are suitable I plan to take them out and show them wild currant and gooseberry bushes and infected pine. Some of the older club members are already familiar with Ribes and blister rust.

When some of the boys are thinking of planting white pine I try to impress upon them the necessity of making sure that there are no Ribes on or near the land they are to plant. In the majority of cases they are keenly interested.

I have been able to reach the parents through the boys in several cases with paying results. Groups of interested boys are good material for future blister rust supporters.

About 100,000 trees were planted in Carroll County in 1925. Practically all of them were white pine. There will probably be a greater number planted this year.

Stephen H Boomer,
Carroll County, N.H.

PRESIDENT PROCLAIMS AMERICAN FOREST WEEK

President Coolidge has designated April 18-24, inclusive, as the 1926 American Forest Week, according to an official proclamation. He gave full weight to the evils resulting from impoverished and idle forest land, but declared that a change is taking place in the attitude of landowners toward the country's forests.

Secretary of Agriculture Jardine, in making public the forestry proclamation, emphasized the importance of tree crops to the farmer and small landowner, declaring that one-third of all forest land in the United States is in small woodlots. He also pointed out that the observance of American Forest Week has reached nation-wide proportions and that the annual campaign is directed by the American Forest Week, a federation of nearly 100 organizations with Hon. Frank O. Lowden, of Illinois as chairman. The Department of Agriculture is represented on this committee by the Forest Service, the Bureau of Plant Industry, and the Biological Survey.

A new feature of this year's observance is the formation of forest week committees in each State and Alaska in order that local forestry problems can be studied and met by States, counties, and municipalities. Canada has issued a proclamation calling for the observance of a Forest Week this spring at the same time it is observed in the United States.

Clip Sheet from U.S. Department of Agriculture, No. 403.

Note: Our men are now busy with plans to participate in this meeting and we expect to derive much good from it.

STATISTICS ON PRODUCTION OF

SUGAR PINE LUMBER, LATH AND SHINGLES

AS REPORTED BY MILLS.

(In M. feet board measure)

Year	Calif. and Nevada	Oregon	Total both states.
1920	141,134	4,772	145,906
1921	132,332	1,234	133,566
1922	183,291	10,776	194,067
1923	207,878	20,678	228,556

This data has been compiled from bulletins of the U.S. Forest Service and the Bureau of the Census.

Roy G. Pierce.

- - - - -

LONG-BELL LUMBER COMPANY TO PLANT WHITE PINE

AND OTHER TREES IN WASHINGTON.

Lumber Company Has Nursery.

Longview, Wash., Dec. 10 - Experimental planting and development of a Nursery owned by the Long-Bell Lumber Company and situated near Ryderwood, seat of logging operations 30 miles north of this city, was begun recently and is the first step in the reforestation program which the company has outlined for the winter of 1925-26. California redwoods, white pine and Port Orford cedars will be experimented with, and in addition the native fir, cedar and hemlock will be planted.

From American Nurseryman, Jan. 1926. p. 13.

ACTUAL VS. "PAPER" WHITE PINE REFORESTATION.

Missoula, Mont. - - R.H.Weidman, director of the Northern Rocky Mountain Forest Experiment Station, gives an interesting instance of the deceptive nature of reforestation statistics when uncorroborated by eye-witness testimony.

Tallies made last summer on land in the Coeur d'Alene National Forest in northern Idaho which was cut over 16 years ago recorded the number of seedlings on adjacent north and south slopes. On the south, or ordinarily less favorable slope, 1,490 seedlings to the acre were counted. On paper this appears a very good growth, promising a creditable stand of young timber.

The north slope had 141,000 seedlings to the acre, of which 122,600 - - an overwhelming proportion - - were hemlock, ranked almost as a "forest weed" in this locality. Only 8,200 were white pine. The "paper estimate" would be that this condition is a hopeless one.

The facts, Mr. Weidman asserts, are just the contrary. Seedlings on the south slope, though sufficient in number, occupy only two-thirds of an area over-run by a dense growth of brush. They are stunted and their age indicates that seeding-in has practically ceased. On the north slope opposite, however, the white pine is sturdy and well-spaced, has attained 5 and 6 feet in height, is continuing to seed-in, and with its natural ability to out-grow hemlock will soon overtop the multitude of less desirable trees and eventually form a very good crop of white pine timber.

THERE ARE ONLY A FEW OF US LEFT.

Truth is said to be stronger than fiction; at least, it is often more surprising. Such was the case last Fall, when, without preamble or warning, and in such quick succession as to fairly bewilder us, came the announcements that Commissioner John M. Corliss and Blister Rust Control Agents Stephen H. Boomer and Denis B. Keane had definitely decided to abandon the carefree existence of the bachelor, to embark upon the tempestuous sea of matrimony.

Accordingly, on October 28th, Miss Agnes K. Nawn of Concord became Mrs. Corliss; on November 16th, Miss Jean Taylor of West Newton, Massachusetts, became Mrs. Boomer and on November 23rd, Miss Gertrude Sullivan of Manchester became Mrs. Keane. The members of the Forestry Department and the Blister Rust organization tender their most sincere congratulations.

From NewsLetter - New Hampshire Forestry Dept. for Feb. 1926.

- - - - - - -

A 29 year old planting contains 22,240 ft. round-edge lumber.

Myron R. Watson, extension forester, writes of a 29-year-old stand of white pine in East New Portland, Somerset County, Maine, which contains 22,240 board feet of round-edge lumber to the acre. Wild stock from neighboring woodlands were planted at intervals of 6 feet in rows 10 feet apart, on a lot 67 by 284 feet, and there are now 556 trees in the lot. Part of the stand has been pruned to a height of 12 or 14 feet, the remainder is untouched.

One old lumberman on seeing this plantation exclaimed, "I never believed before that timber planting was worth while".

The Forest Worker - January 1926. p. 34.
Forest Service, U.S. Dept. of Agric. Washington, D.C.

KANSAS HAS ESTABLISHED NEW BLISTER RUST QUARANTINE AFFECTING

SHIPMENTS FROM OREGON

Quarantine Notice No. 2.
(Supplementing and Modifying Quarantine Notice No. 1.)
White Pine Blister Rust.

The existence of the dangerous imported disease of white pine trees known as the White Pine Blister Rust (Peridermium strobi Kleb.) in several of our eastern states has been confirmed by federal authorities, who are now advising a protective quarantine. In addition to the known infected areas other localities are suspected of harboring the disease.

Believing that the five-leaf pines, currant and gooseberry plants of Kansas would be endangered by the shipment of all five-leaf pines, currant and gooseberry plants, and all other species and varieties of the genera Ribes and Grossularia known to be carriers of this dangerous disease, into the state from all the states east of an including the states of Minnesota, Iowa, Missouri, Arkansas, Louisiana, and the counties of Tillamook, Clatsop, Columbia, Washington, Yamhill, Polk and Lincoln in the state of Oregon, an absolute quarantine is hereby established, prohibiting the shipment into this state from the above-described territory of all five-leaf pines, currant and gooseberry plants, and all other species and varieties of the genera Ribes and Grossularia known to be carriers of this dangerous disease.

Hereafter, and until further notice, by virtue of chapter 108, article 36, General Statutes of 1915, shipment into Kansas from above sources of the species of pines, currant and gooseberry plants, and their varieties hereinbefore named, is prohibited.

Issued by the Kansas State Entomological Commission, Topeka, September 26, 1917. Amended January 29, 1926.

- - - - - - -

Miss M.A. Thompson, in charge of quarantine work in the Washington Office reports that shipments are quite heavy at this time of the year; Mr. L.W. Hodgkins having inspected 771 shipments in one day. Several violations have recently been reported.

O F F I C E   C O M M E N T S

INSTRUCTIONS CONCERNING SHIPMENT OF INFECTED
BLISTER RUST SPECIMENS

February 9, 1926.

MEMORANDUM FOR EMPLOYEES

Gentlemen:

The sending of blister rust material involves a certain element of danger of spreading the disease into uninfected localities unless it is properly treated and prepared for shipment. In order to avoid this danger by establishing uniformity of practice among our employees and fixing responsibility for the treatment and shipment of such material, the following procedure has been agreed upon by this office and the Office of Forest Pathology:

"When a request is received for blister rust material to be used for teaching or as a museum or demonstration specimen in an uninfected locality, acknowledge the letter, collect the desired material, and forward the letter with the material to Dr. Haven Metcalf, Office of Forest Pathology, Bureau of Plant Industry, Washington, D.C. The Office of Forest Pathology will then assume responsibility for killing the material and seeing that it is forwarded to the party requesting it in such condition that there will be no possibility of spreading the disease. When microscopic or other special preparations are called for, the request should be directly referred to Dr. Metcalf, who will undertake to see that such requests are complied with when practicable."

Employees of this Office are requested to follow the above instructions when they receive inquiries for such blister rust material.

Truly yours,

S. B. Detwiler

Senior Pathologist in Charge.

P E R S O N A L S

Mr. Ralph A. Sheals was appointed Field Assistant, effective March 10. He will be engaged on quarantine inspection work.

Mr. Hubert G. Bartow and Philip S. Simcoe were appointed Agents, effective March 1. Bartow at Tacoma, and Simcoe at Spokane, Washington.

The Washington Office has been having its turn with the grippe and other nuisances, this past month. Nearly half of the Office being sick at one time or another.

Mr. Warren V. Benedict's headquarters have been changed from Portland, Oregon to Spokane, Washington - effective March 1.

Mr. Wm. G. Guernsey was appointed Agent, Spokane, Wash. effective March 1.

Mr. Ernest E. Hubert was appointed collaborator at Moscow, Idaho, effective February 15.

Agent E.M. Brockway of Massachusetts was sick with pneumonia during the latter part of February and early March. We believe he is well now (March 15) for a good letter has been received from him dated March 10.

Mr. Amihud Grasousky was appointed Agent, Berkeley, Calif., March 1.

Mr. H. P. Avery, Head Clerk in the Washington Office, will leave for the Midwest about March 20, to engage in quarantine inspection work.

Mr. Wm. C. Thompson was appointed collaborator, effective March 9. His headquarters are at St. Paul, Minnesota.

4

BLISTER RUST NEWS

APRIL 1926.

Volume X *Number 4.*

U.S. DEPARTMENT of AGRICULTURE
Office of Blister Rust Control.

C O N T E N T S - V O L. 10, No. 4   Page

Agents Work
  Agents Have you Picked Your Foremen Yet? 96
  Bits of News From Southern Grafton County, New Hampshire 95
Blister Rust Situation
  Mr. Detwiler Reports on his western Trip 107
Cooperation
  New Hampshire Towns Vote Funds for Cooperation in Blister Rust Control 93
  Rockingham County, New Hampshire, Backs up Blister Rust Control Program 103
  The Society for Protection of New Hampshire Forests is Boosting
    Our Local Control Program 108
Education
  Agent Tarbox Sends in First Suggestions for New Scenario 117
  Cheshire County Paper Furnishes Good Publicity 103
  Colored Blister Rust Illustration Proves Useful in Colleges 121
  Cullen Believes in Putting Before the Public the Facts Concerning
    Blister Rust 94
  Office of Blister Rust Control Arranges an Exhibit for the Sesqui-
    centennial 93
  Press Notice for " The Pines" 108
  Why Are Some Exhibits More Successful Than Others 101
  Why Not Pickle Your Own - specimens? 112
Forestry
  Forestry Economics Should Provide Solution for Situation at Wells,Me. 115
  Forest Taxation Law Incentive to Farmers 109
  King White Pine 118
  Property of Maine Town Decreased as Timber Lots Were Cleared 113
  State's Demand for Pine Seedlings for Reforestation Increasing 104
  The Quest of the Blight-Resistant Chestnut 119
  Timber Stripping or Skinning Must Cease if Maine's Rural Prosperity
    is Retained 116
  What To Do - Suggestions for a Solution of the Problem at Wells . . . 117
  White Pine Has Interesting Historical Background 105
Office Comments 122
Personals 123
Poem - It's All in the State of Mind 92
Publications 128
Quarantine Notes. 124,127
  State Plant Quarantines Declared Illegal in Opinion of Supreme Court . 125
Ribes 128
Technical Study
  Description of Experimental Work Underway at North Hudson, N.Y. . . . 97
Western Work 107
  Report of Work of the Western Office for February 1926 106
  Western Blister Rust Conference Holds Special Meeting 110
State and Provincial News
  British Columbia 107   New Hampshire 93,94,95,96,102,103,104
  California 106   New York 97-100,118
  Idaho 106   Oregon 106
  Mass. 109   Washington 107,125
  Maine 113-117   West Virginia 127
  Mich. 104   Wisconsin 121
  Montana 106   Wyoming 127

UNITED STATES DEPARTMENT OF AGRICULTURE
BUREAU OF PLANT INDUSTRY
WASHINGTON, D.C.

T H E   B L I S T E R   R U S T   N E W S.

Issued by the Office of Blister Rust Control
and the Cooperating States.

VOL. 10, NO. 4.   NEW HAMPSHIRE NUMBER   APRIL 1926.

IT'S ALL IN THE STATE OF MIND

If you think you are beaten, you are;
If you think that you dare not, you don't;
If you think you'd like to win, but you think you can't
It's almost a "cinch" you won't.
If you think you'll lose, you've lost;
For out in the world you find
Success begins with a fellow's will.
It's all in the state of mind.

Full many a race is lost
Ere even a step is run,
And many a coward fails
Ere even his work's begun.
Think big, and your deeds will grow.
Think small, and you'll fall behind.
Think that you can, and you will;
It's all in the state of mind.

If you think you're outclassed, you are;
You've got to think high to rise;
You've got to be sure of yourself before
You can ever win a prize.
Life's battles don't always go
To the stronger or faster man;
But soon or late the man who wins
Is the fellow who thinks he can.

        Lefax Magazine.

Golly, wish I could write like that! Those lines are full of truth.

Read 'em again, Agent, and see if you don't get a new dose of inspiration.

          Ribee Bill

NEW HAMPSHIRE TOWNS VOTE FUNDS FOR COOPERATION

IN BLISTER RUST CONTROL.

With the exception of four towns who are holding postponed annual town
meetings and two cities who will take action before long, the returns are
practically complete for the results of town meetings. Eighty towns and
cities have appropriated $32,375. From the four towns and two cities in
question it is reasonable to expect $2,200. If expectations materialize we
shall have $34,575 as the total appropriation from eighty-four towns and cities.
This compares with $32,725 from seventy-eight towns and cities in 1925. As has
always been the case, some of our towns in Ribes eradication, which might have
been completed this year, failed to appropriate, while on the other hand we
have six towns which have never before made any appropriations and several
which have not appropriated funds since 1918.

Several large corporations have also added to the town appropriations,
namely; the Parker Young Company in Lisbon, and the International Paper Company
in Marlow.

L. E. Newman, N.H.

- - - - - - - - - - - -

OFFICE OF BLISTER RUST CONTROL ARRANGES AN EXHIBIT FOR

SESQUICENTENNIAL EXPOSITION.

The Office of Blister Rust Control has been chosen as one of the
offices in the Bureau of Plant Industry, to arrange an exhibit to represent
the Department of Agriculture at the Sesquicentennial exposition in Philadelphia.
This exhibit features the most important phases of blister rust and its control,
in both the Eastern and Western states.

CULLEN BELIEVES IN PUTTING BEFORE THE PUBLIC THE

FACTS CONCERNING BLISTER RUST.

The Following One-page Mimeographed Sheet Was Distributed to the Farm Bureau Mailing List In Strafford
and Belknap Counties, New Hampshire.

A GREAT STATE ASSET IN DANGER!

White pine has paid from 1/3 to 1/2 of the total tax revenue in rural
New Hampshire towns. It has helped educate children, paid off mortgages,
kept thousands of people employed and saved the abandonment of many farms.
Commercially it is the best species of second growth timber in our state, producing a higher yield in a shorter time than any other tree. Pine will grow
on a variety of soils, has a ready market and is comparatively easy to log and
transport.

HEAVY BLISTER RUST INFECTIONS ON UNCONTROLLED AREAS

Desirous of obtaining definite knowledge as to the amount of damage
being caused to white pine from Blister Rust on land not cleared of currant
and gooseberry bushes, the State Forestry Department has made detailed examinations of certain pine lots where currant and gooseberry bushes were known
to be present. On these areas every tree was counted and examined for infection. The examination revealed that from 21% to 96% of the trees were
either dead or dying from blister rust.

During the month of September 1925, a strip line 2 1/3 miles long and
16 feet wide was made in Landaff, N.H. The purpose of this strip line was to
determine the percentage of pine trees infected as it was known that currant
and gooseberry bushes were plentiful. It was found that 43% of the entire
number of pine trees were infected with blister rust.

BLISTER RUST CONTROL PROVEN SUCCESSFUL

The State Forestry Department does not maintain that it is possible to eradicate all of the currant and gooseberry bushes, but it does maintain that 95% or more are removed by the State crews and the remainder are not sufficient to cause serious commercial damage.

The condition of lots worked 5 to 8 years ago is the best test of control. Very few new infections have been found on land cleared of currant and gooseberry bushes 5 to 8 years ago. One lot on which every large tree was infected has seeded in to young pine since the currant and gooseberry bushes were removed 7 years ago. EVERY YOUNG PINE IS FREE FROM RUST, proving that the removal of the currant and gooseberry bushes stopped the spread of the disease.

YOUR MONEY IS SPENT TO ADVANTAGE

The money appropriated by a town for blister rust control is used entirely for this purpose. There is no supervision cost as this item is taken care of by the State and Government. The men employed receive on an average of $3.50 per day out of which they must pay board and room. All records are on file at the State Forestry Department, Concord, N.H. and open to inspection. For further information regarding this matter address Blister Rust Control Agent, Snow Block, Rochester, N. H.

- - - - - - - - - - - -

BITS OF NEWS FROM SOUTHERN GRAFTON COUNTY, N.H.

Agent George F. Richardson sends in the following news items of interest:

"I don't think that I have written about the fine showing that the slides made this winter at the meetings. They showed things up fine, and I worked up a lecture to go along with them. If there was another speaker, he would talk. We would then wind up the meeting by showing 'The Pines' and have a general discussion of blister rust and woodlot problems.

While I have not fully made plans for the meetings this summer, I am thinking of showing slides at some of the meetings, and holding the meetings while the crews are at work in the towns. I will also try to draw on a number of the surrounding towns for each meeting.

Another idea that I have, if it works out, is to hold meetings in cooperation with the American Legion, and some of the other clubs.

- - - - - - -

Kane and I came out very well, we think, at the town meetings. We each got six towns and his total was $2400 from towns, while mine was $3400. Both of us expect to sign up some private work so will have enough to keep us going.

- - - - - - -

A bit of good news in one way, but bad in another, is that Agent Curtis is now working for the Pillsbury Flour Mills Company, at Syracuse, as Advertising Manager, at a good salary, so I cannot expect him back this summer."

- - - - - - -

Geo. F. Richardson.

AGENT, HAVE YOU PICKED OUT YOUR FOREMEN YET?

If not, This Form Letter May Assist You.

United States Department of Agriculture
Bureau of Plant Industry
in cooperation with
New Hampshire Forestry Department.

Blister Rust Control   Exeter, N. H.

Mr. John Doe
Blanktown, N. H.

My dear Doe:

This is simply to call your attention to the fact that the Blister Rust field season is close at hand.

Are you planning on coming back this season; if so, what date can you report?

Please advise me immediately as I am making my plans now and want to provide for as many of the old men as care to return.

Yours very truly,

(Signed) K. E. Barraclough
Blister Rust Agent.
Rockingham County.

DESCRIPTION OF EXPERIMENTAL WORK UNDERWAY

AT NORTH HUDSON, N.Y.

During the past summer we have been basicly engaged in gathering field
data of Ribes, of control work, and of pine infection, at North Hudson, N.Y.,
on the Experimental Control Area. Although much data has been accumulated
along various phases of the experiment underway on the area since its establishment in 1921, summarization has been necessarily held up pending the
taking of re-examination data after a lapse of time sufficient to permit the
making of comparisons and the drawing of conclusions as to the natural reaction of pine and Ribes to control work. The 1925 data are expected to
produce some results for publication this winter, but as the field season has
just closed, no summary work has been carried to completion. Therefore I have
no results to offer to you, but will touch briefly upon the lines under investigation on this area.

The Experimental Control Area is a tract of land set aside by the New
York Conservation Commission for the carrying on of cooperative experiments in
control work. It is located in the Schroon River valley in the town of North
Hudson, Essex County, N.Y., and comprises some 1771 acres. The elevation of
the tract varies from about 950 to 1606 feet above sea level. The bulk of
the area is under forest cover, but only partly of pine type. White pine
occurs in rather definite groups aggregating about one-third of the total
acreage; birch, aspen, other hardwoods predominating over the rest of the area.

The tract is near the optimum center of the range of Ribes rotundifolium;
other species in order of distribution are: Ribes glandulosum. R. cynosbati,
R. triste, and R. vulgare,

All land in pine needing protection was examined for Ribes, chiefly
by the crew method. In 1921, the first year, 145 acres were eradicated by

crew; in 1922, 290 acres; and 1923, 135 acres. Added to this total of 570 acres eradicated by crew, are about 100 acres covered by scout or by one or two man method, giving a total area eradicated of 670 acres.

In every case, eradications were followed by a data crew, by whom each bush pulled was examined and the following data was recorded: Height, live stem and percent of leaves infected.

Previous to eradication, study plots varying in size from .9 to 1.2 acres were laid out in the blocks to be eradicated. Seven plots totaling 7.8 acres were laid out and studied in 1921, seven more plots totaling 7.8 acres in 1922, and one of 1.2 acres in 1923. Two plots, total area one acre, were studied in 1921 but not eradicated, being located in an area reserved for the study of the rust under undisturbed conditions. Pines on all these plots have been examined for infection, and each tree tagged and plotted on a map to permit connecting up of future data. Detailed Ribes data were likewise secured before eradication, and the bushes numbered and plotted on large scale maps. This past summer, all survivors were staked, each stake bearing numbered aluminum tags designating a particular bush, for positive identification of individuals in the future.

Studies falling into four classes are underway at North Hudson:

1. Eradication of Ribes.
   (a) Study of factors determining time (cost) per acre.
   (b) Efficiency of eradication.
   (c) Decrease of cost of eradication through use of picked men and methods (comparative crew eradication experiment and detailed analysis of one year's eradication work are completed).
2. Ribes ecology and susceptibility.
   (a) General relation of number per acre, and size (height and live stem) to natural factors such as type.

(b) Ribes infection and susceptibility.

(c) Ribes growth and comeback after eradication.

(d) Natural growth and replacement of Ribes under blister
rust conditions where no eradication has been done.

3. Effectiveness of eradication.

(a) Effectiveness of eradication and amount of Ribes
safe to leave.

(b) Minimum width of protective strip and factors
influencing same.

(c) Comparison with uneradicated area for infection
since eradication.

4. Damage by blister rust.

Many possibilities for studies, the basis having been
established when original pine data was taken and tree tagged. Some are:-

(a) Relation of number and size of Ribes to amount of
infection resulting.

(b) Rate of killing of pine by blister rust.

(c) Rate of canker growth, percent of recovery, etc. etc.

I will not go into the details of these experiments. The list includes possibilities as well as studies actually being made, and some may not
materialize while others may be added. Suffice to say that there is still a
great deal of work to be done on the studies undertaken, the tendency will be
to reduce rather than add to this list.

Relative to the study of Ribes growth and comeback after eradication,
we have fairly reliable original (before eradication) measurements on over
5000 bushes, over 1000 of which are still under observation. Many of the
original measurements were made in 1921, the rest in 1922 and 1923. In
1923 after completion of all eradication, all the survivors found were

again measured, and this year the same process was repeated. The data for the three examinations have been transferred to tabulating machine cards by use of which we hope to shorten materially the task of summary and analysis during the winter at Washington.

It is hoped that this data will throw some light on the problem of "when and where do we re-eradicate", but they cannot be expected to answer the question for all types, all conditions and all states. The number of plots on which the results will be, based, is limited and the plots all located in pine types, which, although of first importance, are not the only ones to be considered in eradication.

A.E. Fivaz, Agent.

Discussion

Spaulding: I would like to ask what basis is being used to figure damage?
Fivaz: No damage studies have as yet been carried beyond the point of securing basic information on infection and of tagging the trees for future work. No basis for damage computations has been developed.

Note: The above paper by Mr. Fivaz was delivered at the Eleventh Annual Blister Rust Conference at Springfield, Massachusetts, on December 9 and 10, 1925. It has been presented in the Blister Rust News because of the requests for information concerning the work being carried on at North Hudson.

WHY ARE SOME EXHIBITS MORE SUCCESSFUL THAN OTHERS?

There may be many reasons why some exhibits are more successful than others, but from observations, I am convinced the procedure of the man in charge is the important thing rather than the exhibit itself. I have seen some excellent exhibits which failed to secure results. On the other hand, I think of a rather mediocre exhibit which produced numerous contacts and many cooperators. The exhibit, in this case, consisted merely of some freshly cut Ribes and infected pine placed in the truck body of a Ford car parked in front of an exhibit hall. In addition to the specimens, several signs and a panel were displayed on the truck.

The day I saw the exhibit, it was raining. Yet people stopped to inspect the exhibit. Why? Because the Agent in charge saw to it that they did. By offering a circular with a friendly word, he attracted attention, and in most instances, the prospect stopped and glanced at the truck. Then some such remark as this — "If you're an owner of pine or currants, you should be interested in blister rust", usually brought the person over to the car. In most cases, it only took a few moments to get the prospect's name and a request that the Agent examine his pine lot. Other people passing heard the Agent talking and came over to the car without special solicitation. The Agent's enthusiasm and sincerity produced the desired results, the exhibit only helped. This is not an argument for less carefully arranged exhibits, but rather a suggestion that we put more of ourselves into the exhibit.

E.C. Filler

THE SOCIETY FOR PROTECTION OF NEW HAMPSHIRE FORESTS -

IS BOOSTING OUR CONTROL PROGRAM.

A recent 3-page printed circular letter was issued in February 1926, by the Society of New Hampshire Forests, addressed to the Selectmen in towns in New Hampshire, and to members of the Society. Particular attention was called by the President, Mr. Allen Hollis and the Secretary, Mr. Philip W. Ayres to two main lines of action which were to be brought up at the town meetings, March 9. That part of the letter relative to blister rust control is as follows:

"The White Pine Blister Rust is a very dangerous disease that spreads from currant and gooseberry bushes to White Pine trees, and kills the trees. Widely prevalent throughout New Hampshire, it will destroy all Pine trees, young and old, conservatively estimated at a value of fifty million dollars. Currant and gooseberry bushes, both wild and domestic, must be eliminated. The cost per acre is very small, from ten to twenty cents.

Enclosed you will find a list of towns in New Hampshire that made appropriations for control of this disease in 1925; also a list of towns in which the entire area has been scouted for the elimination of currant and gooseberry bushes.

If your town has not been completely scouted, will you urge the citizens to make appropriation at Town Meeting? The State adds 25 per cent to every town appropriation for Blister Rust control."

The list of towns appropriating funds for 1925 is so long, (78 in all) that it has been omitted. A total of the towns appropriating for last year amounts to $32,600. An interesting list and comment is given concerning the

TOWNS IN WHICH SCOUTING FOR THE ELIMINATION OF CURRANT AND GOOSE-
BERRY BUSHES HAS BEEN COMPLETED

Bartlett	Hampton	Merrimack	Plaistow
Bow	Hebron	Milford	Portsmouth
Derry	Hollis	Milton	Randolph
Durham	Jaffrey	Nashua	Richmond
Franklin	Keene	Nelson	Rollinsford
Fremont	Litchfield	Newfields	Stratham
Greenville	Madbury	Newmarket	Somersworth
Hamstead	Manchester	Peterborough	Tilton
			Wilton

Note!! If you think of buying land for a pine plantation, these towns have shown great energy in eliminating the Blister Rust disease.

ROCKINGHAM COUNTY, NEW HAMPSHIRE, BACKS UP BLISTER

RUST CONTROL BY TOWN APPROPRIATIONS.

Twenty-two Towns in the County Have Signified Their Intentions of Cooperating in the Protection of White Pine from Blister Rust, During 1926.

The amounts varied from $100 to $400. In only one town, Auburn, was there an appropriation left over from 1925 and the amount of $100 will be used this year. All others made appropriations this spring. The following is a list of towns that have voted money for the control work:

Town	Amount	Town	Amount
Atkinson	$100	Newington	$200
Auburn	100	Newmarket	400
Chester	400	Newton	400
Deerfield	400	N. Hampton	400
Epping	400	Northwood	400
Exeter	400	Nottingham	400
Greenland	400	Raymond	400
Hampton	400	Rye	400
Hampton Falls	400	Sandown	400
Londonderry	400	S. Hampton	200
Newfields	100	Stratham	400

Nine towns in the county have completed eradication work the first time over. However, four of the nine appear in the above list; Hampton, Stratham, Newmarket, Newfields as doing reeradication work. All towns in the county have carried on blister rust eradication at one time or another since 1917 except the towns of East Kingston and Danville. Some private work, however, has been carried on in Danville.

K.E. Barraclough

CHESHIRE COUNTY (NEW HAMPSHIRE) PAPER

FURNISHES GOOD PUBLICITY.

Agent F.J. Baker, of Cheshire County, has recently forwarded the Office a full page ad on the blister rust and its control. The article is headed, "Save the Forest and You Save Your Town".

An open letter from the State Forester, Mr. John H. Foster, is addressed
to the town of Fitzwilliam. Particular attention is called to the new forest
classification law of New Hampshire and how it helps the woodland owner. A
main feature of the page, occupying a central position, is a topographic map
of the town of Fitzwilliam showing by crosshatching the area where blister
rust eradication work has been carried on, and indicating where badly infected
pine areas are located.

The page in the Monadnock Breeze was donated by a pine owner who is one
of the project leaders in forestry in Cheshire County. This is true patriotism.

It has been suggested that where other agents are in a position to secure
publicity through the local or county paper, that it might pay them to borrow
a copy of the Monadnock Breeze, for March 5, 1926, from Mr. F.J.Baker, %
County Farm Bureau, Keene, New Hampshire, or from the Washington Office.

- - - - - -

NOTES FROM MICHIGAN.

State's Demand for Pine Seedlings for
Reforestation Increasing.

Those numbers of the "Blister Rust News" came as a very welcome surprise and gave me the opportunity of catching up on the Rust situation and
the enjoyment of other topics of special interest.

I had the impression that I could contribute to that "Largest pine"
hunt by producing photos of enormous pines growing north of Gogebic Lake,
Gogebic County, Michigan, but a day's cruise through that territory last
November failed to bring forth the desired results. Dr. Darlington measured
one in this district that was about 5 feet (diameter breast height) and I had
previously seen one I judged to be six feet, but was probably mistaken.

Present indications point to some busy years for Michigan forestry. The
demand for pine seedlings has jumped way ahead of nursery production and is a
welcome change from the inactivity caused by the blister rust scare. Our new
nursery in the Upper Peninsula, and the new Forest taxation law (I must look
into it more closely) should stimulate reforestation on a portion of our
twelve million idle acres.

F.J. Gibbs
Agent in Michigan during 1925.

WHITE PINE HAS INTERESTING
HISTORICAL BACKGROUND.

Josselyn gives us to understand that the wood of the white pine is that
mentioned in the Scriptures as gopher wood, out of which Noah built the ark.
Certainly, if the white pine of Josselyn's day was abundant in the neighborhood
of Ararat in Noah's time he could have done no better. The wood is light, soft,
close and straight grained. You may search the world for one more easily worked or more generally satisfactory. Indeed, the last half century has seen the
good white pine of the world pretty nearly used up, certainly all the best of
it, for wood-working purposes. Fifty years ago it was the cheapest New England
wood, today it is the highest priced; and the old-time clear pine, free from
knots and sapwood, is almost impossible to obtain at any price. In 1832 white
pines were not rare in Maine 6' feet in diameter and 240 feet high. In 1736,
near the Merrimac River, above Dunstable in New Hampshire, a pine was cut,
straight and sound and having a diameter at the butt of 7 feet 8 inches. Could
a man have a few of these on his farm anywhere in New England today they would
be worth more than any other crop the centuries could have raised for him.

Winthrop Packard.

REPORT OF WORK
Western Branch, Office of Blister Rust Control
February 1, to February 28, 1926.

* * * * *

1. Work of State Leaders.

Montana: Mr. Johnson reports that he has finished the compilation of all available white pine data for Lincoln County. This information has been taken in tabular form and has also been mapped by Mr. Johnson.

Oregon: Mr. Goodding has also spent some time in discussing matters pertaining to the new Oregon nursery inspection and scouting work with the Oregon State officials. He and Mr. Melis also made a trip to Mapleton, Oregon, to investigate a reported outlying stand of sugar pine. Mr. Melis visited three National Forest headquarters and secured all available data on sugar pine distribution.

California: Aside from the general office work, Mr. Root made two field trips during the month. One of these was into Alameda, Santa Clara, Santa Cruz, and Monterey counties. Interviews were had with the Horticultural Commissioners or their deputies in each county regarding the general distribution of black currant plantings and the possible possession of blister rust hosts, by the nurseries. A number of the nurseries were personally visited. An owner of a planting of about 1500 black currants in Santa Cruz County was interviewed, resulting in the assurance that these bushes would be removed this spring. This is probably the largest planting along the coast.

Several days were spent in black currant work in Sutter County. No plantings were found.

2. Work at Spokane Office.

Four general types of work have been in progress at the Spokane office during the month of February:

1. Further work on the preparation of type, age-class, and ownership maps of the white pine area of northern Idaho.

2. Study and analysis of reconnaissance data to determine the relationship of the Ribes and timber conditions.

3. First steps in development of plans for the coming field season by the Ribes eradication and reconnaissance leaders. This includes the assignment of temporary personnel, interviewing applicants for summer work and general development of the season's plans.

4. Study of the ratio of leaf area to live stem of Ribes in northern Idaho. A scale has been developed for measuring leaves of Ribes lacustre and is accurate to within 3 percent. This scale has been checked for 1,000 leaves of Ribes lacustre. Work is now underway to develop similar scales for Ribes viscosissimum and Grossularia inermis and at the same time leaves of Ribes lacustre are being measured as rapidly as possible. To date approximately 5,000 leaves of Ribes lacustre have been measured.

Stephen N. Wyckoff, Pathologist.

HISTORY

This is history
> This white pine was born in 1913 ′ ′ ′
> It grew in a pine lot in Egremont ′ ′ ′
> It was attacked by Blister Rust in 1919 ′
> It was killed by Blister Rust in 1925 ′
> It is one of 91 diseased pines in every
> 100 on that lot.

WE WILL BE GLAD TO SHOW
YOU THAT LOT

IS THIS HISTORY REPEATING ITSELF
ON YOUR LOT?

Signs 11"x14" made up in Washington for Mr. W.J.
Endersbee. Others may be made up for you upon request

DEAD *!*

This tree might have produced 500 board feet of
white pine lumber
It would then have been worth on the stump
five dollars of any mans money.
It might have been protected from Blister Rust
at a cost of less than one cent.

BUT THE CENT WAS NOT INVESTED

This tree was killed by Blister Rust before reach-
ing commercial size.
The owner saved the cent but lost five dollars.
He paid taxes on the land on which it grew.
These too he lost when this tree died.

PROTECTION PAYS *!*

MR. DETWILER REPORTS ON HIS WESTERN TRIP.

Mr. S.B. Detwiler has returned to Washington after seven weeks in the West. Besides attending the blister rust conference at Portland, Mr. Detwiler, accompanied by Mr. L.N. Goodding, scouted for pine infection in the Hood's Canal country of the Olympic Peninsula. Rust was found well established on pine at a point about 8 miles south of Quilcene, Washington. One specimen when found on March 5th showed a single blister just breaking through the bark. A possible infection point was found on the Duckabush River; this specimen is being determined.

Mr. Detwiler, with Mr. H.N. Putnam scouted between Nelson and Proctor, British Columbia, approximately 30 miles north of the United States border. Mr. Putnam found three pine infection centers; one at Willow Point, where diseased trees were found late last fall, and two centers near Proctor. Mr. Putnam and Mr. Benedict are continuing to scout in British Columbia territory adjacent to Idaho, cutting out and destroying cankers as found. This work is done as a delay measure, and while it has been repeatedly proved impossible to eradicate the disease in this way, it should result in considerable benefit in checking the spread.

A number of cankers showed a full crop of blisters pushed about halfway through the bark at Willow Point, on March 17, and at Proctor, on March 19. The aecia on cankers observed near Vancouver, British Columbia, on March 21 were in a similar condition of advanced development.

The West has had an unusually mild winter. Geraniums in Portland, Oregon, remained out of doors all winter without freezing, and cherry trees were beginning to bloom on the Olympic Peninsula of Washington on March 3rd.

While in British Columbia, Mr. Detwiler met Mr. Caverhill, Chief Forester
of British Columbia, and Mr. St. Clair, District Forester in eastern British
Columbia. He also attended the meetings of the Idaho Forest Protective
Associations in Spokane, Washington, March 8th to 10th. Mr. Detwiler reports
general interest in the West in blister rust control and that the work is
making excellent progress in spite of many handicaps.

- - - - - - -

The Office of Forest Pathology was represented at the Portland Conference
on February 26, by Dr. Metcalf, Dr. E.P. Meinecke, Dr. J.S. Boyce, and Mr.
Lachmund. Dr. Metcalf returned to Washington after the conference, but is again
on his way west to confer with the pathologists in charge of western field
stations relative to the plans for the season's field work.

- - - - - - -

PRESS NOTICE FOR " THE PINES"

Use This in Local Papers Preceding the Showing of the Film.

The campaign for the control of white pine blister rust, a disease that
has made serious inroads on our rapidly diminishing pine forests and threatens
to do much more damage if not checked, is illustrated in a new motion picture,
"The Pines," just produced by the U.S. Department of Agriculture. The film is
designed to show the dangers of blister rust, the application of control
methods, and the desirability of pine as a crop.

The ravages of the disease are shown, both in "close-ups" and in general
views, and, in contrast, plantations and stands of pine that have been guarded
by the methods worked out by the Department and the cooperating State organizations. Other scenes show the eradication of the gooseberry and currant bushes,
that serve as carriers of the disease, by means of "grubbing crews" in the
forest.

"The Pines" tells the story of a young couple who, coming into possession
of some pine land, did not know what to do with it until they were put on the
right track by more experienced neighbors. Their early struggles, their work
among the pines, and their happy emergence from their trouble, gave an
opportunity to impart some information as to how blister rust is fought, and
the setting, among the picturesque pines, adds not a little to the attractiveness of the film as a whole.

FOREST TAXATION LAW INCENTIVE TO FARMERS.

Massachusetts Imports Half of Timber Used
Now and Future Demands Immediate Action.

- - - - - - -

Forestry is something that is being urged more and more year by year
and we see individuals falling in line one after another, but there are still
a large number to be convinced.

There is a tremendous area of land in the United States which has been
cleared for farming but which under present conditions is not of agricultural
value. Three-fifths of our former timber supply is gone. Twenty years ago
New England was self-supporting. Now she imports one-third and Massachusetts
imports one-half. The future holds an appalling outlook if present day methods
continue and 90,000 workers in New England alone will be affected, as wood
working industries employ this number.

If an individual feels that he cannot afford to plant more land to
trees then more scientific management of his already existing woodland will be
greatly to his benefit. Improvement cuttings will be a great benefit to the
pine that are left, cutting out dead and dying trees, inspecting land for wild
currant and gooseberry bushes to prevent spread of white pine blister rust,
piling and burning brush, - - all these things will be money well spent and
will result in a greater income from the land.

Idle land can be planted for about $18 an acre and at the end of 35
years, should produce 20-30 M board feet per acre worth eight to twelve dollars
a thousand. In the meantime, have land classified under new Massachusetts
forest taxation law, and if this isn't an incentive to any farmer to plant idle
land, then there never will be one.

This putting of our forests to work ranks among the major industries of the country. Forestry is really the backbone of agriculture. The United States produces more than half of the world's supply of wood and used 95 per cent of it at home.

* * * * * *

Let's put all our idle acres to work and thus improve all our daily needs and every industry and make this a better world in which to live.

From the Plymouth County Farmer, March 1926.

WESTERN BLISTER RUST CONFERENCE HOLDS
SPECIAL MEETING.

A special meeting of the Western Blister Rust Conference was held at Portland, Oregon, on February 26, 1926, to consider means for meeting the emergency caused by the rapid southward spread of the rust on the Oregon coast. The rust advanced 90 miles in a single leap to cultivated black currants in 1925, and the distance from this infection point to the northern end of main body of sugar pine is only 170 miles. The conference considered the various aspects of the situation and was of the opinion that the western 10-year program should be revised to include more extensive activities looking to the development and application of local control in the sugar pine regions of Oregon and California. The conference also recommended that allied work in investigations of the behavior of the rust in the west, and in eradication of cultivated black currants be speeded up.

The attendance at the conference was mainly from the states of Montana, Idaho, Washington, Oregon and California. The gathering was representative, including state foresters, 9 state plant quarantine officers, forest schools, various forest protective organizations, and lumbermen.

The resolutions passed by the conference are as follows:

R E S O L U T I O N S

ADOPTED BY WESTERN WHITE PINE BLISTER RUST CONFERENCE

PORTLAND, OREGON - FEBRUARY 26, 1926.

I

"Moved that this Conference accepts and approves the report presented (by the Executive Committee of the Conference), setting forth in detail the need of an expanded program for blister rust control in the West and the estimates showing the required items and cost for supplemental work amounting to $73,500 above the original 10-year program estimates for the fiscal year 1927."

II

"Careful study of the white pine blister rust situation in the Pacific Northwest shows conclusively that a serious emergency exists by reason of the spread of the disease southward into Oregon, thereby threatening, in advance of expectations, valuable sugar pine stands of southern Oregon and California.

In view of this it is earnestly believed that the ten-year program must be speeded up to meet this emergency and after due consideration it is the belief of this Conference that an additional sum in the amount of $73,500 is required, over and above the amount estimated for the fiscal year 1927, for this purpose.

We, therefore, respectfully request that this additional sum be made available at the earliest possible moment through an emergency appropriation, or if this is not possible, at this time, that this added sum be included in estimates of the Department of Agriculture for the fiscal year 1928. And we further urge that in the event Congress fails to appropriate $175,000 as called for under our original ten-year program, that especial effort be made to successfully present to Congress need for this increase, effective for the fiscal year 1927.

It is the sense of this Conference that this resolution, together with a detailed statement of the need for additional funds be sent the Secretary of Agriculture and Chief Bureau of Plant Industry for such action as in their judgment seems desirable."

III

"The Conference recognizes the fact that ultimate control of white pine blister rust in the forests of western United States is dependent upon information to be secured on the one hand by the Bureau of Plant Industry as to the proper methods and costs of local control, and, on the other hand by the Foresters as to future yield and value of present stands of reproduction which stand in the path of the disease. It will be necessary for each and every owner of white pines including the Forest Service as the administrator of the National Forests to reach a definite decision on whether or not blister rust local control is to be applied to each and every pine growing unit of land. Each unit of forest land must be judged on its own

merits and values. In order to make this decision it will be necessary that
the owner balance the future value of these reproductive stands against the
cost of local control. It is the belief of this Conference that such information on the future value of reproductive stands is not now available. The
Conference therefore requests that the Forest Service immediately undertake
adequate studies of yield and financial possibilities of present and future
reproductive stands of western white and sugar pines to the end that the effect
of adequate blister rust control on these pine areas be known. In order that
this information may be speedily obtained it is suggested that the Chief
Forester, Forest Service, confer with Chief of the Bureau of Plant Industry as
to ways and means of having Congress appropriate such sums as are required
for as many years as are necessary for the completion of these studies by the
Forest Service."

IV

"Resolved that the Secretary be instructed to transmit the resolutions
of this Conference to the Secretary of Agriculture, Chief of Bureau of Plant
Industry and Head of the Forest Service, with a letter setting forth the
emergency situation and conveying the point of view and belief of the Conference
that delaying the work called for is bound to increase the losses sustained
by the advance of the disease into the regions menaced."

- - - - - - -

WHY NOT PICKLE YOUR OWN - specimens.

A number of requests have been received from Agents, for pickled
specimens of the blister rust showing the disease on white pine in the aecial
stage. Unfortunately the Washington Office has no large collection which can
be forwarded to the field men. It is suggested, for that reason, that each
of the Agents collect specimens in the aecial stage, themselves, and pickle
them; that is, if they plan to use such material.

Mr. E.C. Filler has suggested the formula 10% glycerin, 2% formalin,
and 88% water. The original formula had 5% formalin rather than 2% and it was
noted that the speciamens became discolored; hence the reduction in the percent of formalin used.

It would be quite expensive to provide from one half dozen to one
dozen museum jars to each of the Agents preserving pine specimens of the blister
rust. A good substitute is found, however, in the two-quart jars used for
canning vegetables and fruits. These are relatively inexpensive.

R.G.P.

PROPERTY OF MAINE TOWN DECREASED AS TIMBER LOTS

WERE CLEARED.

Blister Rust Control is Vital to Town's Future Welfare.

"Town appropriations for blister rust control have been harder to get in York County this spring than ever before, as the results have shown, and perhaps there are other agents who find themselves in the same position.

As a specific instance, I cite the town of Wells. The town appropriated money in 1924, and since then has steadily refused to make any appropriation. I think our good fortune in 1924 was due mainly to the presence of our State Leader, Mr. Frost, and to his able speaking while at the town meeting.

Therefore I was greatly interested in the news item which appeared in the Portland Press-Herald this morning regarding the town of Wells. It seems to me that the facts stated in the item hit the nail squarely on the head, and show better than anything else that I have seen, the difficulties which face some of our country towns and show, as well, the difficulties which face a Blister Rust Agent who tries to work in these towns.

WHAT TO DO, IS WELLS PROBLEM

"Wells, March 12. - With a debt that is near the limit and $142,000 just appropriated at the town meeting, the town fathers of Wells are asking how the money is to be raised. It is asserted by good authority that the assessment cannot be over 50 mills, owing to conditions. The farmers have sold their timber lots to the Portable mills so that the assessments have been materially reduced and the thing is continuing so that the valuation is coming down with leaps and bounds. There is no manufacturing in town to be assessed. The hotels are up to full valuation.

The extensive beach property comes in for the largest part of the taxable property. "What shall we do?" is the question being discussed throughout town. Another town meeting to reduce the appropriation is talked and another side wants the State Assessors called in and a new valuation of the town is possible as it is asserted with much authority that there are several pieces of property that are not even taxed and that equalization is almost a thing unknown.

The railroad property has been reduced in taxable value
during the last year, Chick's station and High-pine being
abandoned, as well as the little station at the Elms. Most of
the sawed lumber now in town will be shipped before the
Assessors get together April 1st, or thereby; this is done to
escape the high tax rate.

Farmers are feeling the possibilities and say they do
not know where to get off. Many of the appropriations were
made by very small majorities and the vote in many cases was
made by those paying the smallest taxes. Citizens are anxiously
waiting the next move of those in authority to see how the enigma
will be solved."

Portland Press-Herald - March 13, 1926.

Of special interest is the statement regarding the absence of timber lots
in the town, with the resulting loss of taxes, and the fact that operators try to
haul everything out of town to escape the high tax rate.

Since much timber has been cut in the town, it should follow that there
ought to be large areas of young growth, and such is the case. During the summer of 1924, Mr. Lambert and myself covered 18,000 acres in Wells, and would
oftentimes traverse a solid block of a thousand acres or more in extent consisting entirely of one stripped lot after another. It is clear that the salvation
of this town lies in securing maximum returns from its forest lands.

Now it is a truth that the best insurance possible for future timber sup-
plies in this town (outside of protection from fires and equitable taxation) is
the preventing of Pine Blister Rust. But it takes a wise group of men to look
into the future in that way, and the logical thing for them to do, as they see
it, is to cut expenditures at any cost. When this is done, blister rust appropriations fall by the wayside along with many other worthy projects.

It would seem to me that this problem offers a fertile field for discussion
and exchange of ideas between Blister Rust Agents far and near, through the
columns of the News Letter. To this end, I would like to see the enclosed newspaper item and this letter printed in the News Letter as an opening gun; the
question being - "what to do?"

E.E. Tarbox - Maine.

FOREST ECONOMICS SHOULD PROVIDE

SOLUTION FOR SITUATION AT WELLS, MAINE.

The case of Wells Township, State of Maine, is a striking result of
America's neglect of forest economics. Foresters have made little headway in the
basic problem facing the profession, not because forest economics is a tough nut
to crack, but because few strong hammers have been pounding whole-heartedly at
the subject. Today is a new dawn and the situation of Wells, forerunner of many
other forest towns, urges immediate attention to the problem of forest economics.
Will foresters awaken and tackle the job?

There is some stirring about - the Clark-McNary Act provides for the study
of forest taxation, and that branch is now in the capable hands of Dr. Fairchild
of Yale. The Pack Forestry Prize for 1926 will be given for the best contribution
to progress in forestry, and is especially aimed at economics. Mr. Tarbox brings
this subject to wide attention at an opportune moment; I hope he will capitalize
his opportunity of being on the ground and in touch with the facts. The detailed
case of Wells, well thought out, would make an interesting and worthwhile article
for American Forests and Forest Life. And a study of forest economics is the
next step - - winning the Pack Prize is a long feather in any forester's cap,
aside from $500 in his jeans.

Mr. Tarbox hits the nail squarely when he states that forest protection,
including blister rust control, is an essential step the town must take in recovery. Since the town valuation of Wells is largely forest valuation, which
when depleted takes years to replace, it is evident that no short-sighted policy
can be successfully followed by the town government. I believe that the town
will arrive at this conclusion in considering the question - "What to do". Then
the Blister Rust Control Agent, supported by definite and accurate information
on Ribes, pine, and infection in Wells, will have to establish the place of
blister rust control in the long-term plans to be followed.

A.E. Fivaz.

TIMBER STRIPPING OR SKINNING MUST CEASE IF MAINE'S
RURAL PROSPERITY IS RETAINED.

The situation as described at Wells, Maine, is common to that in many other rural New England white-pine towns. Constructive suggestions on how to meet this difficult situation would be welcomed, not only by Messrs. Frost and Tarbox of Maine, but by other State Leaders and Agents. The problem which confronts Mr. Tarbox, is how to secure town cooperation in Wells.

Suppose that the forest area of the town were in such condition that a definite proportion of the area were cut every year. The timber from this area would furnish taxable property which could be levied on to meet town needs.

The reasons why this situation does not hold in Wells may be among the following:

1. - The lack of proper state timber land legislation.

2. - The lack of a proper appreciation on the part of the pine owners, that their forests, especially their white pine, should be considered as a crop from which a harvest could be taken from one part or another, periodically; and that it would also be to their interest, as well as to that of the timber buyer, if the forest area were left in good condition; that is, containing either young trees up to a certain diameter, or a given number of seed trees per acre.

3. - The lack of appreciation upon the part of the town officials that their aim should be the building up of the forest capital in the town to as high a state as possible. This would provide a larger annual production of timber upon which taxes could be levied. A fair consideration should be given, not only to the resident owner of timber property, but to the out-of-town owner in making their appraisements for taxation purposes.

4. - The lack of knowledge upon the part of the timber buyer or portable mill owner that it would be to his advantage to leave the woodlots which he cuts in more productive condition; and that there is less profit, or no profit, in cutting trees of small sizes, (the minimum diameter, below which it is un-economical to cut timber, would be determined by studies carried on in each of the states). One long-headed lumberman in central Massachusetts finds that it is to his advantage not to cut white pine less than 12" in diameter. By restricting his cutting to the larger trees, he makes a larger profit and is able to return to the same lot for a recut in 10 to 15 years.

It may not be within the province of the Blister Rust Agent to deal directly with any of these matters except as incidental to his furthering the blister rust control program. It is in his power, however, to suggest to proper authorities, both town and state, those matters which would aid him in securing town cooperation in Ribes eradication.

R.G. Pierce.

WHAT TO DO

Suggestions For a Solution of the Problem at Wells, Me.

1. Suggest to the State Forester the desirability of an economic survey in Wells, on the order of the Land and Economic Survey in progress in Michigan. The survey would no doubt show large opportunity for more profitable utilization of land and for better forest practice.

2. Suggest to the State Forestry Association that a serious effort be made to establish a large Town Forest in Wells. The Association could profitably assist Wells in financing this forest, since it is a striking opportunity to demonstrate the value of forestry to the entire state.

3. Intensify blister rust control educational and service activities with private owners in Wells, and do all that is reasonable to assure eradication of Ribes through private effort. Even though the town cannot appropriate any funds, and individual owners cannot afford to hire crews, it is still possible for the owners to do the work themselves if they are shown how. Impress them with the fact that the pine and protection from blister rust help them to solve the tax problem.

S.B. Detwiler.

AGENT TARBOX SENDS IN FIRST SUGGESTIONS FOR NEW SCENARIO.

Agent E.E. Tarbox recently sent in a good plot for a new motion picture. We congratulate Mr. Tarbox on his original ideas; also for being the first Agent to submit suggestions for the new scenario.

It seems to be the general opinion that we will need a new motion picture film of a popular nature, for educational use. Well-worked-out scenarios or good ideas for them will be greatly appreciated. I have a hunch that there are some very good play-writers among the Blister Rust Control men; it simply remains to have their talent discovered. Tarbox has already made the start, who is going to be the next?

R.G.P.

KING WHITE PINE

This is the title of a mimeographed publication of the New York State College of Agriculture, at Ithaca, issued in February 1926. It contains a series of lectures given by members of the staff of the Forestry Department of the College at Ithaca, during Farmers Week. This is a very interesting series of lectures and is worthy of serious study by anyone dealing with white pine.

The lectures given were as follows:

White Pine Still King in The Empire State.
(A description of the special exhibit)

What White Pine Has Meant to New York State.
Ralph S. Hosmer

Life History of White Pine.
J. Nelson Spaeth

The Growth and Management of White Pine in New York State.
C.H. Guise

Bringing Up White Pine.
S.N. Spring

Measuring the White Pine Crop.
J. Bentley, Jr.

White Pine — The Wood of a Thousand Uses.
A.B. Recknagel

Hand-Planted White Pine.
J.A. Cope

Protecting the White Pine From Blister Rust.
Dr. H.H. York

THE QUEST OF THE BLIGHT-RESISTANT CHESTNUT

The killing of two birds with one stone is much talked of, yet seldom accomplished. Difficulties confront him who would perform this feat. If we of the Office of Forest Pathology endeavor to point out to Mr. Blister Rust Agent, the benefit to both of us, were he to occasionally pause in his arduous task of uprooting Ribes, and rest his aching back by unbending it long enough to make a hasty mental note of the condition of the chestnut about him, he might be unkind enough to remark that everyone knows that pine and chestnut generally grow on different soil types, and seldom hobnob together in mixed stands. Still, a few questions about resistant chestnuts in that vicinity, to a landowner who is not especially interested in blister rust, may sometimes pave the way for a blister rust discussion. It is good psychology too, since everyone knows about the losses from chestnut blight, and it will often stimulate the owner to wonder if his pines will go just as his chestnuts did.

Our plea to Mr. Agent, for assistance in the quest of the blight-resistant chestnut, is not made with the idea that his official duties permit of any time for searching for chestnuts. Rather it is on the ground that practically no extra time will be required, since the area is covered for other purposes and the number of chestnuts worthy of being reported will be so very, very few. Only a tree of very marked resistance is worthy of being reported, that is, a tree which has survived the blight in good condition after the chestnut growth of that general region has been dead for 5 to 15 years. The most resistant trees so far located, namely, the ones found by Dr. Graves near New York City, have been in groups, indicating probably that

there are blight-resistant strains of the American chestnut rather than individual trees.

For many years the Office of Forest Pathology has been seeking an immune, or very resistant chestnut. Records have been kept of all the chestnut
trees reported as unusually resistant to the blight. These trees, which include both native and introduced species, have been inspected as opportunity
permitted, and the more promising kept under observation, or propagated at
the government experimental station at Bell, Maryland.

Various species and strains of introduced chestnut have also been
under observation. Introductions by nurserymen, private individuals, and the
Office of Plant Introduction are included. No species of true chestnut
(Castanea) is known to be immune to the chestnut blight. Considering each
of the following classes as a whole, the American chestnut is by far the
most susceptible, the European chestnut less susceptible, and the Japanese
and Chinese species the most resistant. Individuals and strains within a
species show considerable variation in susceptibility or resistance to the
disease.

It may be that our ideal chestnut, a good old American chestnut which
will thrive despite the blight, grows in some woodlot which Mr. Agent will
go over this year. If so, a report of its exact location to some member of
this office will be greatly appreciated. Dr. Perley Spaulding, pathologist
of the Northeastern Forest Experiment Station at Amherst, Mass. is carrying
on the work on resistant American chestnuts in New England and New York in
cooperation with the State Departments. The work on all exotic chestnuts

and on American chestnuts south of New York is being handled from Washington.

R. P. MARSHALL and G. F. GRAVATT

March 29, 1926   Office of Forest Pathology.

- - - - - - -

COLORED BLISTER RUST ILLUSTRATION PROVES USEFUL

IN COLLEGES.

A recent letter from a teacher in the Department of Botany, Milwaukee-Downer College, Milwaukee, Wisconsin, reads somewhat as follows:

"Your placards posted in local stations, warning people of danger of fire to our forests, and of diseases threatening pine trees, struck me forcibly last summer.

There was a splendid color chart of 'White Pine Blister' showing the disease on pine and currants and its progressive changes . . . . .

In teaching elementary work with all illustrations of textbooks at hand, nothing makes quite the impression that one good colored plate does. I am anxious to get hold of one of the placards and if you will tell me where it can be secured I shall much appreciate it."

OFFICE COMMENTS

USE OF ENVELOPES

There has been brought to the attention of the Interdepartmental Board on Simplified Office Procedure several instances of the extravagant use of envelopes in the Government services.

Large Kraft envelopes are often used to mail out a few sheets of mimeographed material that could possibly be mailed in an ordinary white envelope; envelopes of a quality better than necessary for the purpose are often used; envelopes of a size much larger than necessary are very frequently used; many field personnel receive material almost daily that is not of immediate interest and might well be held and mailed out to them at stated periods, making one envelope do the service of several.

The Interdepartmental Board on Simplified Office Procedure believes that by proper administrative attention and study on the part of those charged with mailing out material, the extravagant use of envelopes as indicated above can be much curtailed and a quite considerable saving made in the aggregate.

- - - - -

March 13, 1926.

Frank L. Wells,
Assistant Chief Coordinator,
Secretary.

- - - - - - - - - - - -

REGARDING THE PURCHASE OF BOOKS

Gentlemen:

My attention has been called to a circular letter being distributed by the MacMillan Company, in which they urge the purchase of books by field men, and suggest further that they will be glad to ship books to the field men upon approval.

While books may be purchased for field use from appropriations available for our investigational activities, these purchases may only be made upon request through the Washington office. All letters of authorization specifically preclude the purchase of books. Where library facilities are not available and a field man requires books for his work, he should take the matter up with the head of his office in Washington, and any books purchased must be upon requisition, supplemented by a statement showing that the book is for field use, and where it is to be filed. If purchased, upon arrival it will be carded by the Bureau Library and turned over to the office for forwarding to the field.

I shall appreciate it if you will see that this memorandum is promptly called to the attention of your field men.

Very truly yours,

Wm. A. Taylor
Chief of Bureau.

P E R S O N A L S

Mr. O. C. Anderson, Agent, Providence, Rhode Island, writes that he is making his radio debut during American Forest week, (April 18 to 24 incl.) from Station W J A R Outlet Company, Providence. He will talk on Forest Protection.

Miss Evelyn Gallison, stenographer, resigned on March 31. Her headquarters were at Montpelier, Vermont.

- - - - - - -

Mr. Ralph H. Hutchinson, Agent at Saratoga Springs, New York, will leave the blister rust control work to become Field Agent in Forestry (Extension Forester) with field headquarters at Orono, Maine, on April 15, 1926. Mr. C. E. Baker will take over the work of Mr. Hutchinson.

- - - - - - -

Mr. Myron R. Watson, formerly engaged in blister rust control, has left the Extension Service of Maine to go with the Travelers Insurance Company.

Mr. Torfine Aamodt was appointed collaborator, effective April 1. His headquarters are St. Paul, Minnesota.

- - - -

Mr. Detwiler returned to the Washington Office on April 3, from a trip to the Western states.

- - - - - - -

Mr. Noble Harpp's headquarters were changed from Hudson, New York to Warrensburg, New York, effective April 1.

QUARANTINE NOTES

QUARANTINE WORK FASCINATES NEW INSPECTOR

Somewhere in the Middle west

March 24, 1926.

Dear Blisters:

I arrived Monday night. Messrs. Hodgkins and Lambert met me. Lambert left for his district last night. Mr. Hodgkins took me the "rounds" yesterday and today, and they are some "rounds". Have to be at the station at 6:30 a.m. and inspect there until after ten, then across the city two miles to the freight depots. After that it is back to the station and inspect until about three. we do not have anything to do then until 6:00 o'clock when we have more inspection until 8:30 or 9:00 p.m. This has been the program so far. I certainly am enjoying all this. There is something about the work and this city that is very fascinating to me.

Sincerely,

H. P. Avery.

Two days later: We inspected 2100 packages today. Please send me two bars of castile soap. H.P.A.

– – – – – – –

NOTES FROM THE FRONT.

Violations of Federal Plant Quarantines 26 and 54 are being reported from the Middle and Far West, though since it is now the middle of the shipping season no comparative statement can be made as to increase in violations.

In the Far West, one of the main difficulties is in the prevention of the shipment of the flowering currant, particularly the red flowering currant, (R. sanguineum). This currant grows abundantly in western Washington and Oregon and is particularly admired for its flowers.

M.A.T.

STATE PLANT QUARANTINES DECLARED ILLEGAL IN OPINION

OF SUPREME COURT.

As the outcome of a complaint filed by the State of Washington against
the Oregon-Washington Railway & Navigation Company for violation of a State
quarantine against importation of alfalfa hay in unsealed box cars from the
State of Idaho, the Supreme Court has rendered the opinion* that with the
existing Federal law in force, State quarantines of trees and plants in interstate commerce, are illegal.

Citing certain sections of the Federal Plant Quarantine Act which
authorize the Secretary of Agriculture to promulgate quarantines, the decision
states:

> It is impossible to read this statute and consider its scope with-
> out attributing to Congress the intention to take over to the Agricultural
> Department of the Federal Government the care of the horticulture and
> agriculture of the states, so far as these may be affected injuriously by
> the transportation in foreign and interstate commerce of anything which
> by reason of its character can convey disease to and injure trees, plants
> or crops. All the sections look to a complete provision for quarantine
> against importation into the country and quarantine as between the states
> under the direction and supervision of the Secretary of Agriculture.
> * * * * * * * * * * * *
> In the relation of the states to the regulation of interstate
> commerce by Congress there are two fields. There is one in which the
> state cannot interfere at all, even in the silence of Congress. In the
> other, and this is the one in which the legitimate exercise of the state's
> police power brings it into contact with interstate commerce so as to
> affect that commerce, the state may exercise its police power until
> Congress has by affirmative legislation occupied the field by regulating
> interstate commerce and so necessarily has excluded state action. * * *
> * * * * It is suggested that the states may act in the absence of any
> action by the Secretary of Agriculture; that it is left to him to allow
> the states to quarantine, and that if he does not act there is no
> invalidity in the state action. Such construction as that can not be
> given to the federal statute. The obligation to act without respect
> to the states is put directly upon the Secretary of Agriculture when-
> ever quarantine, in his judgment is necessary. When he does not act, it
> must be presumed that it is not necessary.

In order to allow the States to establish quarantines on materials
entering the State or being transported through it, a resolution amending
Section 8 of the Plant Quarantine Act, was introduced in the House of Representatives on March 8, 1926, and amended by Senate Joint Resolution 78,
to read:

"Provided further, That until the Secretary of Agriculture shall have
made a determination that such a quarantine is necessary and has duly
established the same with reference to any dangerous plant disease or insect
infestation, as herein above provided, nothing in this Act shall be construed
to prevent any State, Territory, Insular Possession, or District from promulgating, enacting, and enforcing any quarantine, prohibiting or restricting the
transportation of any class of nursery stock, plant, fruit, seed, or other
product or article subject to the restrictions of this section, into or
through such State, Territory, District, or portion thereof, from any other
State, Territory, District, or portion thereof, when it shall be found, by the
State, Territory, or District promulgating or enacting the same, that such
dangerous plant disease or insect infestation exists in such other State, Territory, District, or portion thereof: Provided further, That the Secretary of
Agriculture is hereby authorized, whenever he deems such action advisable and
necessary to carry out the purposes of this Act, to cooperate with any State,
Territory, or District, in connection with any quarantine, enacted or promulgated by such State, Territory, or District, as specified in the preceding
proviso: Provided further, That any nursery stock, plant, fruit, seed, or
other product or article, subject to the restrictions of this section, a
quarantine with respect to which shall have been established by the Secretary
of Agriculture under the provisions of this Act shall, when transported to,

into, or through any State, Territory, or District, in violation of such
quarantine, be subject to the operation and effect of the laws of such State,
Territory, or District, enacted in the exercise of its police powers, to the
same extent and in the same manner as though such nursery stock, plant, fruit,
seed, or other product or article had been produced in such State, Territory,
or District, and shall not be exempt therefrom by reason of being introduced
therein in original packages or otherwise."

This joint resolution passed the Senate March 27 (Calendar day, April 1),
1926. This measure became a law April 13, 1926. M. A. Thompson.

- - - - - - -

NEW BLISTER RUST QUARANTINES.

Two new blister rust quarantines have been brought to the attention
of the Office. One of them concerning West Virginia is an amendment to
Quarantine No. 1 relating to the white pine blister rust, dated March 20, 1925.
Under this quarantine West Virginia prohibits the shipment into the state, of
all species and varieties of live five-leaf pines and all currants and gooseberries (Ribes and Grossularia) which are known to be carriers of the aforesaid
disease, from all the states east of and including the states of Minnesota, Iowa,
Missouri, Arkansas and Louisiana and also from the state of Washington.

The state of Wyoming on the 18th of June 1925 declared a white pine
blister rust quarantine, known as Quarantine No. 2. Under this quarantine they
prohibit the importation into the state of five-leafed pines, and currant and
gooseberry plants from the infested territory, namely: the State of Washington,
and all states east of and including Minnesota, Iowa, Missouri, Arkansas and
Louisiana; and the province of British Columbia, Canada.

PUBLICATIONS

Blister Rust

    Pierce, Roy G. - Currants and White Pine.
    The Country Gentleman. April 1926, p. 96.

Ribes Industry

    Card, F.W. - Bush Fruits, 1925.
        Gooseberries - p. 282-283. The total area devoted to
gooseberry culture in the United States in 1909, according to census report, was 4,765 acres. This was nearly
2000 acres less than 10 years before when the amount
reported was 6,752 acres. New England and the Mountain
divisions show an increase; all others a decrease, though
in the Middle Atlantic Section it is so slight as to be
negligible. The East North Central division leads with
1,482 acres in 1909. This is closely followed by the West
North Central division with 1,232 acres. It outranks the
currant in the South Atlantic and East South Central divisions, but falls behind it in the West South Central
section. The total production is placed at 5,282,463 quarts
valued at $417,034 an average price of nearly 8 cents a quart.

        Currants p. 264.
        The total area devoted to currants in the United States
as reported in the census of 1910 is 7,862A. The total production is given as 10,448,533 quarts valued at $790,431. The
Middle Atlantic section leads in production with an area of
3,239 acres. The smallest area is found in the East South
Central division which reports only 16 acres. This is followed
by West South Central and the South Atlantic sections with 46
and 80 acres respectively.
        The total area under cultivation 10 years before (in 1899)
was 12,865 acres. This shows a decrease of 5,003 acres, or
about 39% within that decade. All small fruits show a decrease
during that period but with none of the others is the percentage
so great. - - - - - Since the currant crop is one easily grown,
this seems to indicate that the demand is not keeping pace with
that for other fruits.

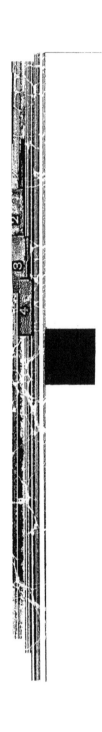

BLISTER RUST NEWS

May 1926.

Volume X

Number 5.

U.S DEPARTMENT of AGRICULTURE

Office of Blister Rust Control.

C O N T E N T S - V O L. 10, No. 5.

Page

Agents Work
Berkshire Bits 133
Blister Rust Agent Attends Tree Grafting Demonstration 143
Conference of New York Agents Held in Albany 134
Connecticut News 137
Massachusetts Agents Have Conference and Field Trip. 153
Notes on Two Meetings in Connecticut 133

Blister Rust Situation
Two New Towns With Infected Pines in Norfolk County, Mass. 139
White Pine Blister Rust Control in Massachusetts. 136

Cooperation
Blister Rust Agent Finds Cooperation in Plymouth County, Mass. 149
Public Interest and Cooperation. 138

Editorial
Associate Editors Appointed for Blister Rust News. 132
Hello Agent. 131
Staff. 130

Education
American Forestry Week at Pittsfield, Massachusetts. 146
Blister Rust Control on the Air in Massachusetts 142
Circular Letter and Franked Card Used in New York Work 147
Forestry Week in New York State. 147
Maine's Many Meetings Mean Much. 151
New Set of Lantern Slides Available. 144
News Items, Writing. 132
Notes From Southern Worcester County, Massachusetts. 146
Our Job. 149
Selected Readings in Psychology. 160
The Initial Interview. 138
Two Title Slides Suggested by Massachusetts. 140
White Pine Blister Rust Control in Massachusetts 136

Forestry
A Few Notes on White Pine from the Entomological Viewpoint 157
Ancient Pine Felled by Winchendon Woodsmen 156
Rhode Island Forestry Association Formed 151
White Pine Uses. 155

Personal. 164
Publications. 168
Quarantine Notes. 162
Warning to Tourists. 163

State News.
Conn 133,137,141,145,166,167   New York 134,139,144,147,148,163,166
Maine. 136,143,151,165   Rhode Island. 151
Mass. 133,136,139,140,142,143,144   Vermont. 164
146,149,150,152,153,154,156,164,165   Western States. 162,165
Minnesota. 164   Wisconsin. 162
New Hampshire. 135,162

Technical Studies
Blister Rust Infection Study 150

E D I T O R I A L   S T A F F

Roy G. Pierce . . . . . . : Editor - Washington, D.C.
E.E. Tarbox . . . . Assoc. Editor - Maine.
Thos. J. King. . . .   "   "   New Hampshire
S.V. Holden . . . .   "   "   Vermont
W.J. Endersbee. . .   "   "   Massachusetts
O.C.Anderson. . . .   "   "   Rhode Island
J.E. Riley, Jr. . .   "   "   Connecticut.
George H. Stevens .   "   "   New York
H.J. Ninman . . . .   "   "   Wisconsin

UNITED STATES DEPARTMENT OF AGRICULTURE
BUREAU OF PLANT INDUSTRY
WASHINGTON, D. C.

T H E   B L I S T E R   R U S T   N E W S.

Issued by the Office of Blister Rust Control
and the Cooperating States.

VOL. 10, No. 5.   MAY 1926.

Hello Agent!

Here goes the bell for the fifth round of this here blister rust
control campaign. The News starts the round auspishusly with a new board of
live Associate Editors. Back 'em up, Agent, and we'll all make the News a
knockout.

While the Ribes are taking the count this season, don't forget that
"Service" is the motto in the Washington Office corner. Don't be bashful about
making your wants known, the Service Department can help you serve the pine-
owning public.

Brother Roop delivers one straight from the shoulder concernin' kids
and blister rust control. Clark, McNerney, Riley, and others are also appealing
to the risin' generation. Getting immediate response from their Dads, but, Oh
Boy! when them kids grow up into pine owners, won't they make the Ribes family
sick! What do you suggest toward a B R C circular for the young'uns? In
the meantime, don't forget the hundreds of young minds in your district that
are being shaped by what they read, see, hear and do - is blister rust control
on the program?

Out of the corner with a rush, ole timer!

Yours for hard hittin' !

Ribee Bill

ASSOCIATE EDITORS APPOINTED FOR BLISTER RUST NEWS.

The following Associate Editors have been appointed in the various
states to assist the Washington Editor in securing material for the Blister
Rust News. However, it is not intended that they should be responsible for
writing all of the material themselves, but that they secure news items from
their associates and have general supervision over the kind and amount of materi
sent in. It will be appreciated by the Washington Office and your Associate
Editor if as many as can will submit any items which they think to be of
interest. The following are the Associate Editors: Maine - E.E. Tarbox;
New Hampshire - Thos J. King; Vermont - S.V. Holden; Massachusetts - W.J.
Endersbee; Rhode Island- O.C. Anderson; Connecticut - J.E. Riley, Jr.;
New York - George H. Stevens; Wisconsin - H.J. Ninman.

- - - - - - - - - -

WRITING NEWS ITEMS

It is generally agreed that news items are one of the most effective
features of the educational work. Much excellent material regarding blister
rust has been published. However, on the whole, our efforts in this respect
have been rather sporadic. When the inspiration came, we have written an
article for this or that paper. The result has been overemphasis in some
cases and underemphasis in others. Also, we have made little use of weekly
and monthly papers.

We need to utilize each worthwhile agency by adequately distributing
our efforts in supplying blister rust news. To do this, plans have to be
made in advance, which will insure each agency receiving a minimum number
of articles at specific times during the year. Circumstances may arise which
make it advisable to increase the number of items in certain papers over the
minimum figures. However, if we have a definite plan of procedure, we will
be less liable to overemphasize and will be sure of utilizing all favorable
facilities. The same idea can be applied to all other phases of the educational work. First plan, then work your plan.

E.C.Filler

NOTES ON TWO MEETINGS IN CONNECTICUT.

Children Urged to Plant Areas to White Pine Rather Than to Plant Single Trees on Arbor Day.

On April 19, at Thompson, a motion picture show was given under the auspices of the Thompson Grange. Five films were shown, including three from the Department of Agriculture. Mr. J.E. Riley, Jr. gave a talk and answered questions on white pine blister rust. There was a good-sized, appreciative audience.

On the evening of April 28, I spoke to the Abington Grange on White Pine Blister Rust. A half hour of questioning followed the talk and considerable interest was shown. One member suggested the advisability of getting school children to plant areas to white pine on Arbor Day, rather than setting out one or two trees, as an observance of the day.

H.J. Miles.

- - - - - - - - - -

Agent Brockway of Plymouth County, Massachusetts, recently had a request to examine a lady's fir trees as/she said they were badly infected with blister rust. During Forest Protection week nine posters were put up, eighteen articles inserted in newspapers, and three lectures were given by Mr. Brockway.

- - - - - - - - - -

BERKSHIRE BITS

Ice-cutting was resumed in the Berkshires May 5.

Aecia was first seen in this County, this year, April 23,

Wild Ribes eradication work was started May 10.

One cooperator was secured and 1000 white pines were planted as a result of activities during American Forest Week.

80,000 acres made safe for growing white pine is the goal for 1926 in Berkshire County.

CONFERENCE OF NEW YORK AGENTS, HELD IN ALBANY.

The annual spring conference was held in Albany, April 25, and 26.
Those present at the conference were: Messrs. A.F. Amadon, State Leader;
E.C. Filler, in charge of the Boston Office, Ed Littlefield, Pathologist;
H.L. MacIntyre, Supervisor of Gypsy Moth; Dr. L.H. Pennington, New York State
College of Forestry, Syracuse; Mr. Clifford R. Pettis, Supt. of State Forests;
and Dr. H.H. York, State Forest Pathologist; and Agents, Chas. E. Baker,
James Kennedy, H. Henry Knowles, Benj. H. Nichols, Duncan Rankin, George E.
Stevens, Harry Williams and Major E.E. Woodward. Dr. York gave a few intro-
ductory remarks about the work and then introduced Mr. MacIntyre who gave a
most interesting talk on the Gypsy Moth situation in the State, touching
on the early history of the spread of the moth to this State, describing
briefly, its life history and functions, methods of control, operating of
crews, etc.

We were fortunate to have with us, Dr. Pennington who talked on
"The Early History of the Spread of the White Pine Blister Rust Disease To
and Within the State of New York", and gave some results of his experience in
the Pacific Northwest that were of especial interest. Mr. Filler spoke to the
group on extension methods and explained the value of window and fair exhibits
and demonstrations.

Mr. Amadon gave some interesting results of data compiled from 1921 to
the present time, showing the effect of Ribes per acre on cost. He discussed
new forms to be used in the state and explained basis of cooperation with
pine owners.

Mr. Pettis described the new Fisher Bill recently passed by the legislature that relieves the tax burden on reforested land; and pointed out the good effect it would eventually have on securing blister rust eradication. Mr. Pettis also told about some of the early history of blister rust in the state and spoke of destroying the nursery stock and some of the older plantations in order to control the disease. Mr. Littlefield outlined the investigative work being carried on in connection with Ribes, their growth and dissemination.

Dr. York lead most of the round table discussions and talked on several phases of educational work, and spoke of means by which results of cooperation could be increased through more publicity in newspapers, window displays, unique exhibits at fairs, demonstrations, etc., and urged all agents to use every avenue possible of spreading the gospel of blister rust control. He concluded by saying that it was the continual publicity put before the people that had the greatest effect on securing cooperation and ultimate eradication, and he cited several incidents to substantiate this.

George E. Stevens.

- - - - - - - - -

LECTURE WITH SLIDES FOLLOWED BY "THE PINES" DRIVES HOME NECESSITY OF BLISTER RUST CONTROL.

"The Pines" (motion picture film) and the lantern slides were used at a number of meetings in this district and I believe that a lecture given with the slides, followed by "The Pines" makes the best program and drives home the results better than any other way. If there are two speakers I think the slides and talk should come first, then talk by second speaker, and movie last. The lantern loaned by the Boston Office is especially good.

K.E. Barraclough.

WHITE PINE BLISTER RUST CONTROL IN MASSACHUSETTS.

The Massachusetts Department of Agriculture, through its Division of Plant Pest Control, continued during the year 1925 its participation in the state wide campaign to prevent the further spread of the white pine blister rust - a serious plant disease which is fatal in its attack upon white pine trees. The control of this disease is accomplished by the elimination of currant and gooseberry bushes which are the alternate host plants of the fungus which causes this disease. During the year, the department rendered assistance to 1,763 land owners in making examinations on 194,851 acres of land, 110,892 acres of which are producing white pine. The cooperating owners expended the equivalent of $5,554.15 in this protective work. From these lands, 706,830 wild and 33,610 cultivated currant and gooseberry bushes were eradicated at a total average cost of 11 cents per acre.

The stage of the disease as it appears on white pine, has been recorded in 187 towns in Massachusetts up to November 30, 1925. These figures indicate that the disease is generally distributed throughout the state in local centres from which there is likely to be a spread unless the alternate host plants are promptly eliminated.

From - Annual Report of the Commissioner of Conservation and State Forester for the Year Ending November 30, 1925. p. 6.

- - - - - - - - - -

During American Forest Week I showed "The Pines" is Sanford, Springvale, and Biddeford, to approximately 3500 people. The picture was well liked.

E.B. Tarbox, Maine

- 137 -

CONNECTICUT NEWS

Good Meetings Held

We hoped to stage a series of talks and motion picture shows here in Connecticut this winter, but were badly handicapped by a state law prohibiting the use of motion picture projectors unless operated by a licensed operator and projected from a booth that has been inspected for each showing by the state police. A talk with the state police showed that the law was not a dead letter law and we had to either comply with the law or quit. We compromised by cutting down the number of shows and by complying with the law for those we did hold. Four Grange entertainments were staged and one school showing made. One lantern slide lecture and a couple of talks without pictures were given. Two more picture shows are scheduled this month. On the whole the meetings were well attended and some concrete results have been secured.

Crew Work Started

This surely is a backward season! Haven't observed any fruiting cankers yet and it was not until April 28 that we found wild Ribes in leaf. Cultivated currants and gooseberries have been in leaf for a week or two in favorable locations. However, wild ones are leafing out now and crew work was started today, May 6th.

No large central camp will be operated this summer. Instead, a floating state crew will eradicate those scattered areas requiring crew work, in an effort to complete first eradication in the towns of Salisbury, North Canaan and Canaan. We hope to increase the volume of private co-operative work.

J.E. Riley, Jr.

PUBLIC INTEREST AND COOPERATION.

Public interest in blister rust control work has been exceptionally good, as is indicated by 460 towns and 12,437 individuals cooperating in this work during the period 1922-1925. The majority of the owners of cultivated Ribes destroyed their bushes without compensation. During 1925, 59,458 cultivated bushes were uprooted, yet the states only had to pay for 1300 plants, or 2.2 percent. A total of $514.55 was paid in claims for compensation to the 49 owners of these cultivated Ribes. This indicates the excellent cooperation which the public is giving to blister rust control work.

K.K. Stimson.

- - - - - - - - - -

THE INITIAL INTERVIEW.

The most difficult parts of an interview are the approach and the securing of desired action. After exchanging a few casual remarks with the prospect, it is often difficult to get effectively started on the subject of blister rust. Some of the Agents have solved this problem by always carrying a good specimen of the disease on pine. Even while they are making general statements, the eyes of the prospect are continually roving toward the specimen. Then an opening shot; such as, "Here is a good specimen of the blister rust" immediately gets the conversation on the right track. The remark - "Here is a sure way to tell blister rust" almost always gets attention; we all like to be experts. Now is the time not to be over-anxious. Give the prospect time to ask questions. Our job is to guide these questions and to satisfactorily answer them.

Finally the climax is reached and perhaps you have suggested that his pine lot should be given free inspection. Still the prospect sits tight. What then? Well, every man has his own procedure so tell us how you do it.

E.C.Filler.

INTERVIEW, INSPECTION, AND ERADICATION WORK HELD UP

IN NEW YORK STATE THIS YEAR.

Weather and Late Season to Blame.

The early start in Ribes eradication which featured the work in former years, is being held up this year due to weather conditions and the backward season. A year ago, a crew was at work in Harpp's District pulling Ribes on the 27th day of April. This year eradication crews in the southern districts will not commence work before the middle of May and it will be along toward the first of June before crews will commence operations in the northern districts.

In many sections of the northern districts there are still three and four feet of snow back in the woods with drifts running up over the height of an automobile. Some of the town roads are still blocked in places, to say nothing of the side roads which are still but a sea of mud. The continued cold, rainy, and cloudy weather has kept these roads in poor condition and has not given them a chance to dry out. However, the Agents are all prepared and just as soon as conditions are favorable for interview, inspection, and eradication work they will open and renew their attack against the blister rust disease in the state.

G.E. Stevens

- - - - - - - - - -

TWO NEW TOWNS WITH INFECTED PINES

IN NORFOLK COUNTY, MASS.

Things are now shaping up in this District O.K. for Ribes eradication. I have recently found blister rust in two new towns in Norfolk County, and in town forests at that. The town in each case is cooperating to remove wild Ribes. People in the vicinity are removing cultivated Ribes.

E.M. Brockway

```
              I S   A   T R E E

                G R O W N "

              Calvin Coolidge.
```

```
        •    FOR FURTHER INFORMATION
             REGARDING THE CONTROL
                  .OF THE
      W H I T E   P I N E   B L I S T E R   R U S T
             GET IN TOUCH WITH
                 YOUR LOCAL
    B L I S T E R   R U S T   C O N T R O L   A G E N T
           YOU CAN LOCATE HIM
          THROUGH THE OFFICE OF THE
                C O U N T Y
  A G R I C U L T U R A L   E X T E N S I O N   S E R V I C E
```

In the January 1926 number of the Blister Rust News, on page 15,
a number of title or word slides were suggested, to be used with picture
slides to prevent monotony. As yet only two suggestions for slides have
come in; both of them being from the Old Bay State.

If you can use any of the slides to advantage which were suggested
in the January Number, or if you have others which you like better, the
Washington Office will be very glad to hear of it and to make them up for you.

N.B. Do not put this off until two days before your lantern slide lecture.

R.G.Pierce

- 141 -

FORESTRY WEEK IN THE PRESS OF LITCHFIELD COUNTY, CONN.

Peter Pine Planter had an article in the papers of Litchfield County
entitled "Encouraging Grandpa to Plant Trees". The article was addressed
to the city and town boys who love to come out to the old farm at vacation
time. It called their attention to the scarcity of labor and ready cash
for nursery stock on many farms in spring time. A word was spoken as to the
many discouragements which the farmer grandfather meets and a suggestion
was offered that the strong young city fellow take enough of his spending
money to buy five hundred or a thousand little trees and spend a little of
his idle time helping the old gentleman set them out somewhere in the old
pasture where the hardhack and alders and birch are spoiling the grass.
The city must not try to lay burdens on the country which they themselves
will not so much as touch with their little fingers.

In another timely article, Peter Pine Planter addresses the city and
town sportsman who come out to the country for trout. He shows how the
destruction of the forests has caused floods and droughts which have spoiled
the fishing. He points the way to a restoration of good fishing and suggests
personal service with a mattock. There is no reason why the farmer should
pay taxes and carry the financial burden, that city sportsmen may come out
once a year and free of charge secure the season's crop of trout, in many
cases not even saying "Thank you". The sportsman who comes with five hundred
or a thousand little trees and helps set them where they will finally shade
the stream and keep it cool will improve his welcome and will be actually helping improve conditions. There is too much a spirit of Forestry which says:
"The Government must do so and so", "The State must do so and so". There is
an opportunity for many city people at small expense to get some personal
blisters in the Conservation Crusade.

BLISTER RUST CONTROL ON THE AIR IN MASSACHUSETTS.

Through the courtesy of Mr. Harris A. Reynolds, Secretary of the
Massachusetts Forestry Association, and Chairman of the Massachusetts
American Forest Week Committee, State Leader Perry was privileged to
give a talk on blister rust on April 22 through Radio Station W E E I,
The Edison Electric Illuminating Company of Boston. Although this
talk was scheduled at 2.45 p.m., an hour when few people have the time
or the inclination to listen-in, Mr. Perry knows from the following
letter, that he at least had an audience of one.

***** *****************

April 25, 1926

Dear Sir:

I was listening to the talk over the radio
about the pine tree blister rust. Now I have lots of
white pines on my farm, very many small trees growing
up, and the rust is very bad among them. We do not
know of any currant or gooseberries with 900 feet of
any pines. If there are wild ones, how are we to find
them. Should like to know what you think about it. I
live in Billerica on a back road near the Burlington
line.

Yours truly,

(Signed)

Oscar H. Bicknell,
Woburn, R.F.D.,
Mass.

****

Needless to say, Mr. Bicknell will receive the SERVICE which was
offered "over the air" and since there is no Agent located near this
town at present, the State Leader will have an opportunity to shake
hands with "his audience" and incidentally find out if he still knows
Ribes from young maples, viburnums, etc., after hibernating all winter
at 136 State House, Boston.

BLISTER RUST AGENT ATTENDS TREE GRAFTING DEMONSTRATION.

A Good Day's Work Accomplished for Blister Rust Control.

One of the Maine Agents has recently sent in a statement which has a
lot of meat in it: "Tuesday I attended a tree grafting demonstration with
the County Agent, in a town that has never yet made an appropriation. We
worked all day and had a meeting that evening. This was not a demonstration,
it was the real thing as this man had about five hundred trees girdled by
mice, and all the neighborhood was working to save the orchard by bridge
grafting. I worked like a Trojan all day waxing grafts.

This may seem like a queer place for a Blister Rust Agent to be, but
during that day I made contacts with five men owning probably 1000 acres of
pine, and they all want their pine scouted, and are agreeable to eradicating
alone if the town shows no signs of cooperating. Motto: "The longest way
round is the shortest way home - - sometimes". I didn't try to push my
business in the least. Someone would ask what my business was and I would
tell him. Conversation would ensue, and the result would be as I have stated
above. This man would go away to work and sooner or later a second man would
drift over saying: "I hear you are the Blister Rust man, etc. etc. - - cooperation."

- - - - - - - - - -

Agent Brockway of Plymouth County, Massachusetts, has been requested
to exhibit for the fifth time by the Committee at Marshfield Fair this coming
summer. One member said that Brockway's Blister Rust Exhibit had the best
educational feature of any in the hall last year.

NEW SET OF LANTERN SLIDES AVAILABLE.

Including Map, Chart, and Word Slides.

The Washington Office has a new set of four slides as follows:

2771 - (Graph or Chart) - Lumber cut of White Pine of the Six Leading States 1909 to 1923.

2983 - (Map) White Pine Range and Areas Protected from Blister Rust in Northeastern States 1917 to 1925.

2992 - (Word slide) "A Tree Saved Is a Tree Grown"-Calvin Collidge.

2896 - (Map showing distribution) - White Pine Blister Rust 1909 to 1925.

Requests may be made for individual slides, or by the set, as desired.

- - - - - - - - - -

THE PINES

Three films arrived on time for use during American Forest Week and "The Pines" in particular made a great hit. Numerous people have stopped me on the street and commented on it. The three slides came last Monday in time for all week. They are very attractive and nicely gotten up. So far I have one cooperator as a result of the films. This man is trying to get more pines to plant.

W.J.Endersbee.

- - - - - - - - - - -

HEARD IN LEWIS COUNTY, N. Y.

A woman, one day last year, asked my foreman if the Gypsy Moth laid eggs on pine trees that when they hatched out, if that was blister rust.

RILEY OF CONNECTICUT PUTTING THROUGH
PROGRAM OF EDUCATIONAL WORK FOR YOUNGSTERS.

Exhibits for School Superintendents

We are fortunate in securing the cooperation of the State Board
of Education. Mr. Russell F. Lund, Supervisor of Elementary Agriculture in
the State Department of Education, has invited us to prepare a blister rust
exhibit for the meeting of school superintendents at Hartford in the fall.
Just what the display will consist of has not yet been worked out, but the
exhibit will be there when the time arrives. Other exhibits are to be displayed in some of the rural schools and we hope to arrange for a field day
with the school children in Salisbury.

Work With Boy Scouts

The splendid cooperation of the Boy Scout organizations is most
encouraging. Scout Executive Arthur D. Marsden of Waterbury, has granted
us permission to use one of the cottages at the Scout Camp at Mt. Tom. The
state crew has made this their headquarters for the month of May while
working in the towns of Litchfield and Warren. Mr. Marsden has also
approved of a permanent blister rust exhibit in the Scout Museum Room.

Attends Demonstration Planting with School Boys

Today Ye Editor attended a demonstration planting with school boys
on the school grounds at Washington Depot. It was conducted by a representative of the State Forester's office and the Director of Elementary Agriculture of the State Board of Education. The writer attended in the hopes than
he might be of some assistance and at the same time learn something of the
art of handling school boys! The effort paid ff for no other reason that
he was asked to prepare a blister rust display for Nature Study Exhibit to
be held by the students of the Elementary Schools of Meriden, May 20,21,
and 22.

NOTES FROM SOUTHERN WORCESTER COUNTY, MASSACHUSETTS.

Good Cooperation from Theatre Owners.

I have secured the cooperation of the theatre owners of four towns in
this district, to run films at least once a week as long as we care to supply
them. If I can do this while I am in this district I believe it will help
the work.

I started out to do this for American Forest Week, but they say they
would like one each week. Mr. Arthur Ledoux of East Brookfield has made me
a very generous offer. He will lend his theatre and pay all expenses if I
wish to put on a full show including a talk, on any Wednesday I choose, the
schools to be dismissed one half hour earlier to take it in. Mr. Ledoux
would have to cancel his Wednesday show to allow me to do this. This offer
coming unsolicited, is some cooperation, to my mind. Mr. Ledoux is a pine
owner and is doing some planting this year. We eradicated the Ribes on his
land last year.

E.J. McNerney

- - - - - - - - -

AMERICAN FOREST WEEK AT PITTSFIELD, MASSACHUSETTS.

The Mahaiwe theatre is featuring American Forest Week by showing
films on different phases of forestry. Tonight will be shown "The Pines"
the subject of which is the protection of a forest crop from a serious
plant disease, the White Pine Blister Rust. The County Blister Rust Agent,
Mr. W.J. Endersbee appears in this film which has a plot with sufficient action
to make it interesting as well as instructive. Wednesday and Thursday will
be shown "Trees of Tomorrow" a film dealing with general forestry and stressing
forest fire protection. Friday and Saturday will be seen "The Pack Train"
which is replete with scenic beauty and depicts much of the recreational side

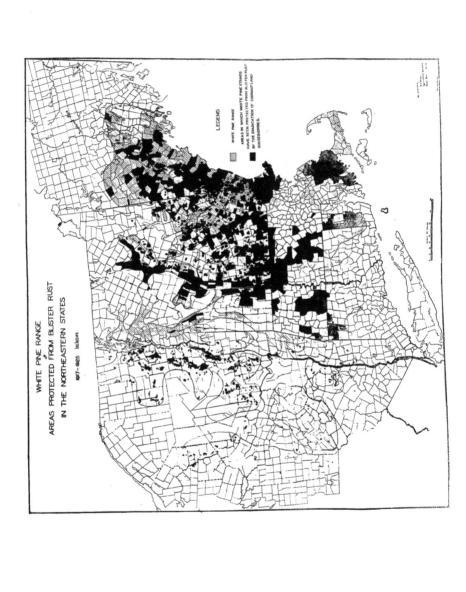

WHITE PINE RANGE

AREAS PROTECTED FROM BLISTER RUST
IN THE NORTHEASTERN STATES

1917-1925   Inclusive

LEGEND

WHITE PINE RANGE

AREAS IN WHICH WHITE PINE STANDS
HAVE BEEN PROTECTED FROM BLISTER RUST
BY THE ERADICATION OF CURRANTS AND
GOOSEBERRIES.

From "The Eagle", Pittsfield, Mass. April 20, 1926.

FORESTRY WEEK IN NEW YORK STATE

Forestry Week was observed as usual in this state with many articles on the subject of Forestry, together with cartoons on reforestation appearing in the local papers throughout the state. Indoor meetings were held in many communities. Where possible, field demonstrations of tree planting were given and of blister rust damage and disease were shown. The cold, backward season, however, made it necessary to postpone many of the field meetings that were planned.

Arbor Day will be observed and in many of the districts plans are underway to hold field meetings in the form of picnics, with school children playing the leading role. There is no doubt that the state will witness this spring, the most ample observance of Arbor Day in its history.

G.E. Stevens

- - - - - - - - - -

CIRCULAR LETTER AND FRANKED CARD USED IN

NEW YORK WORK.

White Pine Blister Rust Information Free

Address_____Date_____

Name_____

Mark (X) before any of the following you desire and fill in where asked. Please note that you are not binding yourself in any way by filling out this card, its purpose is merely for you to indicate your interest and give me some information.
( ) Personal Information from Blister Rust Agent
( ) Pine Inspection
( ) About how many acres of White Pine do you own?

Remarks:-

P. O. Box 116,
Hudson, N. Y.
April 13, 1926.

Dear White Pine Owner:

The purpose of this letter is to call your attention to the fight that is being waged in an effort to control the spread of the White Pine Blister Rust disease in New York State.

White Pine is the most valuable of our softwoods. We cannot afford to stand by and see our White Pines go as did our Chestnuts, when the Blister Rust disease can be controlled by simply getting rid of any wild or cultivated currant and gooseberry bushes that may be within the pine area and from within a safety zone of 900 feet surrounding the pine area. This work can be done at small cost to the pine owner, the average cost for the past season of 1925, in this district, being around 50 cents per acre.

The Federal Government, with the States, has been carrying on an extensive program of control for the past four years and thousands of acres of White Pine have been protected. Last year 35,000 acres were eradicated of currant and gooseberry bushes for the protection of White Pine in New York State.

Spring is here and we are making plans for an even more vigorous campaign for 1926, and we are asking you to cooperate in this matter of conserving the White Pine of the State. We do not wish to appear to pester pine owners in order to get them to help protect their own White Pine. It's up to them if they want the service the State and Federal Governments are offering. There is no compulsion, but we do want you to lend a hand willingly.

The State Conservation Commission will furnish you with a trained man, free of charge, to help you with the eradication work. I am the Forester in charge of Blister Rust control for this district comprising these counties of the lower Hudson Valley. My services are free for the asking and can be had by simply filling out and mailing the enclosed card which requires no postage.

Don't fail to read the enclosed folder, which tells all about Blister Rust, and to fill out and mail the card. My headquarters are in the Farm Bureau Office in the Court House, Hudson, N. Y. If you are in town drop in and talk it over.

Very truly yours,

Duncan G. Rankin
Blister Rust Control Agent, U.S.D.A.

DGR:C

- - - - - - - - - - - - -

EARLY DATE FOR AECIA.

Agent McNerney of Southern Worcester County, Massachusetts reports finding aecia on pine at Webster, April 8 - with pustules just showing. This is the first report of aecia this season.

E.C.F.

BLISTER RUST AGENT FINDS GOOD COOPERATION IN PLYMOUTH CO., MASS.

Scouting started May 4 in the town of Hingham, Plymouth County, Massachusetts. Very few wild currants are being found but there are "oodles" of wild gooseberries and a great deal of infection is also being found. Many owners have been lined up to work their own land and owners are also pulling out their cultivated bushes in grand style. This kind of cooperation makes an Agent feel as though he were really accomplishing something.

- - - - - - - - - - - -

OUR JOB

Miles, an inexperienced lad of 18, recently won the 26 mile marathon at Boston. Why? He had good legs and wind to be sure, but he had something even more important - confidence. At all times during the race, he was sure he was going to win. Belief in yourself and the worthwhileness of your job is sure to produce results. It is impossible, for example, to secure cooperation in control work, unless you have first convinced yourself of the real value of ribes eradication.

If we are continually wondering whether we are in the right job, ours is a divided personality. Part of it is working on one job and part on another. Under such circumstances, we can't do well by either job. Success only comes when we get squarely behind our job and give it the best we have.

A man may be handicapped by an ordinary personality and little education and still be exceptionally successful in securing cooperation. Why? He believes so thoroughly in his job, that his sincerity and enthusiasm carry absolute conviction. With this kind of faith in ourselves and our jobs, success and happiness lie just around the corner.

E. C. Filler.

Blister Rust Infection Study

The special field study, being conducted by the blister rust control agent, to determine the general increase in infection, by recording canker data on the first ten infected trees examined in various pine stands, is already beginning to show results. Roop, Boomer and McNerney were the first agents to submit such records to the Boston Office. McNerney's study in the town of Sturbridge, Worcester County, indicates a large volume of recent infection. This is especially significant, as not much blister rust was known to exist in this part of New England. The town of Sturbridge borders on the Connecticut line and is only a few miles northwest of Rhode Island. The following information was copied from one of McNerney's cards.

Tree Number (Use * to denote killing canker on tree.)	Estimated Tree Height, in feet	No. Cankers by Age Classes		
		Up to 1917	1918 to 1921 Incl.	1921 to Date
1*	7	0	2	2
2*	18	0	17	156
3*	10	0	7	81
4*	3	0	5	0
5*	10	0	12	66
6*	7	0	1	32
7*	6	0	5	35
8*	10	0	1	6
9*	6	0	1	27
10	35	0	1	3
Totals	--	0	52	408

Estimated Area of Pine Stand .... 10 acres.........
Estimated Percent of Pine Infected.....10 acres..........

- - - - - - - - - -

A good start has been made in submitting data for this special study. However, to obtain representative figures, it will be necessary to secure information from as many sources as possible. The study will be successful, if every man does his share.

E. C. Filler

MAINE'S MANY MEETINGS MEAN MUCH.

This Department, the Maine Forest Service, has given talks before several clubs, including the Portland Farmers Club, the Boy Scouts of Portland, the Kiwanis Club, and the Rotary Club. I spoke before the Augusta Rotary last night. The Department also has a large window exhibit in the First National Granite Bank here, which includes blister rust.

I find the transparencies attract much attention - they are rather unusual, not very common hereabouts. I could use to advantage another transparency of an enlarged Ribes leaf showing infection, etc.

The weather is warming up some after giving us snow and cold since last October. Expected to start eradicating May 3- but no chance this year.

April 24, 1926.   W. O. Frost.

- - - - - - - -

RHODE ISLAND FORESTRY ASSOCIATION FORMED.

As an outgrowth of the Rhode Island American Forest Week Committee, which went into a detailed and well executed plan of forestry publicity this year, the Rhode Island Forestry Association was founded April 22nd. Mr. Harris A. Reynolds addressed a group of fifty interested men and women on the objects and possible accomplishments of such an organization. Mr. Howard L. Hitchcock was elected President. Mr. T. Pierpont Hazard of Peace Dale, Vice President and Mr. E.K. Thomas of Providence, as Secretary and Treasurer. The next meeting of the newly founded Association will be held April 15th. I confidently look for action from this long needed organization.

O.C. Anderson, R.I.

A STRENUOUS DAY WITH THE BOY SCOUTS

On the anniversary of Paul Revere's ride on April 19, 1926, I had a
strenuous day myself. I left the feathers at 4:30 a.m. and started for East
Brookfield at 5:00. Since I had to start eradication work that day, I put
the men to pulling cultivated bushes. This is a very good way to begin the
season; you get warmed up so nicely.

My next appearance was in Paxton, where the boy scouts were to teach
their fathers sundry things about the forest. Now the boys have 500 acres
that were given to them by the Civics Clubs of Worcester. Having no idea
what to do with their woods they made the mistake of coming to me. Well,
being an author, I sat down and wrote up a plan for them which called for
plenty of labor on their part. I'm good at that if I do say it. This plan
called for cleaning up the logging debris, planting, thinning and other
forestry measures. It was a good plan but the boys could not get their
fathers to do much work and of course the boys knew more about it than their
dads. Well there were not more than 700 people out, mostly boys, and they
were just like a herd of wild steers, so there was some little stampede.

I put them to stacking brush and they took to cutting snags. We
expected to burn brush but the wind was just right to burn the whole county
so that was taboo. Intermission for mess. I was 698th in line for mess
when I noticed smoke about half a mile away. I gave the alarm, seized a
shovel and started. With the mob? No - just four. The rest were evidently
a little hungry - there was nothing left to eat when I got back.

The fire out, we herded the gang together and as orator of the day I
took my place before them and expounded on the principles of Forest Protection,
chided them on setting forest fires, told them of blister rust and was well

qualified to tell them of blistered soles but being the guest of the day, I
could not go too far. I then distributed one hundred young pines which they
proceeded to plant, contrary to the directions I gave them.

Returning to East Brookfield at 6:00 p.m. I had but one regret. I
wished Paul Revere had been around so that I could have shaken hands with
him and called it a day. American Forest Week was under way.

E.J. McNerney, Mass.

- - - - - - - - - - - -

MASSACHUSETTS AGENTS HAVE CONFERENCE AND FIELD TRIP

The control agents in Massachusetts met in Boston with State Leader Perry,
for their annual spring conference April 16 and 17. On Friday a field trip was
made through parts of Plymouth County where white pine abounds and where numerous
wood-using plants are supplied entirely from local raw material. A visit was
made in Hanover to one box factory which secures its logs from a maximum radius
of ten miles. This factory uses one million feet a year. Numerous plantations
of white pine were observed in this region, one of them being 25 years old and
estimated to contain 30,000 board feet per acre. Considerable time was spent at
the Pembroke Arms infection area where damage this spring is particularly strikin
in the number of dead pines or the number of pines with advanced stem cankers.
Aecia had not yet appeared on that date.

The Saturday meeting was held in the State House, Boston and was devoted
to discussion of the work of the coming field season. In addition Mr. Filler
gave an instructive talk on the activities of the Bureau, the type of agent who
is being most successful and the more successful ways in which educational
features have been used.

W.J. Endersbee

NEW TYPE OF PUBLICATION NEEDED FOR SCHOOLS,

AND GIRL AND BOY SCOUTS.

Much of our educational work has been focused on illustrated talks
during the past season. One gentleman, a district superintendent of schools,
made it a point to attend two of my talks; one at a men's club, the other
at a grade school. He told me afterwards that he wanted to see how I would
treat the same subject presented to two widely different types of audience.
I asked him if he would kindly criticize any point in my talk that he thought
ought to be improved. He said as far as the talk to the business men and
farmers was concerned he could find no holes in it. So far as the actual talk
to the students was concerned it was given to them in an understandable form
for their age, but considering the fact that a large percentage of the students
were either Girl or Boy Scouts, the printed matter distributed was wholly
inadequate to assist these young people in identifying the plants we wished
destroyed, in which work they would be glad to render assistance.

Since coming to Essex the same criticism has come from a High School
teacher who asked me if I could furnish her with just such material. It
seems clear, therefore, that we should have a supply of colored plates,
correct reproductions of our wild Ribes, with a description of various
plants that look like Ribes but are not.

Agent, what do you think of this? Haven't you found this to be the
case in your district? I am sure the Washington Office would appreciate the
constructive suggestions on a publication which would fill this need.

W.T. Roop, Mass.

WHITE PINE USES

In a recent advertisement of the Weyerhaeuser Forest Products Company, appearing in "American Forests and Forest Life", the following statement is made.

"There is a growing number of lumber-users, foundrymen, pattern-makers, skilled carpenters, and fine artisans of one kind or another - who cannot be satisfied with any other wood than White Pine.

These men know White Pine for its remarkable durability under exposure to the weather - for its fine even texture - its ease of working - its ability once in place, to hold true without warping or twisting or opening at the joints. They have used other woods and know the difference."

This lumber concern had adopted a policy of marking each piece of white pine lumber - "Genuine White Pine".

R. S. Kellogg, in his book "Lumber and Its Uses", lists no less than 112 articles commonly manufactured from white pine, and summarizes the factory uses of white pine as follows:

```
Millwork........................49 percent
Boxes and crates................36    "
Car construction................ 2    "
Matches......................... 2    "
Rollers (shade and map)......... 2    "
Woodware novelties.............. 1    ..
Caskets and coffins............. 1    ..
Other uses...................... 7    ..
```

Arthur Koehler, in the "Properties and Uses of Wood", indicates the annual use of white pine for various purposes as follows:

Board Feet

All industries...3,112,698,017

Planning mill products (sash, doors,
       blinds, etc).............................1,543,545,756
Boxes and crates......................................1,131,969,940
Car construction...................................... 75,382,166

```
Matches and toothpicks..........................73,059,611
Shade and map rollers...........................61,540,000
Woodware (novelties; dairymens', poultry-
   mens', and apiarists' supplies)..............47,744,797
Caskets and coffins.............................33,170,942
Patterns and flasks.............................17,854,635
Tanks and silos.................................17,007,600
Ship and boat building..........................14,256,006
Pump and wood pipes.............................12,524,000
```

(34 other class uses are listed by Koehler, but, in
each case, the amount used is less than ten
million board feet per year.)

E.C. Filler

- - - - - - - - - -

ANCIENT PINE FELLED BY WINCHENDON WOODSMEN

Was Old-Timer When First White Men Arrived on Scene in 1722.

Agent Wm. Clave of Worcester County, Massachusetts has submitted a
news clipping from the Boston Globe of April 17, 1926, which tells of a
white pine which is probably the oldest one known in eastern states during
these later years and which has just recently succumbed to the axe. This
pine was growing in the town of Winchendon, Massachusetts and its age
as estimated by a count of rings was not less than 230 years. It measured
125 inches in circumference at the butt, and stood 116 feet tall. The first
limbs were 54 feet from the ground and the circumference at that point
measured 92 inches. It cut eight 12 foot logs; the first one scaling over
600 feet, the first four 2000 feet and the entire tree over 3000 board
feet of lumber valued at $200.00.

With butt circumference of 125 inches, it is calculated that the
tree had a butt diameter of 39.8 inches.

A Few Notes on White Pine from the Entomological

Viewpoint

It has been estimated that at least 160 species of insects
affect the eastern white pine from the seed stage to maturity. Most
of these are relatively unimportant and but few can be considered
as really primary pests. Two cone insects (one the larva of a
moth; the other a bark beetle) do considerable damage to the cones,
and in some cases seem to be the limiting factor in the production
of seed. The Pales weevil is responsible for the death of a large
percentage of natural reproduction coming in after a logging operation,
and it is practically useless to plant a cut-over area until at
least three years after cutting, because of the ravages of this
insect. Two other insects, the pine bark aphid and the spittle
insect at times do considerable damage to young seedlings and saplings,
but generally they are not considered of primary importance.

The most injurious insect infesting the eastern white pine
is the white pine weevil (Pissodes strobi Peck). Unlike the Blister
Rust, it is a native pest. In some localities very little pine is
being planted now because this weevil does so much damage to the
young trees. The white pine weevil was first described by Peck in
1817, but it was present in the northeast for many years prior to
that date. Since then a number of descriptive articles have been
written, but it was not until a few years ago that we find publications

on the control of this pest by forest management. S.A. Graham,
University Farm, St. Paul, Minnesota, and H.B. Peirson, State
Entomologist of Maine, have done noteworthy work in this line.

At the present time, separate studies of the weevil are being
carried out by the Conservation Commission of New York State and the
Bureau of Entomology in cooperation with the Northeastern Forest
Experiment Station, the State of Connecticut and certain timberland
owners in Massachusetts. This year the states of Vermont and New
Hampshire will also conduct investigations on this insect.

The white pine weevil does not kill the trees, except
occasionally in young plantations where the trees may be killed
back to the ground. The adult females lay their eggs in the terminal
shoots from early April to late June, depending on the locality and
the climate. The peak of egglaying is probably about the middle of
May. The number of eggs laid in each leader averages about 50, but
due to various agencies probably not more than three or four adults
emerge. The flow of pitch around the egg punctures, and larval
tunnels undoubtedly account for the death of many of the young
larvae, and lack of food for more. Parasites, predators and birds
also collect their toll. But even though a very small percentage
of adults emerge, the fact remains that the leader has been killed --
and the result is a crotched or crooked tree. This injury varies
in severity according to the make up of the stand. Pure pine grown

in widely spaced plantations or coming in naturally in sparsely
settled stands will be liable to much injury. Densely stocked stands
may be weeviled, but competition for height growth causes nearly
complete straightening out of the stem. It also seems that white
pine grown in mixture with better hardwoods, hemlock, or pitch
pine, will produce much straighter trees, and there is the added
advantage that the trunks clean themselves of the lower branches
much better in a mixed stand.

The study being carried on by the Northeastern Forest Experiment Station will be completed, it is hoped, in 1927. The writer
would appreciate receiving weeviled leaders from any of the blister
rust agents, who may have a chance to collect them during the
course of their work. Please send them to H. J. MacAloney,
c/o Harvard Forest, Petersham, Mass. They should be collected
by August first, and wrapped carefully to prevent escape of any
weevils which might emerge from the leaders in transit.

The writer will be very glad to send copies of the revised
"Forest Entomology Brief 21" which contains brief information on
the white pine weevil, to any Blister Rust agent. It may help him
a little when he comes across such injury.

H. J. MacAloney,
Assistant Entomologist,
N.E. Forest Experiment Station,
Amherst, Mass.

SELECTED READINGS IN PSYCHOLOGY

1. Dorsey, Geo. M. Why We Behave Like Human Beings.
   Harper Bros. New York, N.Y. 1925.

   Particularly the last three chapters. These may be read first advantageously and should be if the reader is likely to be discouraged by the size of the book.
   Specially useful for the person who may find discouraging the more technical treatments in heavier style of the traditional writer in psychology.
   On the other hand, the somewhat flippant style should not blind the other type of reader to the essential soundness of the presentation.

2. Watson, John B. Behaviorism.
   The Peoples Institute Publishing Co.
   New York, N.Y. 1925.

   A very readable book by the leading exponent of behaviorism in this country. The book represents a series of lectures given under the auspices of the Peoples Institute. In my judgment the author's introduction of the discussion of religion is unfortunate - quite unnecessary, and certain to influence many readers unfavorably toward the remainder of the book. It is suggested that the soundness of the book as a whole is not dependent upon the viewpoint expressed regarding religion.

3. Woodworth, R. S. Psychology.
   Henry Holt, New York, N.Y. 1921.

   A fairly successful attempt on the part of an able man trained in the traditional school of psychology, but sympathetic with the newer dynamic psychology, to write a treatment of psychology from the latter point of view. He still depends largely on the traditional terminology (as Watson does not). This may very well be of some aid to the student familiar with this terminology. To the beginner it represents an unnecessary extra burden of terms.

4. Gates, A.I. Elementary Psychology.
                    Macmillan, New York, N.Y. 1925.

   Another attempt to relate the newer dynamic viewpoint in psychology
to the traditional viewpoints.
   From the Preface: "The results both of introspective and objective
study have been utilized with equal freedom. The book is designed
to be a survey rather than a system of psychology."

5. Gates, A.I. Psychology for Students of Education.
                    Macmillan, New York, N.Y. 1923.

   This is essentially an attempt to present the educational psychology
of Thorndike (the master in this field) in a more readable form than
that of Thorndike. (See next below). For the person able and willing
to master the latter it is strongly recommended.

6. Thorndike, E.L. Educational Psychology. Briefer Course.
                    Bureau of Publications, Teachers College,
                    Columbia University, New York, N.Y. 1914.

   This is an abbreviated form of the author's three volume-
Educational Psychology. The three parts of the former represent
the three volumes of the latter. By the outstanding authority in
the field. Students call it difficult.

7. Thorndike, E.L. Education. A First Book.
                    Macmillan, New York, N.Y. 1912.

   A simple statement of the view that "Education is the production
and prevention of changes."   Very readable.

   The above titles are listed in the reverse order of their direct
application to the problems of teaching - or influencing others.
This has been done with the thought that the person not strongly
motivated to the study of psychology may be stimulated to such study
thru the more popular approach.

Paul J. Kruse
                                        New York State College of Agriculture
                                             Cornell University
                                               Ithaca, New York.

Q U A R A N T I N E N O T E S.

The Western Plant Quarantine Board will hold its annual meeting in
Olympia, Washington, June 9 to 11, 1926, according to Mr. W.C. Jacobsen, of
the California Department of Agriculture, Secretary of the Board. Among the
important features this year will be the attendance of representatives of three
west coast states of Mexico, who have expressed their desire to become members
of the Board. It is believed that the addition of these members will bring about
greater protection to the western states by closing the southern ports to
dangerous foreign plant material through uniform quarantine regulations.

The situation created as a result of the recent Supreme Court decision
relative to State plant quarantines is also one of the important subjects to
be discussed.

M. Thompson

- - - - - - -

Note From Old Timer

Mr. Henry Dorr, Jr., on blister rust control in Wisconsin in 1919, now
with the Medford Lumber Company of Medford, Wisconsin, writes on May 3 -

"How is the blister rust work coming? I presume the inspection work will
soon be starting. The weather here has been unusually cold for this time of the
year. . . . I want to thank you very much for the Blister Rust bulletins you
send me each month as they are very instructive and bring back memories of
yester-years."

- - - - - - - -

"The Fish and Game Club of this locality are having a banquet and enter-
tainment on Monday, May 17th. The committee in charge have asked me to speak
and show movies. I have "The Pines" coming from the State Office but I want
some others that will appeal particularly to sportsmen."

Thomas L. Kane, N.H.

WARNING TO TOURISTS

The promiscuous pulling and transportation of young forest trees is becoming a menace. Alexander Macdonald, State Conservation Commissioner, declares in his report to the legislature, and recommends that all persons transporting trees be required to obtain certificates showing that such trees are free from disease.

The practice of tourists to pull up young trees and carry them away on the running boards of automobiles is becoming alarmingly prevalent and threatens to spread tree diseases throughout the state unless stopped, it is pointed out.

"Nurserymen of New York are required by law to have certificates of inspection from the state, stating that their Nurseries are free from dangerous pests before they are permitted to ship plants of any sort from their Nurseries. There is a federal and state quarantine against bringing pine trees into New York state from New England, the violation of which subjects the offender to a penalty of $100. It is absolutely inconsistent with our present Nursery laws and quarantine to tolerate the haphazard transportation of trees from one part of our state to another.

"New York spends annually more than $200,000 in fighting two very dangerous forest tree pests, the gipsy moth and a fungous disease of the white pine, white pine blister rust. This latter disease will make, if not controlled, the growing of white pine an impossibility, and the gipsy moth will surely destroy shade and forest trees wherever he gets a foothold."

From American Nurseryman - April 1926, p. 95.

PERSONALS

Mr. S. V. Holden had the hard luck of being taken sick with the flu which began on March 17 and lasted until March 28. On top of this Mr. Holden had a severe fall which resulted in an injury to his spine. Here's hoping that an operation will not be necessary.

- - - - - - - - -

A letter has recently been received from Mr. W. F. Peel, former Blister Rust Agent in Minnesota. Mr. Peel states that his work, in the jungles of Liberia where he is engaged in the study of the pathology of rubber plantations, has kept him away from all the news. For those who are interested, Mr. Peel can be reached - ℅ Firestone Plantation, Monrovia, Liberia, West Africa. Mr. Peel was probably the first man to discover the blister rust on Ribes hudsonianum, one of the wild black currants of the Lake States.

- - - - - - -

Mr. E.M. Brockway, Plymouth County Agent has just written in for an extra copy of the December 1925 number of the Blister Rust News; this happens to be the Connecticut number. The City Forester of Brockton, Mass. found this copy so interesting that he has requested this extra copy for himself. We always appreciate the favorable comments passed on the News Letter from time to time.

- - - - - - -

Mr. Francis C. Scofield was appointed as Field Assistant effective May 1, 1926. He is now working in the Washington Office, but will probably be assigned to field work later.

Mr. H. P. Avery recently returned to the Washington Office after a trip in the field where he was engaged on quarantine inspection work. Mr. Avery told the reporter that he appreciated the work attached to quarantine inspection.

- - - - - - - - -

Mr. H. R. Offord has written several interesting letters from London and Paris, telling us of his studies and researches along the line of chemical compounds used to kill weeds. He has had the cordial cooperation of Dr. Etienne Foex of Paris, and Mr. Norris who represents a large German dye syndicate in France, as well as others in France and England. Mr. Offord sailed on April 24 from Naples after "seeing Italy in seven days". He has been appointed Agent, effective May 7, with headquarters at Boston, Mass.

- - - - - - - - -

The following Agents have been appointed in the state of Maine, effective May 3, 1926: Messrs Fred P. Yeaton who was on our work in 1924 -25; Willis S. Kimball, in 1925; Stillman L. Jones who has worked with us each summer since 1923, and Llewellyn R. Moore who is a new man on the work.

- - - - - - - - -

Mr. Harold A. Brischle of Washington resigned as Agent, effective April 14.

- - - - - - - - -

Prof. Dorr Skeels was appointed Collaborator, effective May 13, with headquarters at Missoula, Montana.

- - - - - - - - -

Mr. George S. Doore of Massachusetts has completed his work of assisting the State Leader in Boston and is now resuming his work in Franklin County (effective May 16, 1926).

NEW YORK AGENTS CHANGE HEADQUARTERS

Noble Harpp to Work With "Major" Woodward in Warren County.

Noble Harpp has recently been transferred from Columbia County to take over the work in Warren County. For some time effort was made to appoint an Agent in Warren County to fill the place made vacant by the resignation of Sherburne Fogg who was Agent in that county in 1923 and 192 Mr. Harpp will work with "Major" Woodward in this effort and it is anticipated that Harpp will meet with the same success as he did in securing cooperation in his former district. Mr. Harpp will make his headquarters at Warrensburg.

Warren County is in the center of the white pine belt of the state and some of the best stands of white pine in the northeast are located there; also some of the worst infections occur there.

- - - - - - - - -

Baker Takes Over Work in Saratoga County - Transferred from Essex County.

Charles B. Baker, former Blister Rust Control Agent of Essex County has taken over the work as Agent in Saratoga, to fill the place left vacant by the resignation of Mr. R.M. Hutchinson, recently appointed Extension Forester for the state of Maine. Mr. Baker has had experience along this line, in other parts of the state. He is a graduate from the Forestry School at Purdue University and is well qualified to carry on the work in the new district.

- - - - - - - - - -

CONNECTICUT NOTES

N. A. Norton, who has been with the Connecticut Blister Rust organization since 1923 as a crew member, foreman, and finally scout, is to enter the Yale School of Forestry this year. From May 1st to July 1st, Mr. Norton will scout the unworked portions of Salisbury to determine the areas in need of crew work. We will be sorry to lose Mr. Norton's services but believe he has taken the proper course and we wish him the best of success. May he return to the fold after completing his course.

J. E. Wilfong, Supervisor of the State Blister Rust Camp last summer, will be with us again this year acting as a special state agent. He will scout areas previously worked in Norfolk to determine the need of re-eradication and will also scout unworked areas in the same town for the purpose of eliminating non-pine and non-Ribes lands. "Will's" regular job is instructing boys in mathematics at Swarthmore Preparatory School, but he is ever anxious to get back to the wide open spaces of the Connecticut wilds and we welcome his annual reversion to the more or less primitive.

State Forester Hawes has asked us to scout the state forest in Cornwall and The Peoples' Forest in Barkhamsted and has agreed to have all necessary eradication work done.

Alfred A. Doppell, a graduate of Cornell University, has been appointed forester for the Extension Service in Connecticut. If we have a proper under-

PUBLICATIONS

Blister Rust

Hedrick, U.P. - The Small Fruits of New York.
Part 2 of the 44th Annual Report of New York State
Experimental Station, Geneva, N.Y. Sept. 18, 1925.
Blister rust is largely on page 253 in connection with
the cultivated black currant.

The black currant is little grown in America. Few
Americans born in this country have tasted the fruit, or
ever having done so care for a second taste. The product
is almost never seen in fruit markets, and the growing of
black currants is nowhere in the United States a commercial
industry, although an occasional plantation may be seen in
Canada. Here and there, plants are found in the gardens
of Europeans settled in America or in those of their immediate descendants. The law in many states prohibits the
culture of black currants because the plant is a host for
the fungus which causes the pine blister-rust, a dangerous
disease on certain pines. The black currant, for these
reasons, though probably introduced in the United States
as early as the red, has never become popular.

McCubbin, W.A. - The White Pine Blister Rust situation.
In Journal of Economic Entomology, Vol. 19, No. 2.
pp 350-355. Dec. 1925.

Park, C.A. - Eradication of Cultivated Black Currant In Oregon
in Relation to the White Pine Blister Rust Situation.
Proc. West. Plant Quarantine Bd. Spec. Publ. Dept. Agr.
Calif. 54: 78-80. 1925.

Stillinger, C.R. - White Pine Blister Rust In the West.
Proc. Western Plant Quarantine Bd. Spec. Publ. Dept. Agr.
Calif. 54: 80-82. 1925.

Ribes

Hedrick, U.P. - The Small Fruits of New York.
Several chapters in this monograph are devoted to the
cultivated currants and gooseberries. Quite a number of
excellent colored plates are included, together with
descriptions of various varieties. A statement concerning
the early history and evolution of the cultivated currants
and gooseberries, and statistics on the acreage, yield and
value of currants in the United States. is given on pgs.
243 to 354 inclusive.

BLISTER RUST NEWS

June 1926.

Volume X   Number 6

U.S. DEPARTMENT of AGRICULTURE
Office of Blister Rust Control.

CONTENTS - VOL. 10, No. 6.

Agents Work   Page
    Blister Rust Agent Taking His Cue from a Politician   185
    Five Months' Work in Four   191
Blister Rust Situation
    New Infection Area at Kennebunk Port, Maine   190
    New Spot Infection in Rhode Island   190
    Vermont Notes   190
    Notes from Plymouth County, Massachusetts   191
    White Pine Blister Rust in Pennsylvania in 1925   194
    Practicing Foresters of Connecticut Attend Blister Rust Demonstration .   195
    Eradication Work Started   197
    Need of Reeradication   197
Cooperation
    Just a Little Bit Satisfies   183
    Town Cooperation in Maine   183
    New Type of Curve Worked Out in Maine   184
Editorial
    Making Decisions   170
Education
    Aecia in the Smokeshop   173
    Methods of Getting the Average Pine Owner to Eradicate   174
    Use of Tags an Aid in Securing Blister Rust Cooperation in Warner, N.H.   177
    More About the Initial Interview   178
    Card Used to Secure Cooperation of Out-of-Town Pine Owners   180
    Use of Blister Rust Tags   181
    King Holds Series of Six Meetings   182
    Press in Springfield Aids in Blister Rust Control   186
    A Sample of Replies Received to Personal Letters Concerning
        Cooperative Control Work   189
    Blister Rust Exhibit at Vermont Forestry Association Meeting   193
Eradication
    Late Spring Delays Starting Blister Rust Control Work   188
    Save The Pine Forests   189
Forestry
    Professor Advises Students to Plant White Pine   192
    Importance of the Farm Woodlot   198
Office Comments
    Instructions Regarding Use of Government Bills of Lading   206
    Rattlesnakes   207
    Wash Away Ivy Poison   210
Personals   203
Publications   210
Quarantine Notes   202
State News
    Connecticut . . . . . . .188,190,195-197 Pennsylvania   194
    Mass.. 173,178-179,183,186,188,191,192,193 Rhode Island 188,190
    Maine . . . . 180,183,184,188,190 Vermont 180,188,190,193
    New Hampshire . . . . 177,181,182,186,188 Western States. . 200-203,205,210
    New York. 171-173,174-176,188,189
Technical Studies
    Ribes Investigations in New York State   171
    Native and Cultivated Ribes   187
Work With Young People
    Blister Rust Exhibits in Schools.   196

```
            E D I T O R I A L   S T A F F
    Roy G. Pierce . . . . . . . Editor - Washington, D.C.
    E.E. Tarbox . . . . Assoc. Editor - Maine
    Thos. J. King . . .    "      "      New Hampshire
    S. V. Holden . . .     "      "      Vermont
    W.J. Endersbee . .     "      "      Massachusetts
    O.C. Anderson . . .    "      "      Rhode Island
    J.E. Riley, Jr. . .    "      "      Connecticut
    George H. Stevens .    "      "      New York
    H.H. Ninman . . . .    "      "      Wisconsin
```

UNITED STATES DEPARTMENT OF AGRICULTURE
BUREAU OF PLANT INDUSTRY
WASHINGTON, D.C.

THE BLISTER RUST NEWS.

Issued by the Office of Blister Rust Control
and the Cooperating States.

VOL. 10, No. 6,   JUNE 1926.

MAKING DECISIONS

Many business men owe their success to their ability
of making decisions. People hesitate to make hurried
decision due to lack of self confidence, if not, at times,
carelessness.

A delayed decision delays progress. Ninety-five per
cent of all decisions are correct. Executives must have
keen powers of decisions. There must be no interruption
in the daily regime.

Battles are won by quick decisions which baffle the
enemy. A man gets somewhere if he keeps going. The
man who never knows what to do moves in circles, inter-
rupts others, and is a general nuisance. -

The Agricultural Student.

RIBES INVESTIGATIONS IN NEW YORK STATE.

Methods of eradicating Ribes in 1926 are not the same as those of ten years ago. The difference lies not so much in principles as in technique. Blister rust control, like other forms of forestry practice, is becoming more intensive with each year of development. Continued progress in this direction, however, is possible only in the presence of increasingly accurate knowledge regarding the plants with which we have to deal - in this case, particularly, Ribes.

Considerable valuable information has been contributed to this subject from time to time within the last six or eight years, yet there still remains much to be learned. The need for further work along this line was presented convincingly by Agent Endersbee in a recent issue of the News Letter. Unless the deficiences which he pointed out in our present state of knowledge be remedied within the next few years, it seems likely that they may prove obstacles in the way of making eradication technique all that it could be. And as our acreage of eradicated territory becomes greater, and as more years elapse since these areas were cleaned up, it becomes more necessary to know what is taking place or is likely to take place on them. Hence the need for becoming acquainted with the factors involved in Ribes replacement; their methods of becoming established, their reaction to site and competition, their normal rate of growth.

A few experiments commenced in New York State in 1923 and 1924, which have been continued and extended during the past season, represent an attempt to supply some, though by no means all of the desired information. These experiments have been laid out along three general lines, as follows: (1) Studies of Ribes in their development from seed. (2) Studies of the sprouting capacity of Ribes. (3) Studies on areas which have been eradicated, to determine, (a)

The amount and type of Ribes material remaining after eradication, and (b) The increase which takes place over periodic intervals. The work so far has dealt principally with gooseberries, as these represent the dominant Ribes cover on many of the eradication areas. Some work, however, is being done with skunk currants (R. glandulosum) and wild black currants (R. americanum).

The studies listed under (1) above have been carried on chiefly by sowing Ribes seeds in small plots, or "seed-spots" under a variety of orest conditions, and noting the germination which takes place, the survival among the germinated seedlings, the rate of growth of the survivors, and other conditions such as infection by Cronartium ribicola. About 400 such plots have been established, in three widely separated localities. In addition, about 75 plots are under observation where Ribes fruit has fallen naturally from old bushes. One area is being studied to observe the effect of light burning on Ribes glandulosum.

Sprouting has been studied principally on Ribes which have been root-pruned or pulled in such a way as to offer means for determining the region of growth from which sprouting is most likely to occur, and for observing the rate of growth of sprouts. About 1000 bushes have been so treated. Sprouts which have developed under natural conditions are also being watched.

Studies on eradicated areas are mostly in the form of permanent quarter-acre plots established, usually, a short time after eradication. The Ribes found there, have been measured, recorded, and tagged for future observation. This method makes it possible to obtain an accurate count and measurement of Ribes which may come in here in the future, as well as of those missed originally. Twenty-six plots of this type have been laid out to date.

Investigations such as those just described cannot be expected to take the

place of more extensive, practical field studies such as the checking operations
carried on in direct connection with the work of eradication. These aim to
collect a large mass of reasonably accurate data for the purpose of keeping track
of the work as a whole. The more detailed studies, on the other hand, aim to
establish a scientific basis for the consideration of Ribes in future working
plans. They have purposely been distributed over a considerable territory in
order to eliminate local factors, and thus make the results applicable in as
general a way as possible.

                                        E.W. Littlefield
                                        Asst. Forest Pathologist
                                        Albany, New York.

                    - - - - - - -

AECIA IN THE SMOKESHOP.

This town has a smoke shop which is little more than a hole in the wall
but it is perhaps the most popular gathering place for both smokers and non-
smokers. The proprietor is an elderly German named "Dorf". Friday I purchased
some cigarettes from Dorf who asked about blister rust. I replied by showing
him a small pine fruiting profusely with aecia. He listened to my story of the
disease, put the pine in a glass jar on the counter and said, "we will leave it
here".

Saturday a clothier told me he would destroy 75 red currants which he
planted two years ago. During the week two reporters, four merchants and two
school boys asked me for further information about the disease. They had all
seen the aecia in the smokeshop. Since then several farmers have told me they
too saw the specimen. It developed too that Dorf had "spieled" on the ravages
of the disease and had not only urged, but demanded, that currants be destroyed.

June 1, 1926.   W.J. Endersbee, Massachusetts.

METHODS OF GETTING THE AVERAGE PINE OWNER TO ERADICATE

First of all, find out just about how much white pine acreage, worth protecting, the man owns and, in a diplomatic way, find out if the place is clear. Try to understand the man and his surroundings as much as possible; also his standing and ability in the community in order to help you to get someone else to clean up the Ribes when you get him. Take it for granted that you are to get everybody in the community to eradicate if financially able.

Never leave a man with "no" for an answer, unless it is more than just "no", and he has a real good excuse to hold you off for awhile. Never go away leaving anyone with the idea that he is not going to eradicate sometime if his pine needs to be cleaned up.

Talk with the man on any subject he wants to talk about - Ford cars, cow testing or what not. If you don't know much about what he wants to talk about, talk a little on it anyhow whether you say much or not, but do not tell anything that isn't true and that you can not back up. Then talk something that you can talk; -"blister rust", as soon as convenient. Explain the disease, how it spreads, control measures, basis of cooperation, how much you would judge it would cost him per acre to eradicate, etc. Impress upon him the variation in the cost prices per acre on account of amount of Ribes, kind of men, and everything that enters into it; also how the crew is handled to cover the ground systematically and get 95 or 98 percent of the Ribes.

One of the best things I have, or rather a comparison that seems to make the blister rust control methods plain, is the old story, "Chestnut Blight". It is very easy for anyone to see that spreading from tree to tree it couldn't be controlled. Coming back home, blister rust can very easily and, in most cases, very reasonably be controlled.

Impress on the man when trying to get blister rust eradication as well as when talking reforestation, that the state is only helping in this matter and not going to run his business, or have any hold on his place afterward. However, when doing or getting work lined up, don't be afraid to let him know in a courteous way that you know your business and are bossing and giving good supervision over all that is going on. Maybe this man is a public spirite or a prominent man in the community, and if he is, don't hesitate to let him hear that in an easy, off-hand, but plain way. Judge your man as well as possible, get his confidence in some way, because if he doesn't like your cut, and unless he is exceptionally anxious to eradicate, you won't get him to act.

Be business-like but let your prospect know about the others who are doing the work, or have done, or expect to do it. Ask him to assist you in securing information about other pine owners nearby that possibly you haven't seen as yet. By the way, above all things, don't try to scare the man in any way about blister rust. Make it plain that the blister rust is not going to kill all his pine in one year but do impress on him plainly that the measures taken to control the disease are proof of its not spreading any farther. Also bring out the point that if he ever wants to sell the land, what a different attitude most buyers would take for the better if the land had been cleared of gooseberries and currants. Be sure to tell him that if a good job is done, it will not have to be eradicated again for six or seven years and maybe not then.

Whatever the case may be, just talk "horse-sense" and if you can't make it plain so he understands it in one way, try another, but satisfy yourself before you leave him that he understands something about it and above all things, why we are eradicating and how. If the pine owner thoroughly understands the basis of cooperation and is financially able, you will have no

trouble in getting a big percentage of these men to eradicate. If a pine
owner says that he is not financially able to eradicate, satisfy yourself that
this is true before you make any progress in trying to get the man to eradicate.
If this is true, think up some basis of their working together or something of
that sort for we have to get the gooseberries and currants out and hanging up
to dry.

When talking to a pine owner don't, of course, talk too fast, but put
your little job across just as quickly as you can and do it right. Don't
linger and hang around unnecessarily. In most cases make everything as business
like as possible. Have some kind of a definite understanding about starting a
foreman to work, but never tie yourself to any certain day or time to start
unless necessary to do so to get the work. If this is the case, make it a point
to have the foreman there promptly. By having some of the men ready to eradicate when you can conveniently, makes you feel more at ease about having a
place for a foreman that might get through unexpectedly on some other job. I
have found in most cases that this keeps the ball rolling better.

As I see it, there are no limits to the reasonable things one can
think of in making arrangements to eradicate and in getting a man to destroy
his bushes, if he is financially able. Every man is different and has to be
approached in a different way. It is up to us to get them, so let's do the
best we can. One good way to get eradication is to get people to plant white
pine where white pine can be planted to the best advantage; and follow up for
the destruction of currant and gooseberry bushes. So, let's go. Nearly
12,000,000 trees of all species were planted last year in this state. That
record will be beaten this year, so let's determine to also beat our Ribes
eradication record of last year.

Noble Harpp, New York.

USE OF TAGS AN AID IN SECURING BLISTER RUST COOPERATION IN
WARNER, MERRIMACK COUNTY, NEW HAMPSHIRE.

Shortly after Town Meeting, the Chairman of the Board of Selectmen of Warner, came into the Office and discussed the Town Meeting activities, particularly those concerning the securing of the Blister Rust Appropriation. In 1925 the opposition to this article was so strong that there was not a single vote in favor of it. During the fall of 1925 the writer scouted various sections of the town for infection on pine, aroused a sufficient number of leading men in the town as to the necessity of continuing the work, that the article passed in 1926 without a single vote against it. The Selectman advised that the opposition in 1925 was based purely on misrepresentation by the opposition and that our work in the fall of 1925 had overcome this.

An additional aid in securing town cooperation was the tagging of trees as we found them, both throughout the woodlands and along the roadsides. Many people who had formerly opposed or were lukewarm, noticing the tage on the trees, got out of their carriages or machines to determine the reason for them. They remained sometime examining the tagged trees and saw for themselves the effects of blister rust on the pine, decided for themselves that it could do all that we claimed for it, and changed their attitude with reference to the town's voting money for control work. Mr. Johnson, the Selectman previously mentioned, said "I hope you will continue this work of tagging trees, at least in my town." We will.

T.J. King, N.H.

Prosperous Communities. Growing forests producing annually and regularly makes business and draw other industries.

(From News Letter, New York State College of Forestry.)

MORE ABOUT THE INITIAL INTERVIEW.

Mr. Filler's article on the initial interview which appeared in the May
issue of the News Letter was interesting and prompts me to relate certain parts
of my own experiences, observations and conclusions on this subject. My experiences at least are undoubtedly common to other Massachusetts agents and
others who work under a policy similar to the one in vogue in this state. We
may, however, differ on observations and particularly on conclusions.

Ringing door bells from May to October gives rise to thought as to the
surest ways to get the doors opened. By deliberate experimentation I find that
a blister rust specimen of liberal proportions is the surest way at my disposal.
During May the fruiting specimen has done most of the talking on the initial
interview. Would that aecia were produced during all the summer months. I shall,
however, continue to carry the most wicked looking specimen I can secure. I
have also learned what not to do or what not to appear. Not long ago my wife
saw a man with books in his hand approach our house. She said, "here comes a
book agent, you go to the door." He turned out to be the assessor, but had my
wife been alone he would have found no one at home. A few days later I experimented. Stopping the car in front of a house, I approached with a circular
and note book in hand and rang the bell. There was no response, yet I know there
were people in the house. I repeated this procedure in two other places where I
knew people were at home, with the same results. I have decided not to try to
sell books.

The blister rust specimen has become my most common and most successful
means of approach and in most cases I make it direct by saying "Good morning,
Sir, I thought you would be interested in seeing some blister rust." Thus far
the prospect always has been interested.

Securing action is the most difficult part of the interview. With me
the goal in each interview is to secure a definite appointment to do the

necessary work on each property. For the purpose of appointments I carry a
diary which I call a schedule book. The interview is complete and successful
only when each person's name is entered under some date in that book. I tell
the prospect how we cooperate and who has taken advantage of our offer of aid.
I produce the book and tell him the first open dates that he may choose from
and at the same time read the names of his neighbors who are listed. This
system has been 100% successful to this extent, that no pine owner has failed
to give me a promise to do the work at some time. In about a third of the
cases I get a definite date. About half the owners give me an approximate date
where I record their names with the understanding that I will see or phone them
on or before that date. The remaining promises are very indefinite as to time.
One put the time at sometime this fall, another for next year. Others have
promised to phone me when they would be able to do the work. Some of these
have already kept their word.

This system has so far been sufficiently satisfactory for my needs. I
now have, on June 1, work scheduled for three men for the next ten days. There
is an even greater amount of work listed under approximate dates. Within ten
days I expect to have a keep five foremen busy on jobs which I arrange for.
Each job averages about two days work for one foreman. This system does not
eliminate follow-up work and I believe there is no system that will do that.

W.J. Endersbee — Massachusetts.

* * * * * * * * * * * * *

Increasing Revenues. Growing forests are producing wealth every hour
of the day and the night.

(From News Letter, New York State College of Forestry.)

CARD USED TO SECURE COOPERATION OF OUT-OF-TOWN

PINE OWNERS

No. _____   Date_____ _____

Bl. _____

Dear Sir:
     I authorize you to carry out the control measures
necessary to prevent the spread of Blister Rust on my
property in _____. The total cost to me is not to
exceed $_____and it is understood that the Town
Foreman will supervise my labor without cost to me.

                Signature_____

                Address _____

                _____

    A supply of the above cards has recently been run off in the
Washington Office at the request of Mr. Solon D. Conner, Agent at Portland,
Maine. This is a sample of the SERVICE that the Washington Office can
render.

- - - - - - - -

BLISTER RUST COOPERATION WITH THE UNITED STATES MORGAN HORSE FARM

    Cooperation has been arranged between Vermont Forest Service and the
Bureau of Animal Industry which maintains the Morgan Horse Farm at Middlebury,
Vermont. The farm has an area of about 1000 acres of which about 250 acres
are in white pine. The Ribes will be eradicated to protect the white pine.

DEDUCTIONS FROM ALEXANDRIA TOWN MEETING.

I attended Town Meeting in Alexandria last March. Rather a peculiar situation developed here. There was the usual discussion pro and con on the Blister Rust Article. Then the vote was taken. The motion was lost 14 to 13. There were 78 voters in the hall at the time the question came up.

I believe that some persistent educational work in this town this year on the value of the pine to the town, and the necessity of conserving this valuable forest crop, will win for blister rust control in the town meeting next year.

G. F. Richardson, N.H.

- - - - - - -

USE OF BLISTER RUST TAGS

As the result of a discussion at the last meeting of New Hampshire Agents, I have talked with a number of pine owners on the value of tagging infected trees. They feel that we should use a greater number of tags. They also feel that the tag suggested at the meeting of the Agents which would include a short description of the disease on one side would be a big improvement over those now used.

G. F. Richardson, N. H.

- - - - - - -

It is often the case that a Chairman becomes confused in the introduction of a speaker to an audience. The following was heard recently –
"Motion pictures on Blister Rust will be shown by Mr. B. - - -, the Blister Bust Agent."

- - - - - - -

First uredinia on Ribes in the Massachusetts Berkshires were observed by W.J. Endersbee on June 8. The first uredinia in A.J. Lambert's district in Maine, were reported on R. hirtellum and R. glandulosum on June 12.

KING HOLDS SERIES OF SIX MEETINGS

Fruiting Specimens of Blister Rust a Valuable Aid.

Mr. T. J. King, Agent in Merrimack County, has recently forwarded the Editor a series of six programs for field meetings in his district. The meetings were held on consecutive days at different timber lots throughout the county. The total attendance at these meetings was 100. Mr. King talked on the white pine blister rust and its control. The wood-lot problem, including thinning, pruning, weeding, and utilization, was discussed by Mr. Fletcher, Extension Forester of the Dept. of Agriculture. Activities of the New Hampshire Forestry Commission, including Planting, Town Forests, and Classification Law, were discussed by Messrs. Newman, Tripp, Watson and Hale. Mr. King writes "This is the most successful series of meetings I have ever attempted. A real interest was shown in the meeting by farmers, members of rural Agricultural Class, and Boys Clubs.

Fruiting specimens of the blister rust were taken to the meetings and these were especially successful in gaining attention since it turned out that very few had seen blister rust in the fruiting stage.

Mr. Fletcher, the New Hampshire Extension Specialist, commenting upon the damage to the pine from blister rust which he had seen at Andover stated "It is plain to be seen that any plan of forest management relating to white pine must have as its first step, protection from the white pine blister rust".

Edit: The holding of the meetings just at the time of the blister rust fruiting stage was a happy thought and the idea might be taken advantage of by the other Agents in future years.

JUST A LITTLE BIT SATISFIES

One of our first cooperators this season was finally coaxed from his plough to go over his land, 116 acres in all. After spending the greater part of the day in the woods and finding nothing to pull on he was rather inclined to be bored. On the last four-acre piece covered, the scout pointed out to him a young pine about six feet tall, with the top dead and a fruiting canker on the stem.

"Well, now then," said Mr. Cooperator, "if all that blister rust man told me is true, where is the currant or gooseberry bush that infected that tree?"

After a close search one gooseberry bush about fifteen inches tall was found about forty feet from the tree. You can be sure that this area was checked over in quick time, but no other bushes were found.

One more citizen convinced of the reality of blister rust!

William Clave, Massachusetts.

- - - - - - -

TOWN COOPERATION IN MAINE.

To date, June 5, forty-seven town have appropriated $7,716.00, by counties as follows:

Oxford County - 18 towns appropriating $2800.00

Cumberland County - 12 towns appropriating $2006.00

Androscoggin, Sagadahoc and Kennebec Counties - 9 towns
        appropriating $1750.00

York County - 9 towns appropriating $1159.

Inquiries regarding blister rust are coming in from non-appropriating towns - what to do with them regarding eradication is a problem. Blister rust is surely spreading in unprotected areas.

W.O. Frost, Maine.

NEW TYPE OF CURVE WORKED OUT IN MAINE.

White Pine Blister Rust Control Work From 1922 to May 1926

By W.O.Frost - State Leader

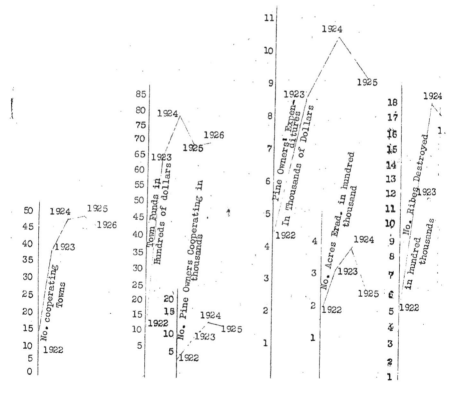

BLISTER RUST AGENT TAKING HIS CUE FROM A POLITICIAN.

"I remember hearing a prominent politician once remark when he was
questioned regarding his prowess as a vote getter, 'Well, I attribute my
success to one rule that I have closely followed. Whenever I found an enemy
in the camp I never rode him or tried to make it disagreeable for him. I put
myself out to make things so congenial and comfortable for him that eventually
this unexpected friendly treatment got him, and he came around to my way of
thinking. Play into the hands of your adversaries (apparently), your friends
can take care of themselves'.

I thought this statement over quite a bit and decided to try the stunt
last summer on a chronic kicker against blister rust, Mr. B. This man had been
stating his views at Town Meeting for two years and had given the blister rust
an annual blasting. Some time in August I paid him a social call and talked
every subject but Blister Rust. I continued these visits for some time, never
failing to heap words of praise on him for his success as a dairyman and general
farmer. When I felt that his chest had expanded to its limit and he was in a
happy frame of mind I had a heart to heart talk with him about our work.

The crew had already completed its work in this town for the summer,
but Mr. B. felt so tickled about everything I had said that before our visit
ended, he made up his mind to cover his own pine lot with his hired help and
the foreman the State provided. As a fitting climax, Mr. B. proved to be one
of the best boosters I had at the last Town Meeting and aided materially in
securing a town appropriation. Everyone in town wondered at his change in
attitude and inquired from me the reason why it all came about. I've never
let out the secret until this day and only to you and other agents. Try the
stunt yourself sometime, but be sure and buy a good brand of plug tobacco
before you pay the visit. I found out that it came in handy."

T. J. Kane, N.H.

PRESS IN SPRINGFIELD AIDS IN BLISTER RUST CONTROL
Public Spirited Owners Near Parks Remove Bushes.

Early in the year, a campaign was instituted in the Springfield, (Mass.) press to educate the citizens of the city who lived in the vicinity of the municipal parks in the life-history of blister rust, and the consequent neces-sity of removing their cultivated Ribes. Later in the season, a complete census of these bushes near the parks was taken. When all the data was complete the press campaign was brought to a climax by an article telling briefly and plainly what was to be done — and why. The cooperation of the Department of Parks of the city government was an active feature of the campaign.

With the press campaign behind him, and with all the data in his pos-session, the Agent made a personal call on the owner of every cultivated Ribes bush in the removal zone. Some of his experiences were amusing, needless to say, and highly gratifying. Out of about two-score persons interviewed, only two made any objection to the removal of their bushes. Of such is the power of the press.

One lady has a nice group of flowering currants growing in her front yard. When the Agent broke the sad news to her that the bushes would have to come out, she said; "Oh, I can't let those go. They were set out twenty years ago by my mother; she set them out two years before she died". It took half an hour of earnest solicitation before Mrs. X agreed to the removal of the shrubbery; before she could be brought to see that the currants were a menace to the pine forest of the great park used by thousands of her fellow-citizens every year.

R.E. Wheeler, Massachusetts.

NATIVE AND CULTIVATED RIBES OF THE EAST

In the East there are 13 native species of wild currants and gooseberries, all of them, as far as known, being susceptible to the blister rust.

The habitat of these species varies from very dry, stony sites to moist swamps. In the Northeastern and Lake States currants and gooseberries are usually found in all sites where white pine grows; that is, both hosts of the blister rust thrive in practically the same localities and usually several species may be found on the same area.

Native Species of Currants

Ribes americanum - Mill. - wild black currant
" aureum - Pursh - yellow flowering currant
" glandulosum - Grauer - skunk or fetid currant
" hudsonianum - Rich. - Hudson Bay or northern black currant.
" lacustre -(Pers.) Poir. - prickly stemmed or swamp black currant or swamp gooseberry.
" triste - Pall. - swamp red or wild red currant.

Native Species of Gooseberries

Grossularia cynosbati (L.) Mill. - prickly berried gooseberry
" curvata (Small) Cov. & Britt.- Georgia gooseberry
" echinella - Cov. - spiny gooseberry
" hirtella - (Michx.) Spach - Northern or smooth gooseberry
" missouriensis - (Nutt.) Cov. & Brit. - Missouri gooseberry
" oxyacanthoides - (L.) Mill.- hawthorn gooseberry
" rotundifolia - (Michx.) Cov. & Britt. - Eastern wild gooseberry.

Cultivated Species

Ribes alpinum - (L.) - Alpine currant
" aureum - Pursh - yellow flowering currant
" nigrum - (L.) European black currant
" odoratum - Wendl. - yellow flowering currant or spice bush or Missouri, buffalo, or golden currant.
" vulgare (Lam.) common red or white currant.
Grossularia reclinata - (L.) Mill. - common garden gooseberry

R. G. Pierce

LATE SPRING DELAYS STARTING BLISTER RUST CONTROL WORK

Reports received on the beginning of Ribes eradication may be of interest:

Maine

Owing to backward season, eradication work started later than in past years. The first eradication being carried on in the town of Kittery, on May 10.

W.O. Frost.

New Hampshire

"Eradication work was started on May 5 in two towns - North Hampton and Canaan."

L.E. Newman.

Vermont

"Eradication started by W.E. Bradder at Rutland, Vermont, May 6. Rose began work at Hartford, May 13, and Holden at Charlotte, Vermont, May 18."

S.V. Holden.

Massachusetts

"First field work this year in Massachusetts was started on April 16 in Whitman, (Plymouth County) but the first Ribes were removed on April 19, in East Brookfield, (Worcester County)."

C.C. Perry.

Rhode Island

"Eradication work commenced in Rhode Island this season on May 3rd in the town of Burrillville with a crew of five scouts under the direction of Mr. Byron W. Carr, acting as foreman."

O.C. Anderson.

Connecticut

"The first Ribes eradication this year was on the E.C. White estate at Litchfield, May 6."

J.E. Riley.

New York

"The first eradication crew in the field began work May 12, in the town of Watson, Lewis County."

A.F. Amadon.

SAVING THE PINE FORESTS

New York State Plans to Cover 40,000 Acres This
Year For Control of White Pine Blister Rust.

Eradication work in New York State is approximately one month late in
starting this year. In 1925, the work started April 16th and by May 1st there
were 26 crews at work on private land. To date, there are but 16 crews at
work, yet in spite of the handicap of the late spring, it is planned to cover
40,000 acres of land or thirty percent more than in 1925. It is also planned
to eradicate approximately 3000 acres in the 10,000 acre tract on Tongue
Mountain, Lake George, which was recently acquired by the State for park purposes. There are also in this tract, 700 acres of open farm land which the
State will plant to white pine as soon as the land has been cleared of Ribes.

On the east side of Lake George, William T. Knapp, one of the largest
land owners, is completing the eradication of Ribes on 2,547 acres begun three
years ago. Just as soon as Mr. Knapp was convinced that the removal of all
currant and gooseberry bushes was necessary to the protection of his white
pine he started control work and has continued ever since. This summer he
plans to cover 500 acres and to complete the Ribes eradication next year.

- - - - - - -

A SAMPLE OF REPLIES RECEIVED TO PERSONAL LETTERS CONCERNING

COOPERATIVE CONTROL WORK

Personal Letter Suggesting Cooperation Brings Good Response.

A few of the replies are as follows:

"Our white pines were set out in an old pasture where there was
nothing but grass so we think they are safe from the disease.
However we would be pleased to have you look them over and see
if they are doing well."
* * * * * * *

"In reply to your recent letter, I have only 1000 nursery pine
planted and I have noticed no rust or blister although they are open for
inspection any time you wish."
* * * * * * *

"I would like a tree inspection as I have around twenty-four
hundred white pines."

George E. Stevens. New York

NEW INFECTION AREA AT KENNEBUNK PORT, MAINE.

Concerning this area, there must be in the neighborhood of three or four hundred acres of woodland of all types and description. The heaviest infection noted was on about eight acres, I should judge. Infected trees vary in size from trees of twenty or thirty years down to small reproduction. Infection is of all ages, from 1917 up to 1924.

Skunk currants are to be found in large quantities around these areas. In places the currants are growing in through the pine in profusion. Some of the lots in this area are covered with birch with young pine scattered around under the birch, and infection seems very plentiful.

As this is a coast town there is planty of fir and spruce to be found in places along with the pine, but this type seems to offer no protection to the pine as far as blister rust is concerned.

E.E. Tarbox, Maine.

NEW SPOT INFECTION IN RHODE ISLAND.

A large spot infection was found in North Smithfield, May 6th, in one of the largest white pine stands. There are several trunk cankers dating 1919 found near wild black currant bushes growing throughout the stand. Over 50 limb cankers were found on one tree.

O.C. Anderson.

- - - - - - -

VERMONT NOTES

We have several eradication crews going now (June 1). Am finding pine infection in nearly every stand in the Burlington district. Cooperation is coming fine.

S.V. Holden.

NOTES FROM PLYMOUTH COUNTY, MASSACHUSETTS.

8000 Gooseberries on One Lot

One lot of 300 acres belonging to O.O. Smith, Hingham, has just been worked and over 8000 wild gooseberries pulled, and about 200 currants. About one third to one half of pines are diseased. Other neighboring owners are now starting crew work.

New Infection Area From Imported Black Currants

A new infection area was discovered in Hingham, on Derby Street, near South Weymouth. Infection will run 85% and started wholly from cultivated black currants imported from England.

Radio Talk Pulls Black Currants

One lady in Hingham heard C.C. Perry's lecture on Blister Rust during Forest Protection Week and went out and pulled out eight black currants.

E.M. Brockway.

- - - - - - -

FIVE MONTHS' WORK IN FOUR

Normally, the Ribes eradication season is about five months long. This year, the late spring has cut the time by at least a month. Consequently, to accomplish as much control work as last season, we must do five months' work in four. (Also, in 1925, there was a decrease of 17.2 percent in the acreage cleared of Ribes over 1924.) To attain the desired results this year will require every available employee on the firing line throughout the summer months. It means greater efforts by each man in the organization, increased cooperation, additional crew men, more checking, and better planning and organizing of all phases of the control program.

E.C. Filler

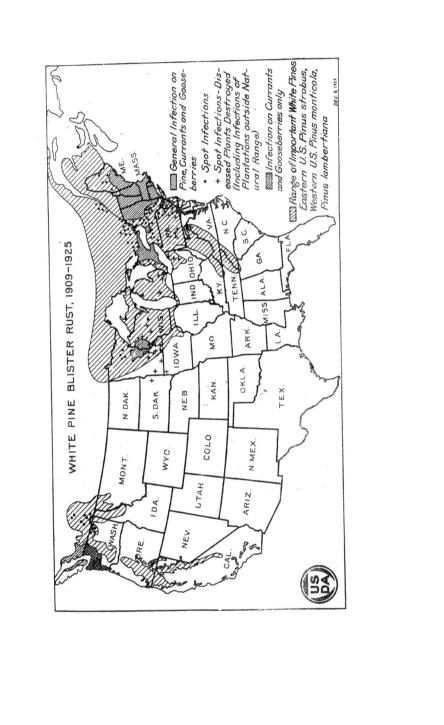

WHITE PINE BLISTER RUST, 1909–1925

General Infection on Pine, Currants and Gooseberries

• Spot Infections
+ Spot Infections–Diseased Plants Destroyed (Including Infections of Plantations outside Natural Range)

Infection on Currants and Gooseberries only

Range of Important White Pines, Eastern U.S. Pinus strobus, Western U.S. Pinus monticola, Pinus lambertiana

DEC. 8, 1925

PROFESSOR ADVISES STUDENTS TO PLANT WHITE PINE

Economics Teacher Tells Boston University Pupils That
They Can Do a Big Service to the Country and Profit at
the Same Time - Warns of Blister Rust.

Added proof that the foresters who urge more and better practice in
timber land management are developing a plan which is advocated by economists,
was given recently in a lecture by Professor Roy J. Honeywell of the economics
department of Boston University College of Business Administration in which
he stressed the need of conservation and advised his students to buy waste
land for reforestation.

Professor Honeywell spoke of the fast depleting available timber land
of the United States, and outlined how the lumber had shifted about the country.

In spite of the efficient State and Governmental organization for
eliminating diseases, preventing and checking fires, promoting conservation
and advocating reforestation, the inroads of the ruthless waste of the past
have been so great that we will undoubtedly be faced with a serious shortage
in a few years.

"This offers a chance," said Professor Honeywell" to do a big public
service and at the same time probably make a fortune. Lumber is practically
indispensable. It is practically certain that there will be bigger demands
for lumber in fifty years than there is today, due to the growing shortage.
It so happens that white pine, which is perhaps the most useful of all woods,
is the easiest to grow.

"White pine will grow on almost any kind of waste land, in fact, land
that practically nothing else will grow on. It requires very little attention
and it grows fast. Waste land can be bought very cheap. The trees, several
years old, can be obtained from the State and set out at a very reasonable

cost.

"It requires, generally, about thirty years to get usable timber, which should yield a big profit. White pine is fortunate in another way, it has comparatively few enemies and requires little care. A yearly cleaning out of the underbrush is the greatest expense, and I have been told that this can be done for only a little over a dollar an acre.

"There are only two principal enemies of white pine – Fire and Blister Rust. Both can be controlled. Fire prevention, due to more adequate fire patrol and keeping out the underbrush, is gradually becoming a fact. Blister rust can be prevented or eliminated by State and Government men who will make free inspections and eliminate the disease when private pine owners will cooperate.

"The study of forest conservation and the careful consideration of both the service as a citizen and the personal gain in investing in forest raising are well worthwhile. Should you be unable to realize personally on the crop, you will always have the satisfaction that you have done a good work for posterity."

G. Stanley Doore, Mass.

BLISTER RUST EXHIBIT AT VERMONT FORESTRY
ASSOCIATION MEETING.

The Vermont Forestry Association held its first annual meeting at the Long Trail Lodge, near Rutland on May 26. The meeting, according to the Secretary, was a good one. Agent W.E. Bradder had a small exhibit of blister rust present and answered questions concerning the rust and its control.

Editor: The idea of having a blister rust exhibit and an Agent present to discuss the subject at the annual meetings of the state forest associations is a good one.

WHITE PINE BLISTER RUST IN PENNSYLVANIA IN 1925.

Scouting for the blister rust was carried on in Wayne County, Pennsylvania in 1925 in cooperation with the Pennsylvania Bureau of Plant Industry under the direction of Dr. W. A. McCubbin. Paul B. Smith, Agent was engaged on this survey during July and August. Mr. Smith sums up the situation in Wayne County as follows:

> Blister rust has been found in various parts of the county except the southern section. The host in every case, excepting one, is the black currant; the one exception is the wild gooseberry. One new infection was found at Laurella in the central district. In some cases, rust areas located previously and again inspected this year show no infection. This condition was found by Dr. McCubbin and the writer near Poyntelle. Bushes near Galillee where infection was known have been destroyed. Rust is still found at:
> 1. Callicoon – pines and black currants.
> 2. Rileyville – black currants.
> 3. Laurella – "   "
> 4. Damascus – pines and wild gooseberries.

Dr. McCubbin writes confirming Mr. Smith's observation that there has been little spread southward of the disease beyond the points at which it was noted in 1922 –

> "I also noted that in at least two locations where rust was found by me in both 1921 and 1922, there was no rust on these cultivated black currants during the present year. In this connection it is worthy of note that the first lot of pines found with infection in 1921 on the Delaware River opposite Callicoon, N. Y., now show no infection. I cut off most of the cankered branches at that time and there are indications that the owner has removed branches since then. But I found this season no new infection on any of these twelve or on a lot of 50 or more young pines nearby.
> On the other hand, pine infection was found in young second growth near Damascus and rust on adjacent wild Ribes in a field. The indications are that the rust has been present here for a number of years, since there was one young pine, evidently dead for several years, which has been killed by blister rust. The location found by Mr. Smith at Louella also had young pines entirely killed."

CONNECTICUT NOTES

The first uredinia to be discovered this year in Connecticut were found June 2, in the town of Salisbury on R. cynosbati. Uredinia on R. vulgare and R. hirtellum were found June 13 in the town of Washington.

- - - - - -

BLISTER RUST CONTROL DISCUSSED AT CONNECTICUT FORESTRY
ASSOCIATION MEETING.

The Connecticut Forestry Association's summer field meeting was held May 15, on the estate of Alain C. White. About 150 members were present and enjoyed a varied program including a trip through the extensive plantation, followed by a picnic lunch in a pine grove. Here talks were given by Dean Graves, of the Yale Forest School; Dr. Perley Spaulding, of the Northeastern Forest Experiment Station; Mr. John W. Titcomb, State Superintendent of Fish and Game; Prof. Fred R. Fairchild, in charge of the special forest tax investigation being made by the U.S. Forest Service; and Mr. W. O. Filley, Forester for the Connecticut Agricultural Experiment Station. Fire fighting methods were demonstrated by men from the State Foresters' organization. A blister rust exhibit attracted considerable attention and two and sometimes three men were kept busy answering questions. A short talk was given by the State Blister Rust Leader. In introducing the speaker Dean Graves spoke of the economic importance of control work and emphasized the seriousness of the blister rust menace to western timber.

- - - - - - -

PRACTICING FORESTERS OF CONNECTICUT ATTEND
BLISTER RUST DEMONSTRATION

The monthly field meeting of the practicing foresters of Connecticut was held in Salisbury, June 2, and was devoted to a study of blister rust conditions in northeastern Connecticut. Two heavily infected areas were visited where

Ribes had been destroyed in previous years; old infections were numerous, but

while a surprising number of seedlings had come in during the last few years,

no new infections originating subsequent to eradication were found. An

informal talk on the life history of the disease, control measures, and present

status of the control work was made by W.O. Filley who conducted the trip.

Several blister rust men were present to assist Mr. Filley. Another area that

had not been eradicated showed sixty to eighty-five percent infection; many

of the infections being of recent origin. Among those attending were

representatives of the State Department of Education, the Supervisor of the

Salisbury Association (nature study in the schools), State Forester's Office,

Connecticut Forestry Association, Connecticut Agricultural Experiment Station,

Recreation and Wild Life Commission.

- - - - - -

BLISTER RUST EXHIBITS IN SCHOOLS

A blister rust display consisting of colored panels, posters, specimens

of diseased pines, growing specimens of several cultivated and wild Ribes,

well labeled, so assembled as to tell the story of blister rust control was set

up at the school childrens' nature study exhibit in Meriden, May 20-24. It

was visited by thousands of children and teachers and the general public. It

was made self explanatory and no blister rust representative was present. We

are informed that considerable interest was shown in the display. One concrete

result was a request for a similar display at the school childrens' exhibit in

Lakeville, June 8. Here Agent Clark was in attendance and gave a talk to the

assembled children and their parents.

It is believed that school work is an important part of our educational

rust on currant and gooseberries is to be made a part of the garden study work
in Salisbury. It is planned to arrange a field trip with the school children
for the purpose of identifying trees and common tree pests, and blister rust
will be especially studied.

- - - - - - -

ERADICATION WORK STARTED

Eradication work was started in Litchfield, May 6. Two private cooperation jobs served as a training course for foremen and state crew men.
On June 15 the crew started state eradication in the town of Salisbury.

The Ribes on the Mohawk State Forest are now being eradicated with men
supplied by the State Forester under the direction of a foreman furnished by the
Agricultural Experiment Station. Agent Clark is supervising the work.

- - - - - - -

NEED OF REERADICATION

Mr. L. W. Hodgkins spent the greater part of the week of May 24 training
R. A. Perry and N. C. Norton for scout work. Various parts of Salisbury were
visited and their reports show an immediate need of reeradicating areas worked
five years ago. This need of rescouting in northwestern Connecticut after
five years is borne out by numerous observations made by the state leader and
others and is further emphasized by Mr. Endersbee's report on the results of
1920 and 1921 eradication in Colebrook. The survey of previous eradicated areas
that is to be made in Norfolk this summer by J. E. Wilfong will afford more
data on this subject of reeradication.

- - - - - - -

Mr. Fivaz spent a couple of days in New Haven with the State Leader,
discussing progress of the crew efficiency experiment and making plans for
supplementary experimental work along this line.

J. E. Riley, Conn.

IMPORTANCE OF THE FARM WOODLOT IN

FINANCING THE FARMER

By E. H. Thomson
President, Federal Land Bank of Springfield

In most of the Northeastern states wood and timber occupies a substantial part of the farm area. Probably in no other district in the country
is this resource so interwoven with the farm business, not only in its plan
of management but as a part of the regular farm income. It is due to this
fact that the Federal Land Bank of Springfield in its work of financing
farmers in the Northeastern states has been brought into intimate contact with
the problems arising from the consideration of wood and timber on farms.

The purpose of the Federal Land Bank of Springfield is to furnish long
term first mortgage loans to farm owners. These loans are made up to about
one-half the value of the land and buildings and at a low rate of interest and
on a long term basis. No other form of mortgage loan so well fits the needs of
agriculture.

The Springfield Bank, organized in 1917, is one of twelve such Federal
Land Banks in the country, and has loaned approximately 42 million dollars to
the farmers in New England, New York and New Jersey. The capital of the bank
is largely owned by the farmers and it obtains its loaning funds in the investment market through the sale of Federal Land Bank bonds secured by the
first mortgages on farms.

It is the policy of the Federal Land Bank of Springfield to regard
wood and timber as a crop. This crop differs from other crops only in the
length of its growing and marketing period. From the standpoint of security
or credit wood and timber on the farm has many advantages.

It permits the utilization of and furnishes an income from lands that would be a liability on many farms because of the soil, topography and rugged conditions common to much of this area. It is a crop adapted to this type of country. It fills in the waste spaces and balances out the farm.

It is a crop that has steadily increased in value while other farm products have been subject to ruinous prices in some years. It also bids fair to continue to gain in value.

A third feature and one that is given altogether too little attention is the fact that wood and timber readily responds to care and improved methods of management. The farm woodlot even with little or no attention has assumed an important place on most farms so that with increased attention its field of use and value is greatly enlarged. That is, if the returns today from 40-acre woodlot warranted a valuation of $1,000 this same lot can be nearly doubled in value, as measured by income received - assuming that prices and costs remain the same - by better care and improved methods of forest management. This is a big factor when it comes to paying off a long term mortgage. Such methods would be of little use to a farmer who has his mortgage to pay off in from three to five years but they are of inestimable value to the man whose mortgage is paid over a 34-year period.

(The remainder of this article will be reproduced in the July and August issues of the Blister Rust News)

From Journal of Forestry, Vol. 24, No. 4, April 1926. p.347

- - - - - -

Mr. W.J. Endersbee attended the Connecticut Forestry Association meeting in Litchfield, May 15.

REPORT OF BLISTER RUST CONTROL WORK IN THE WESTERN

STATES, MAY 1 to MAY 31, 1926.

Work of State Leaders.

Montana: C. H. Johnson reports the eradication of 25 cultivated black currants in Ravalli County and 66 in Missoula County during May. He has also made a field study of the Ribes species occurring in the white pine stands in Montana, preliminary to reconnaissance work during the summer.

Oregon and Washington: L. N. Goodding, accompanied by Patty, spent the month of May in scouting for pine infection in western Washington. Infected pines were found in 8 localities, all on or near the Olympic Peninsula. Infection occurred only on young trees, and only in the vicinity of R. bracteosum.

California: The following report by Root covers all phases of the work in California.

"Experimental local control work in California will commence June 1st. At this time the camp will be established and preliminary work started preparatory to getting the project under way in "full swing" by June 15th at which time the camp will have its full quota of men.

"The area decided upon for this project is in the Stanislaus National Forest in Tuolumne County where sugar pine reaches its optimum range. The wild currants and gooseberries will be removed on a cutover area where a good stand of second growth timber is coming up, and on an area of virgin timber. Three species of wild Ribes will be found, the Prickly Fruited Gooseberry, G. roezli, the Sierra Nevada Currant, R. nevadense and the Squaw Currant, R. cereum.

"The first camp site will be located about twenty-five miles northeast of Sonora on the north fork of the Tuolumne River, not far from the main highway traversing this country. Autos can quite easily reach the camp site so men and provisions can be readily transported.

"This project, the first of its kind in California, will employ about twenty-five men. For the first two weeks, there will be about eight men in camp, during which time satisfactory Ribes tools or implements for grubbing out the bushes will be developed. It has been found that these bushes do not pull as easily by hand as do those of the white pine regions of northern Idaho.

"Mr. P. E. Melis will have immediate supervision of this work and make his headquarters in Berkeley. Mr. W. V. Benedict, recently transferred from Spokane, Washington, to Berkeley will be in charge of the Methods Study. His duties will consist of checking all areas worked for missed bushes and making plot studies to determine the most efficient methods of performing the different phases of the work. Mr. P. O. Hanson, a graduate of the University of California, will assume

duties with this office, July 1st, with headquarters in Berkeley. His work
will consist largely of a _Ribes_ survey of sugar pine areas to determine the
ecological relationship between _Ribes_ and sugar pine. In the study of
ecology in general, light is conceded to be a factor which influences plant
growth. Just wheat influence this has upon Ribes growth in white and sugar
pine stands will be studied by Mr. A. Grasovsky who at present is located at
the University of California. He is perfecting a photometer or light
measuring instrument which may prove to be of practical value in determining
areas where we may or may not expect to find wild currants or gooseberries.

Black Currant Eradication

"This phase of the control work will start about July 1st. Four men
will be put into the field, the same number as last year. It is hoped the
following counties will be covered this season: Yuba, Sutter, Yolo, Napa,
Solano, Marin, El Dorado, Amador, Calaveras, Alpine, Tuolumne, Mono and
Mariposa.

Educational

"Permission has been granted to install a permanent Blister Rust
exhibit in the museum in Balboa Park in San Diego and in the museum in
Exposition Park in Los Angeles. It is hoped these may be permanently
placed by the end of the year."

Quarantine Inspection

During April, 6 violations of Federal Quarantine 54 and 4 of Washington State Quarantines were intercepted. During May, however, only a single
violation of Quarantine 54 was intercepted.

QUARANTINE NOTES

THE AUTO A MENACE IN BLISTER RUST CONTROL.

From California State Department of Agriculture News. May 1, 1926.

That other states besides California recognize the automobile as a serious problem when it comes to transporting plants which may be the carriers of disease, and have followed the California method of protection, is attested by the following statement made by George A. Root, State Leader in Blister Rust Control.

> "The interstate bridge at Portland, Oregon has proved to be a very serious problem from the standpoint of the transportation of the blister rust from Washington into Oregon. On Sundays many motorists have been carrying the Red Flowering currant, Ribes sanguineum from Washington into Oregon. A short period last spring revealed over 100 such cases. On Sunday, March 21st of this year, 108 such cases were intercepted. This work is being done by the State Board of Horticulture of Oregon since the Federal Horticultural Board does not have the necessary authority to do this type of work."

A Federal quarantine prohibits the movement of all currants and gooseberries out of the State of Washington, as well as all five-needled pines. California forests besides being afforded the protection of this quarantine are further being protected by the removal of all cultivated European black currants, the worst offender in the spread of this disease.

Mr. George E. Stevens' headquarters have been changed from Lowville, New York to Albany, % Conservation Commission. Mr. Stevens is now acting as Assistant State Leader of the New York work.

Mr. Gilbert B. Posey, in charge of the Western control program with headquarters in the District of Columbia, started June 2nd on a three months' trip to study conditions in Pennsylvania, Michigan, Wisconsin, and the Western States.

Mr. Julian F. Cannon, Clerk in the Washington Office, left on May 30 for Spokane Washington, for the purpose of installing in our Western Office a computing and analysis machine similar to the one in the Washington Office.

Mr. Arthur F. Amadon, New York Blister Rust State Leader has been appointed a collaborator of this Office. Mr. Amadon has taken a position as forester with the New York Conservation Commission but will continue to handle the blister rust control work as formerly.

Mr. H.G. Strait of Oneonta, New York has recently been appointed Blister Rust Control Agent in District No. 1, Columbia County, with headquarter at Hudson, New York.

Mr. D.G. Rankin has resigned as Blister Rust Control Agent of District No. 1 and has been appointed a state forester with the New York Conservation Commission. He will be assigned to Chenango County to conduct a forest economi survey.

The State crews which are ordinarily engaged in eradicating Ribes on state land under the direction of Mr. E.T. McAveigh have been engaged this sprin in planting one million trees on the T.C. Luther preserve at Saratoga.

- - - - - -

Mr. Robert S. Caruthers who has been working summers for this Office since 1922, is again working as Field Assistant. He will assist Mr. A. E. Fivaz at North Hudson, New York, with experimental blister rust control work. Mr. Thurston L. Corbett will again work for this Office as Field Assistant, effective June 15, 1926. He has been working for us during the field seasons since 1923. Mr. Corbett will also assist Mr. Fivaz on the North Hudson experimental control area.

- - - - - -

Mr. Torfine L. Aamodt resigned as collaborator effective June 3, 1926. His headquarters were St. Paul, Minnesota.

- - - - - -

Mr. P.A. Walker was appointed Agent in Maine and started work on May 26. He was engaged in Blister Rust Control work during the field season of 1924.

- - - - - -

Mr. A.E. Fivaz left Washington June 8th to begin field work on the North Hudson, New York experimental control area.

- - - - - -

Miss Mary B. Grandfield will fill the vacancy created by the resignation of Miss Evelyn Gallison in the Montpelier office.

Miss Nettie Slocum resigned as clerk May 31, headquarters at Albany, N.Y.

The following men have received appointments, during June, to the fie
force, with headquarters at Spokane, Washington.

Fred R. Allen, Bernard A. Anderson, Charles C. Baker, John C. Baird,
P. Balch, John B. Biker, Raymond H. Bitney, Isaac C. Burroughs, Allen C. Bur
Robert Davis, George A. Felch, Claude R. Fullerton* Edwin G. Greene, Charles
Gregory, Cecil W. Guptill, Cecil W. Hatton* John F. Hume, Edwin L. Joy, Rene
La Rocque, George L. Luke* Wm. H. Lund, Raymond MnKinley, Carl O. Peterson*
Galen W. Pike* Percy B. Rowe* Frederick J. Simcoe, Liter E. Spence, Herman E
Swanson, Guy V. Williams, and Ralph T. Young.

The following appointments outside of Spokane have been made:

Harold L. Beeson, Missoula, Montana; Orley N. Callender, Boise, Idaho
Leland O. Drew, Sacramento, California; Frederick R. Robertson, Boise, Idaho
John E. Spurlock, Sacramento, California; and Edwin E. Stuart, Boise, Idaho.

Edit: The men whose names are starred (*) have worked in previous
seasons on western work.

- - - - - - -

Word has been received that Mr. J.E. Riley, Jr. will receive his M.F.
degree from the Yale Forestry School this month. Congratulations are in ord
Mr. Riley's thesis was on "A Study of Some of the Factors Making up Crew
Efficiency in Control of the White Pine Blister Rust".

```
┌─────────────────────┐
│   OFFICE COMMENTS   │
└─────────────────────┘
```

INSTRUCTIONS REGARDING USE OF GOVERNMENT BILLS OF LADING.

When a shipment is sent you on a Government Bill of Lading the original copy of the Bill of Lading should be sent to you from the Company making the shipment, at the time the shipment is made. When the shipment is delivered to you, turn the Bill of Lading over to the express or freight agent.

Do not pay express charges on shipments sent on Government Bills of Lading.

Frequently these Bills of Lading are sent in to the Washington Office or returned to the Company making shipment and are not on hand when the shipment is received. Such shipments should not be delivered by the Railroad or Express Company until the Bill of Lading is turned over to them.

- - - - - - - - - - -

ECONOMY NOTICE

Your cooperation is desired in reporting to this Office any improvements in organization, economies effected, or better business methods adopted. Every quarter a report on this subject is requested by the Office of the Chief of Bureau. Your cooperation in reporting economies will be very helpful to this Office in the preparation of its report.

H.P. Avery, Head Clerk.

R A T T L E S N A K E S

What to Wear in Rattlesnake Country -

What to Do if Bitten.

In regard to the matter of clothing, the men could wear long leathe
boots or high shoes with leather puttees or canvas leggins which would
probably give protection to the parts covered. They can give some protection to their hands by wearing leather buckskin gloves or gloves made of
a similar material and preferably ones that reach half way or more to the
elbow. They can also help avoid being bitten by using long sticks to pusl
aside the brush in searching for Ribes as they advance in crew formation.
The rattlesnake usually rattles before striking and the noise made by the
crew in advancing and the poking around in the brush ahead of them with
sticks would probably arouse the snake so that it would run away or give
warning in time for them to avoid being bitten.

Snake bites are most often received on the legs, below the knees,
less frequently on the hands or arms. Wherever the bite may be located,
first-aid treatment must be given quickly in order to be effective.

In the case of a bite on the foot or leg below the knee, expose th
limb instantly and bandage or ligature it just above the knee so tightly
to at once stop the flow of blood and prevent as far as possible the dist
utionof the poison to other parts of the body. Anything that can be tie
such as rope, strap, or handkerchief, will answer. A pad of cloth place
under the knee will help to make the bandaging more effective. (The li
ature, however, must be loosened for a short time every thirty minutes t
prevent gangrenous mortification.) Next, sink the point of a clean shar
knife to the bottom of each wound made by the snake's fangs and slit the
flesh parallel with the limb for one-third to half an inch; avoid cutti

across or around the limb which is more likely to sever a blood vessel. Pinch
and rub the flesh about the wound and suck the blood from it for several minutes,
or as long as a free flow of blood continues. This will remove much of the venom.
The blood and poison should be spit out quickly from time to time. No one having
abrasions, open sores, or cuts on the lips or in the mouth should suck a wound,
as these may take up the poison. As a rule, the fangs of a rattlesnake make a
wound from 1/8 to 1/4 of an inch deep, in case the person is bitten through
trousers and underclothing. In opening the fang-marks the cut should go to the
bottom of the wound, the point where the poison is injected. The wound should
then be thoroughly sterilized by the application of potassium permanganate
(permanganate of potash) by spreading the wound open and pouring the crystals
of powder into the cut freely. An application of strong tincture of iodine
will answer if the potassium permanganate is not available.

Keep the limb bandaged for at least an hour after the blood has been
thoroughly sucked from the wound. Then, the bandage can be slackened a little,
provided the patient shows but little effect (depression) from the poison. If
the patient is greatly affected, do not loosen the bandage.

When snake bites are received in a part of the body where a bandage can
not be applied effectively, opening the wound, sucking out the blood and poison,
and sterilizing the wound with potassium permanganate or strong tincture of
iodine is all that can be done before taking the patient to a doctor, which in
all cases should, if possible, be done promptly.

Alcoholic stimulants should in no case be used. In the past, alcohol in
the forms of wine, whiskey, and brandy has been freely administered, although
there has been no foundation for its use except popular belief. Certain investi-
gators demonstrated that the absorbed venom is eliminated in part by the stomach,
and it was thought therefore that the venom could be precipitated by the alcohol
before its reabsorption. Recent experiments have shown that alcohol precipitates

venom but does not impair its toxic properties. By increasing the blood
pressure, and in large doses intensifying coma, alcohol had a distinctly
injurious influence on the victims of poisonous snakes.

The use of strychnine and caffein also should be avoided because of
danger of increasing hemorrhage through the rise of blood pressure.

In case of emergency get in touch with Dr. R.L. Ditmars of the New York
Zoological Garden, New York City, who has a small supply of serum on hand. If
serum is called for, mention should be made of the kind of poisonous snake which
bit the patient since there are three types of poisonous snakes in the United
States which call for three distinct antivenins. There are two poisonous snakes
in the northeastern United States, namely - the copperhead, which has a tail
without a rattle, and the timber rattler which has tail with rattle.

United States Forest Service men in rattlesnake districts use snake bite
cases. These cases can be obtained from The Max Wocher and Sons Co., 29-31 W.
Sixth Street, Cincinnati, Ohio, and probably from the Kny Sheerer Co. 404 West
27th Street, New York City. The cases from the first firm formerly cost about
75 cents each or around six dollars per dozen. The snake bite case is a small
wooden tube about two inches long with a cap at each end. Under the cap at
one end is a sharp lance or scalpel to be used in piercing the wound made by th
snake. On the other end is carried permanganate of potassium.

The Biological Survey has put out two leaflets concerning snakes; one
entitled, "Facts About Snakes" and the other, "Poisonous Snakes of the United
States". Copies of the leaflets can be secured by writing direct to the
Biological Survey at Washington, D.C.

Most of the above information has been secured from data furnished by th
United States Forest Service and the Bureau of Biological Survey.

- -- - -- -- - --

WASH AWAY IVY POISON

Thorough washing soon after exposure to poison ivy reduces the danger of injury, says the United States Department of Agriculture. The poison usually requires some time to penetrate into the tender layers of the skin, and until such penetration has taken place much or all of it can be removed.

Make a thick lather and wash several times, with thorough rinsing and frequent changes of hot water, using ordinary alkaline kitchen soap. Running water is preferable for this purpose. If a basin is used, the water should be changed frequently. Even after inflammation has developed, thorough washing should be tried in order to remove from exposed surfaces of the skin all traces of the poison that can still be reached.

For the inflammation, simple remedies, such as local applications of solutions of cooking soda or of Epson salts, one or two heaping teaspoons to a cup of water, are helpful. Fluid extract of grindelia, diluted with 4 to 8 parts of water is often used. Solutions of this kind may be applied with light bandages or clean cloths. Such cloths must be kept moist and discarded frequently in order to avoid infection. When the inflammation is extensive or severe it is best to consult a physician.

- - - - - - -

PUBLICATIONS

Western White Pine

Nettleton, H.I. - Growth of White Pine (Pinus monticola) on Logged-off
Areas. - Idaho Forestry Bulletin, Vol. III, No. 5, p. 1,2
May 1926.
Edit. A very interesting report on study plots established
by the University of Idaho School of Forestry. Lands which
were logged-off 25 years ago and more are again being cut over
for the white pine.

BLISTER RUST

NEWS

July 1926

Volume X   *Number 7*

U.S. DEPARTMENT of AGRICULTURE
Office of Blister Rust Control.

C O N T E N T S - V O L. 10, No. 7.

                                                                          Page
Agents' Work
    A New Paint for Field Use   219
    From California to Maine Work is Under Way to Protect White Pine.   225
Blister Rust Situation
    Infection Runs Heavy in Pine Reproduction in York County, Maine   215
    Black Currants May Have Been Responsible for Heavy Blister Rust
        Infection at Waterford, Vermont.   217
Editorial
    Imagination   224
Educational
    Success With White Pine Depends Upon a Knowledge of Blister Rust
        and its Control.   218
    New Set of Pine Slides Available to be Used With Blister Rust Slides. . .   220
    Newman Uses Cartoon Effectively   221
Eradication Work
    Ribes Eradication Work to be Started on Indian Reservation at
        Keshena, Wisconsin   220
    New Method of Getting Out the Ribes   221
    Thoroughness of Survey for Common Barberry.   227
Forestry
    Oswego County, (N.Y.) Holds Forestry Field Day at Great Bear Farm. . . .   222
    Importance of the Farm Woodlot in Financing the Farmer.   232
    Forestry Can Restore the Economic Strength of New England   234
    Some Notes on Rotation of Western White Pine and Eastern White Pine . . .   235
Personals   238
Publications.   240
Quarantine Notes.   236
    New Blister Rust Quarantine Proposed to Take Place of Federal Plant
        Quarantines 26 and 54.   213
State and Provincial News
    Illinois.   226
    Indiana   238
    Maine 215-216
    Massachusetts 238-239
    Minnesota   238
    Montana   239
    New Hampshire 214,217
    New York. 217,218,219,221,222,231
    Prince Edward Island (Canada)   238
    Vermont 217,234
    Wisconsin   220
Technical Studies
    Detailed Figures on Pine Infections in Merrimack County, New Hampshire. .   214
Western Notes   237
    Western Office Puts Out Good News Letter.   224
    Some Notes on Rotation of Western White Pine and Eastern White Pine . . .   235
Work With Young People
    Rural School Children Locate Barberry Bushes.   226

SUPPLEMENT TO

THE BLISTER RUST NEWS

Vol. 10. No.6. June, 1926.

C O N T E N T S   Page

A Distinguishing Character of   176
the Wild Black Currant (Ribes
americanum Mill.) With Notes
on R. nigrum and other Ribes
species.

A DISTINGUISHING CHARACTER OF THE WILD BLACK CURRANT (RIBES

AMERICANUM MILL.) WITH NOTES ON R. NIGRUM AND OTHER RIBES SPECIES

By Roy G. Pierce

There is such a similarity in the appearance of the leaves of the eastern wild black currant (Ribes americanum) and the cultivated European black currant (Ribes nigrum) that the finding of a fairly positive means of distinguishing between the two species is of great value. The desira bility of finding an easy means of identification of the two species has been brought out many times in the practical field work of controlling the white pine blister rust.

Throughout the eastern half of this country, the eastern wild black currant, (Ribes americanum Mill.)(synonym - R. floridum L'Her.) is fre quently cultivated. In February, 1925, four new cultivated varieties of R. americanum were offered for sale in South Dakota, under the names of Tonah, Atta, Moto, and Wanka currants. When found in gardens it may be easily mistaken for the European black currant. The latter, however, is being gradually eliminated in this country, on account of tis great suscep tibility to the white pine blister rust (Cronartium ribicola - Fischer). In control areas where currants and gooseberries are being destroyed for the protection of the white pine no currants and gooseberries should be grown. While both the above species are susceptible to this disease and may act as carriers or intermediary hosts through which the rust spreads to pines, yet Ribes nigrum is by far the worse pest because of its very vigorous growth, abundant leaf production and extreme susceptibility to this rust. A very good graphic representation of the relative amount of blister rust infection found on R. americanum and R. nigrum is given by Minnie W. Taylor (1). The accompanying illustrations of the infection on the leaves of the two species, taken from her paper will be of interest.

RIBES AMERICANUM   RIBES NIGRUM

Diagrammatic drawing to show average size, shape and relative amount of blister rust infection of leaves of Eastern wild black currant (Ribes americanum) and European black currant (Ribes nigrum).

While the characteristic ridged stems of Ribes americanum should
readily distinguish this plant from the round-stemmed Ribes nigrum, yet
it is sometimes very desirable to identify the currant from an examination
of the leaves only.

The position of the resin-dotted glands, which are so characteristic
of both species, does afford a fairly positive means of distinguishing
between these two species and is valuable even where leaves alone are concerned.

It is generally known that sessile resin-dot glands, or resin dots
as they are called, occur on the lower surface of the leaves of these two
species. Early in October 1924, a casual ocular observation of fresh material of Ribes americanum from St. Johnsbury, Vermont, made by Miss Alma
Bishop of the Office of Blister Rust Control, revealed abundant reddish-
brown resin dots on the upper side, as well as on the lower side of the
leaves.

R I B E S   A M E R I C A N U M

The early botanists recorded these resin dots on both sides of the
leaves of R. americanum, but in general, later botanists apparently have not
mentioned those on the upper leaf surfaces, in their writings.

The French botanist, L'Heritier who described the wild black currant
of Eastern America, in 1784 as Ribes floridum, noted that the leaves had
glands on both sides. In 1814 Pursh, made the same observation. In 1838-40
Torrey and Gray described the species as having "leaves sprinkled on both
sides with resinous dots." Mrs. A. H. Lincoln in 1852 describes the leaves
of R. floridum L'Her., as "punctate on both sides"; while in the sixth
edition of Gray's Manual in 1889, R.floridum is noted as having "leaves
sprinkled with resinous dots."

Later botanists, however, such as Britton in 1905, Coulter and Nelson
1909, Britton and Brown 1913, Rydberg 1917, Rehder, 1919, all described
this species as having leaves glandular dotted, or resin dotted beneath.
Coville and Britton in North American Flora, in their description of the
species note that the leaves are "glandular dotted, beneath" but in their
key to species (page 195) list R. americanum with R. nelsoni, under the
group, Americana - with the characterization "Leaves with scattered, sessile, amber-colored, wax-like, non-exudating glands on both surfaces". None
of the above-cited descriptions are incorrect but where mention of the
resin dots on the upper leaf surface was omitted an important diagnostic
character was missed.

A study of the leaves of Ribes americanum in the herbarium of the
Office of Blister Rust Control was made by Miss Nina Schnell, formerly of
that Office; Seven hundred and thirty leaves on 53 specimens have been examined from the following sources:

SOURCE	NO. OF LEAVES	SOURCE	NO. OF LEAVES
District of Columbia	7	Nebraska	52
Michigan	20	North Dakota	48
Minnesota	211	South Dakota	43
Montana	174	Wisconsin	175
		Total	730 leaves

In all cases there were resinous dots on the upper-sides of the leaves. In a few cases, these resin dots were very scarce, being less than 10 for the entire upper surface of the leaf. A hand lens with a magnification of 10 diameters was used in the examination of the Ribes leaves in this study.

The above study was supplemented by an examination, by the writer, of some of the specimens or collections in the U. S. National Herbarium at Washington, D. C. One or more leaves were taken into consideration on each of 54 specimens. Their distribution accrding to state or province is indicated in the following:

SOURCE	NO. OF SPECIMENS	SOURCE	NO. OF SPECIMENS
Illinois	6	North Dakota	4
Iowa	2	North Carolina	1
Massachusetts	1	Ohio	2
Maine	2	Pennsylvania	1
Michigan	2	Rhode Island	2
Minnesota	2	South Dakota	1
Montana	7	Wisconsin	2
New York	7	Wyoming	2
New Mexico	2	Alberta	3
Nebraska	3	Assiniboia	1
		Quebec	1

Total specimens examined - -- 54

Resin dots were found on the upper side of every R. americanum leaf examined, as well as on the lower leaf surfaces.

The above observations on the leaves of R. americanum collected from so many sources prove conclusively that the presence of resin dots on both sides of the leaves is characteristic of this species.

R I B E S   N I G R U M

Coville and Britton[12](page 197) state that leaves of R. nigrum are "3-5 lobed thin, sparingly pubescent and resinous dotted − −," not stating whether they occurred on the upper or lower leaf surfaces, or both.

Statements from the eminent English botanists, Sir J. D. Hooker and George Bentham, on the other hand, show that to them, the resin dots on the lower leaf surface only of Ribes nigrum were characteristic of the species; Hooker[13] described the species as "Ribes nigrum L. leaves angled 5-7 lobed glandular dotted beneath, lobes triangular acute, serrate − − − "; and Bentham,[14] wrote "Black Ribes. Ribes nigrum Linn. Easily known by the peculiar smell of the leaves when rubbed, arising from the small glandular dots copiously sprinkled on the under side − −".

A study of the leaves of Ribes nigrum L. has also been made by the writer from specimens in the Offices of Pathological Collections, Forest Pathology, Blister Rust Control, and Economic and Systematic Botany of the Bureau of Plant Industry at Washington, D. C., and from specimens in the U.S. National Herbarium. Six hundred and sixty-three leaves of R. nigrum from one hundred collections of leaves in folders and envelopes were examined from seven countries in Europe, from four provinces in Canada and from eleven states and territories in the United States. The source and number of leaves examined follows:

SOURCE	NO. OF LEAVES	SOURCE	NO. OF LEAVES
Bohemia	6	District of Columbia	73
Denmark	2	Massachusetts	202
England	5	Minnesota	3
France	3	New Hampshire	68
Germany	36	New Jersey	5
Poland	2	New York	69
Sweden	11	Pennsylvania	7
British Columbia	3	Rhode Island	99
Ontario	6	Vermont	10
Prince Edw. Island	2	Washington	25
Quebec	3	Wisconsin	23
		Total − −	663 leaves

All of the above examined leaves of R. nigrum had resin dots on the under surfaces, while in only five out of the hundred collections were there leaves which had resin dots on the upper surface. Two of these collections were from England, one was from Sweden, and two others were from Massachusetts.

The English collections are in the herbarium of the Office of Forest Pathology, under their collection numbers 37141 and 37150. Both collections were made by W. Stuart Moir at Woodstock, England, on October 14, 1920. One of the two leaves of the first collection, and one of three leaves in the second collection had resin dots on the upper leaf surface.

The Swedish collection of R. nigrum is in the herbarium of the Office of Pathological Collections, and was collected by Hj.Moller, August 16, 1894 in S . Asum, Skane, Sweden and is found under the label "fungi Scandinovici, Cronartium ribicola. Dietr. II, III, Ribes nigr." This collection consists of six leaves, one of which had resin dots on the upper leaf surface. This leaf was 33 mm. in width and had over 100 resin dots on the upper surface.

The Massachusetts collections are in the herbarium of the Office of Economic and Systematic Botany, in two folders. The leaves in both collections, though labeled Ribes nigrum, are all relatively small, none being over 50 mm. in width, and are finely serrate, unlike R. nigrum in this character and in the general shape of the leaves. The first collection was made at the Arnold Arboretum in Boston on April 28, and May 3, 1910 by W. F. Wight under No. 4304. Seven of the eleven leaves examined in this collection were found with resin dots on the upper leaf surface. The second collection was also made at the Arnold Arboretum, at Boston, Massachusetts on April 29, 1913, by W. H. Moore. Two of the five leaves examined had resin dots on the upper surface.

It is thus seen that 12 leaves only of Ribes nigrum in 5 collections, out of a total of 663 leaves examined from over 100 separate collections, were found with resin dots on the upper leaf surface. Generally speaking, the resin dots if present on R. nigrum on the upper leaf surface are few while upon R. americanum they are many. On R. nigrum the resin dots are generally yellow in color while on R. americanum they varied from reddish brown to a pale yellow.

Summing up the evidence it may be stated that is is characteristic of R. americanum to have resin dots on both sides of the leaves, while for R. nigrum their appearance on the upper leaf surface is rare.

OTHER SPECIES

There are at least five other species of Ribes having resin glands or dots on the upper surfaces of the leaves, but on account of the distribution of these species, they will not be confused readily with R. americanum. These species include:

1. R. nelsoni, Coville & Rose, whose known distribution is limited to Colonia Garcia, Chiluahua, Mexico.

2. R. viburnifolium, A. Gray, an evergreen shrub, whose known distribution includes lower and southern California and adjacent islands.

3. R. bracteosum Dougl., distributed along the Pacific Coast from eastern Alaska to northern California. This species has large leaves, 3 inches or more across, and 5-7 lobed.

4. R. petiolare Dougl. whose range extends from the interior of British Columbia to Montana, and southward to Wyoming, Utah and Eastern Oregon. The leaves of this species are cordate at base with basal sinus usually deep. This differs from R. americanum in that the latter has leaves with widely open sinus at base. Of 44 R. petiolare leaves examined, only 4 had resin dots on upper surface of leaf.

5. R. nevadense, Kellogg is distributed through the mountains of California, southern Oregon, and western Nevada.

Ribes americanum according to Coville and Britton,[11] ranges from Nova Scotia to Virginia, Nebraska, Wyoming, Montana, Alberta and Assiniboia, also in New Mexico; its leaves are 3-5 lobed and usually less than 3 inches across.

In general, therefore, it may be stated that when black currants, with resinous dots upon the upper leaf surface are found in cultivation, or in a wild state, in the Rocky Mountains and eastward, the species is Ribes americanum, Mill.

[1]Taylor, M. W. - Potential Sporidia Production Per Unit in Cronartium ribicola. Phytopathology Vol. 12, p. 298-300, Fig. 1. 1922.
[2]L'Heritier de Brutelle, C. L. Stirpes novae - - - Fasc. 1, p.4, 1784
[3]Pursh, F. T. Flora Americae Septentrionalis. Vol. 1, p. 164, 1814.
[4]Torrey, John, and Asa Gray, A Flora of North America. Vol. 1, p. 549. 1838-40.
[5]Lincoln, Mrs. Almira H. Familiar Lectures on Botany - - Part 6, p. 155. 1852.
[6]Gray, Asa, Sereno Watson, and J. M. Coulter. 6th Edition P. 176. 1889
[7]Britton, N. L. Manual of the Flora of the Northern States and Canada. 2nd Edition p. 488. 1905.
[8]Coulter, J. M. and Aven Nelson. New Manual of Botany of the Central Rocky Mountains. p.243. 1909.
[9]Britton, N. L. and Addison Brown. Illustrated Flora of United States and Canada 2nd Edition, Vol.2, p.237. 1913.
[10]Rydberg, P. H. Flora of the Rocky Mountains and Adjacent Plains, p.398. 1917.
[11]Rehder, Alfred. Ribes; in L. H. Bailey's Standard Cyclopedia of Horticulture Vol. 5, p. 2959. 1919.
[12]Coville, F. V. and N. L. Britton, Family 13 - Grossulariaceae; in North American Flora, Vol.22, Part 3, p.195, 206. 1908.
[13]Hooker, Sir J. D. The Students Flora of the British Islands, London, ed. 2 Page 141. 1878.
[14]Bentham, George. Handbook of the British Flora - -London. Vol.1, p. 302. 1865.

- - - - - -

Bureau of Plant Industry
        Washington, D. C.
Nov. 11, 1925.

UNITED STATES DEPARTMENT OF AGRICULTURE
BUREAU OF PLANT INDUSTRY
WASHINGTON, D.C.

T H E   B L I S T E R   R U S T   N E W S.

Issued by the Office of BlisterRust Control
and the Cooperating States.

VOL. 10, No. 7.   JULY, 1926.

NEW BLISTER RUST QUARANTINE PROPOSED

TO TAKE PLACE OF FEDERAL PLANT QUARANTINES 26 and 54 -

- COMMENTS DESIRED.

Tentative blister rust quarantine measures have been drafted to
replace the present Federal Quarantines 26 and 54 and to include a portion
of the State of Oregon not heretofore under blister rust quarantine. Copies
of the proposed quarantine are available for distribution to all interested
parties for comment before the measure is handed to the Secretary of Agriculture for approval. Apply to the Federal Horticultural Board, Washington,
D.C. The proposed quarantine would become effective September 1, 1926, and
comments should be sent in by August 1st.

The revised quarantine would embody the modifications discussed at
the public hearing before the Federal Horticultural Board on June 30, 1925,
i.e., permit cultivated red and white currants and cultivated gooseberries to
move interstate unrestricted except from the infected States. From the infected States, movement of these plants would be permitted if certified as free
from disease after September inspection, and if the plants are dormant, de-
foliated, and dipped to the roots in lime-sulphur solution of specified
strength. A certificate from the consignor as well as from the State Nursery
Inspector would be required to accompany each shipment.

The European black currant would be prohibited interstate movement
throughout the Continental United States except within an area comprising
twelve states in the South and Great Plains region, where five-leafed pines are
not native. Within these twelve States, the movement of Ribes nigrum would
not be permitted interstate unless accompanied by certificates from the State
Nursery Inspector and the consignor.

Five-leafed pines would be prohibited interstate movement from each
New England State, New York, Pennsylvania, New Jersey, each of the Lake States,
Washington, and seven counties in Oregon. Also, no five-leafed pines would
be permitted to move from states east of the present Mississippi Valley quarantine line to states west of this line. Within the uninfected area east of the
present Mississippi Valley line, it is proposed that five-leaf pines shall be
certified if moved interstate.

Restrictions of this quarantine may be limited to the infected areas
in a quarantine state when such state shall have enforced control measures
adequate, in the judgment of the Secretary of Agriculture, to prevent the
spread of the blister rust.

                                                        S.B. Detwiler.

DETAILED FIGURES ON PINE INFECTIONS IN

MERRIMACK COUNTY, N.H.

Figures have recently been secured on various infected pine lots in certain of the towns of Merrimack County, New Hampshire. A section of the lots have been examined, and the areas tagged. The figures given below represent the data collected, and are worthy of study.

Town	Area Examined in acres	Species Ribes found*	Number trees examined	Number infected trees	% Infected	Date Oldest Infection	Ribes Eradicated (date)	Yrs. Between First Infec. & date of Erad.
Andover	1/2	G.	206	156	76	1914	1922	8
Boscawen	3/4	G.	191	145	76	1917	1925	8
Bradford	1/4	S.	265	166	62	1917	1922	5
Canterbury	2/5	S.R.B.	492	364	74	1917	1925	8
Hooksett	1/4	S.	1025	503	49.1	1918	1924	6
"	1/4	S.	1521	471	31	1918	1924	6
"	1/4	S.	1601	469	29.3	1918	1924	6
"	1/4	S.	1868	310	16.6	1919	1924	5
Newbury	70.2	S.R.B.G.	7527	789	10.5	1912	1921	9
New London	1/2	S.	76	56	76	1915	1925	10
"	1/4	S.G.	104	81	78	1917	1925	8
"	3/4	G.	127	105	82	1911	1925	14
Pembroke	1/2	G.	399	255	63.9	1916	not	-
Pittsfield	1/8	G.	20	11	55	1917	1924	7
"	1/8	G.	100	63	63	1916	1924	8
"	1/8	G.	104	67	65	1916	1924	8
"	1/8	G.	52	41	79	1916	1924	8
Salisbury	1/4	?	140	90	64	1918	not	-

* G - gooseberry - largely R. cynosbati
S - skunk currant - R. glandulosum
R - red currants - R. triste
B - black currants - R. americanum.

Thomas J. King, N.H.

INFECTION RUNS HEAVY IN PINE REPRODUCTION IN

YORK COUNTY, MAINE.

On April 4 and 5, 1926 we laid out three one-quarter acre plots in white pine reproduction in the town of York, where blister rust is gaining in intensity, and on April 27, a fourth plot in Kennebunk Port. Examination showed that the blister rust is much worse than believed, infection in the three plots running 60 - 36 - and 44% respectively, and 62% in the fourth plot.

Infected trees by plots are as follows:

Plot 1, York, Maine - MacIntyre Lot

> Total number of trees - 239
> Total number infected trees - 145
> Percent of trees infected - 60%
> Infection by years
> 1918-1919--1920--1921--1922--1923
>   16   22   18   11   23   10 percent

Plot 2, York, Maine - MacIntyre Lot

> Total number of trees-447
> Total number infected trees-159
> Percent of trees infected-36%
> Infection by years
> 1918--1919--1920--1921--1922--1923
>   20   8   29   11   20   12 percent

Plot 3, York, Maine - Arthur Shedd Lot

> Total number of trees - 361
> Total number of infected trees-158
> Percent of trees infected - 44%
> Infection by years
> 1918--1919--1920--1921--1922--1923
>   25   9   20   9   27   10 percent

Summary of Three Lots

> Total number of trees - 1047
> Total number infected trees - 462
> Percent of trees infected - 44%

Plot 4, Kennebunk Port, Maine

Total number of trees - 206
Total number infected - 127
Percent of trees infected - 62%
Percent of infected trees which are dead - 20%
Infection by years
1917-1918-1919-1920-1921-1922-1923
  9   32   9   14   13   15   8 percent

Plots 1 and 2 are in a 60 acre timber lot in an opening surrounded by 50-year-old timber. Plot 1 represents the heaviest infection in the area. Tree 5 to 20 years old; height 3 to 20 feet; opening is not fully stocked at present.

Mr. Tarbox says the Ribes on this 60 acre lot were quite thoroughly eradicated; 1480 Ribes, all gooseberries, being removed.

Plot 3 was taken on a sidehill; a narrow strip of growth averaging 10 to 20 years old, and 5 to 18 years of age, fully stocked. A mature timber lot over the wall from this plot has been cut off this winter. Infection on the plot was heavier than the average for the surrounding pine. On this man's property the record shows that we destroyed 6389 Ribes; gooseberries.

Plot 4 was about the same age, height and density as Plot 3. A mature timber lot lays on one side of this plot. This big timber is apparently free from infection.

Age of oldest infection - Plot 4 - 1917 (two or three)
" " " " " 3 - 1916 (one)
" " " " " 2 - 1918 (many)
" " " " " 1 - 1918 (many)

No attempt was made to list all the cankers on any one tree. The percentage of infection figures refer to the earliest date when the trees became infected as determined by the age of the wood on which the cankers examined were found.

W.O. Frost
S.D. Conner
E.E. Tarbox.

BLACK CURRANTS MAY HAVE BEEN RESPRONSIBLE FOR HEAVY
BLISTER RUST INFECTION AT WATERFORD, VERMONT.

June 15, 1926.

Dear Martin:

Last week was spent at Waterford completing necessary field work on the study area. I made a most important discovery regarding the Ribes situation. About twenty years ago, a dozen cultivated black currants were planted on the upper Lee farm, less than a thousand feet from the outside boundary of our study area. These bushes were purchased from a New York nursery. Nine years ago, the present tenant pulled up the cultivated bushes because he was unable to market the black currants. At the time he destroyed them, there were at least eighty healthy bushes. This discovery explains many of the perplexing problems that have arisen in analyzing the field data.

. . . . E.C. Filler.

Mr. C.R. Pettis was out with Colonel W.B. Greeley, Forester, U.S. Forest Service, last week at Axton, New York, and they certainly saw some blister rust as it was in the aecial stage. Before they got through Colonel Greeley was climbing white pine trees to see blister rust "flags" on some of the upper branches.

June 5, 1926.   A.F. Amadon, N.Y.

- - - - - - - - -

Uredospores of Cronartium ribicola were found in Epsom and Allenstown, New Hampshire, on wild gooseberries June 8th and 9th. This is the first report this year of the early summer stage of the blister rust on Ribes in New Hampshire.

SUCCESS WITH WHITE PINE DEPENDS UPON A

KNOWLEDGE OF BLISTER RUST AND ITS CONTROL.

Secretary of American Forestry Association
Collects First Hand Facts on Blister Rust Control.

On the train from Washington to Albany, I met a fellow forester whose
work has kept him largely in the South. In view of the fact that I was to
meet Mr. Detwiler the next day, for a Blister Rust trip through the Adirondacks, it was natural that our talk turned to that subject. My friend brought
up the question of why New York and a number of the New England states are
promoting the planting of white pine so extensively in view of the "terrible
menace" of the White Pine Blister Rust. Had our conversation taken place
after my trip, rather than before, I could have answered his question with
much more wisdom because I was a wiser forester, at least in respect to the
White Pine Blister Rust.

For the forester who desires to get the White Pine Blister Rust properly
placed in his lexicon of forestry, I recommend a field trip with Sam Detwiler,
who is in charge of the Blister Rust Control work of the Bureau of Plant
Industry.

We left Albany early one morning a few weeks ago with Mr. Amadon of the
New York State Conservation Commission, and spent three days on Blister Rust
trails through the Adirondacks. On that short trip I learned more about the
disease and its relation to the practice of forestry than I had in all my
previous reading about it. Mr. Detwiler has a sixth sense for locating blister
rust infection, and if there was any benighted tree in our path that we did not
find it ought to be tagged as a curiosity. The outstanding thing that this
profitable trip brought home to me is that the white pine blister rust, while
a "terrible demon," need not be so terrible, provided foresters understand its

control. Before the first half day of the trip was over it seemed clear to
me that the success of growing white pine begins and ends with a knowledge of
white pine blister rust and its control. I confess that I had been under the
impression that its control was a very difficult, uncertain and rather costly
undertaking, but here again I was made wise and impressed by the simplicity
and cheapness of its control. My reaction, therefore, as a result of the
trip may be summarized about as follows: It appears useless to attempt to
grow white pine and let the blister rust run wild, but it apparently is not
difficult to control the disease. Therefore, by making proper control provisions, the forester may, with assurance, carry on with the good old tree,
White Pine.

July 9, 1926.   Ovid M. Butler.
                                       Sec. of American Forestry Assoc.

    Edit: Field reports are to the effect that Mr. Butler became a blister
    rust addict, scouting from dawn to dewy eve - and even by moonlight.

                          - - - - - - - -

                      A NEW PAINT FOR FIELD USE.

    Mr. Pierre K. Miller, a former member of Blister Rust Control, now
with Finch, Pruyn & Company, Inc., Glens Falls, New York, writes that he finds
his work with the company very interesting. He states that property lines,
instead of being merely blazed lines, are painted with a specially prepared
paint, forest yellow, prepared by the Dupont people, which makes a very
easy line to find in the woods and from some previous experiments it seems to
be the most durable kind and color.

    (From The News Letter, New York State College of Forestry, May 1926)

    Edit: This sounds like something that we need to investigate in connec-
tion with marking our lines in eradication work, and in our investigative work.

220

RIBES ERADICATION WORK TO BE STARTED ON
INDIAN RESERVATION, KESHENA, WISCONSIN.

Mr. H.J. Ninman, under date of June 18, writes from Madison, Wisconsin, that he is headed for the Menominee Indian Reserve to start a crew of Indians on Ribes eradication work. It will be interesting to watch and see whether the red men of today are as keen in wood-craft and in locating Ribes as were his brothers of yester-years.

A later note from H.J. states that on June 22 he succeeded in starting eleven Indians in two crews at Ribes eradication work at Keshena. These Indians are working under the supervision of Mr. G.O. Grapp, the man in charge of nursery work and fire protection at Keshena. The eradication work will come to a close on June 30, because of shortage of funds.

Edit: We hope for a later report on this work, Herman, so we can compare the efficiency of the red men with some of the crews down East.

- - - - - - - - -

NEW SET OF PINE SLIDES AVAILABLE -
TO BE USED WITH BLISTER RUST SLIDES

Believing that a pine owner would benefit more, and be more interested in a well rounded talk on care of white pine than upon blister rust control alone, a number of sets of slides have been made on white pine silviculture. Thanks are due the Forest Service which supplied the negatives of each of these slides.

Each set contains fourteen slides, showing such phases of silviculture as thinning (before and after), pruning methods, and pruned stands, regeneration of forest under old stand, release cuttings, and clearings.

These sets are available from the Washington Office as long as they last.

R.G. Pierce

NEWMAN USES CARTOON EFFECTIVELY

Eight thousand cartoon postcards were recently made up in this Office, at the suggestions of Mr. L.E. Newman. The cartoon of the face of the card was originally drawn by one of the Forest Service men and was worked over by Miss Bishop, artist in the Washington Office, to fit our needs. Credit is due the Forest Service for permission to use and change the original.

If you have not received one of these cards write to Mr. L.E. Newman, State Forester's Office, Concord, New Hampshire, for it. It may help solve some of your problems.

- - - - - - - -

NEW METHOD OF GETTING OUT THE RIBES.

While foreman Beardsley was working at Mr. Rafferties in the town of Ticonderoga they were up against it for help; there being only himself and two other men. They were pulling large bushes and spending a lot of time digging them out. One of the men suggested they use some dynamite as he was familiar with handling it, and thought it would be a time saver. They tried it and it worked fine; using a small stick under each bush, blew the bush out and loosened the dirt so that the roots came out in fine shape. The use of dynamite for large bushes is not only a time saver, but does more efficient work.

B.H. Nichols, Agent
District 7, New York.

Edit: Better be careful if you try Beardsley's method.

- - - - - - - -

HOW A FORESTER GOT RICH

He started poor as a proberbial church mouse twenty years ago. He has now retired with a comfortable fortune of $50,000.00. This money was acquired through industry, economy, conscientious effort to give full value, indomitable perserverence, and the death of an uncle who left him $49,999.50. - Press Item.

News Letter- University of Maryland, State Department of
Forestry, Baltimore, Maryland.

222

OSWEGO COUNTY HOLDS FORESTRY FIELD DAY AT GREAT BEAR FARM
First Held In County - - To Be Made Annual Affair.

The first annual forestry field day in Oswego County was held at the Great Bear Farm Plantation, Tuesday, June 22nd, 1926, under the auspices of the Oswego County Farm and Home Bureau, Pomona Grange and Dairymens' League in cooperation with the N.Y. State Conservation Commission; United States Departme: of Agriculture; College of Forestry, Cornell University; New York State College of Forestry, Syracuse; and United States Forest Service. About 600 farmers, their wives and children were in attendance, besides many foresters from the two colleges who helped conduct groups through the plantations.

An attractive and instructive forestry exhibit was placed on the grounds by Agents George E. Stevens and Noble Harpp. The exhibit included varieties of trees distributed by the Conservation Commission, cross sections of trees taken from plantings in order to show growth and results obtained from plantings tree planting methods, miniature seed bed and specimens and instructions on the White Pine Blister Rust Disease. Much interest was shown by the farmers toward reforesting and in the control of the White Pine Blister Rust disease. The wiping out of the chestnut trees in this section of the state, by the Chestnut Blight, has brought home to the woodlot owners the danger that is possible from other tree fungi.

Many persons were given instructions in Blister Rust Control as well as instructions in tree planting and many names were obtained for inspection of woodlots.

Along a lane that leads to the grounds, through one of the older plantations, were placed posters urging people to reforest their waste and idle lands. Among the more appropriate posters were the following:

```
                    T I M B E R
    THE ONE CROP THAT WILL GROW WHERE OTHERS FAIL
                        A N D
    ONE CROP FOR WHICH THERE WILL ALWAYS BE A
           C O N S T A N T   D E M A N D
```

```
              O S W E G O   C O U N T Y
        HAS 70,000 IDLE ACRES OF LAND
    MAKE THESE LOAFERS EARN THEIR KEEP BY PLANTING
                   THEM WITH
              F O R E S T   T R E E S
```

The program started at 11 a.m. with guides conducting groups through the plantings. At 12:30 p.m. basket lunch and community singing lead by Harry Eppes, the health clown of the Dairymens' League. At 1:30 p.m. the welcome address was given by Mr. F.A. Emerick of Oswego, who planned the Great Bear Plantation twenty years ago. The speakers were: Hon. J.D. Clarke, Co-author of the Clarke-McNary bill and President of the New York State Forestry Association; Mr. Paul D. Kelleter, of the College of Forestrty, Syracuse; Mr. W.R. Mattoon, Forest Service; Mr. C.R. Pettis, Supt. of State Forests; Mr. S.L. Strinings, Master, State Grange; and Mr. Charles Taylor, New York State College of Agriculture, Cornell.

State Troopers had charge of parking of cars and picked Boy Scouts aided in directing the tours and distributing programs.

George E. Stevens, N.Y.

IMAGINATION

According to Dr. Cadman, imagination is the most powerful factor in life, and can be ruled through its power of suggestion. All of the great inventions have been the result of imagination. This quality applied to a steaming tea-kettle resulted in the steam engine. Here's an example from our own work -

Not long ago Endersbee received one of Pierce's clip sheets, which had an article on "Holes in the Stocking". A few days later he had applied this idea to a sign, and had it placed in a store selling stockings. That is making use of the imagination.

Any job is more or less drudgery until it is clothed with imagination. Then it becomes a living reality, something worth our best efforts. My suggestion is - to hard work, add imagination.

E.C. Filler

- - - - - - - -

WESTERN OFFICE PUTS OUT GOOD NEWS LETTER.

The Washington Office is in receipt of a copy of the Blister Rust News Letter for State and Project Leaders, put out by the Western Office, at Spokane, Washington. This is an office news letter, and is intended especially for the blister rust employees in the West. It contains many articles of interest and the Spokane Office is to be congratulated on the inauguration of such a publication.

- - - - - - - -

Mr. E.J. McNerney reports finding telia on wild black currants at Southbridge, Massachusetts, June 16, 1926. This is the earliest report of telia this season.

E.C. Filler.

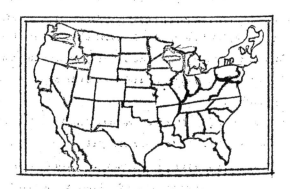

Last March, at its annual meeting, your town, too, made provision for protecting the pine growth.

Control of the White Pine Blister Rust has begun in your town.

YOU SHOULD BE INTERESTED

(1) In seeing the control methods employed.

(2) In learning how the town funds are being spent to protect the pines.

(3) In becoming more familiar with this disease so fatal to pine growth.

The headquarters of the crew may be secured from the Selectmen. Get in touch with the crew foreman and learn from him where the crew will be working the day you plan to go out.

If you are only able to spend fifteen minutes with the crew, nevertheless, go out. It will be worth your while.

REMEMBER: It is not just to criticize public work, unless you are familiar with the details.

Why not call the blister rust foreman to-night!

In cooperation with   New Hampshire Forestry Department
U. S. Department of Agriculture   Concord, N. H.

RURAL SCHOOL CHILDREN LOCATE BARBERRY BUSHES.

Rural school teachers in many districts of the north central grain-growin States are instructing their botany and nature study classes in the principles involved in the Goverment's campaign against the common barberry bush, says F.E. Kempton, In Charge of Barberry Eradication, United States Department of Agricultu By instructing the pupils in a practical method of preventing the spread of stem rust to small grains these teachers have not only aroused interest in the scienti fic study of plant life, but have materially aided in a project conducted for the benefit of agriculture.

Barberry material and literature recently displayed in a school in La Sall County, Ill., so fascinated one ten year old girl that she immediately became interested. The next day, while passing through a wooded area, she found a common barberry bush growing on the bank of a creek in an almost inaccessible spot at least a mile from the nearest road. It was a bush 12 feet high and moderately infected with rust. There also were a number of seedlings close by.

The county had been surveyed in 1923 to locate all common barberry bushes and a resurvey had been made in 1924. In all probability this bush still would be undiscovered had this school girl not become interested in the common bar- berry and its method of spreading rust to the grain fields.

The spores carried by the wind from common barberry bushes have been known to infect distant grain fields.

From Clip Sheet No. 419, United States Department of Agriculture.

Edit: The above item should be of particular interest to all of us engaged in the control of the white pine blister rust. The fact that this small girl took such deep interest in barberry eradication and understood it so well, is but another proof of the beneficial results which can be gained by having blister rus and methods of its control presented in the school room, especially in rural districts.

THOROUGHNESS OF SURVEY FOR COMMON BARBERRY

By F.E. Kempton,
Office of Cereal Investigations, Bureau of Plant Industry
Department of Agriculture.

In surveys for eradicating all common barberries thoroughness means searching out and killing the last barberry bush, sprout, and seedling in the area designated for survey.

The methods of survey and of eradication have been modified and improved from time to time as new facts have become known.

The visiting of the many thousands of properties in the 13 States of the eradication area is by no means a small undertaking. The inspection of every one of these properties in such a manner that every barberry bush, seedling, and sprout is found and destroyed becomes a tremendous task.

This campaign of eradication was begun with little real knowledge of the distribution and abundance of the common barberry in these 13 States. It was known that this shrub had been transported westward from New England by settlers and that both the green and purple varieties had been sold and planted as ornamental shrubbery. Numerous hedges and single bushes had been observed in cities, towns, and on large estates. The occasional spread of common barberries to waste lands had been recorded.

With this rather meager knowledge, methods of survey naturally were not planned with the same ideas of thoroughness that are demanded after eight years of experience in searching out and eradicating this pest.

In the eradication area there are many types of city and small-town properties, large estates, large and small farms, and ranches. On any of these at one time or another common barberry may have been planted. There are numerous woodlands, forests, planted woodlots and wind breaks, wooded banks of streams, shores of lakes, brushy pastures, and hillsides, to which common barberry bushes or seedlings may have escaped from cultivated common barberry bushes fruiting on near-by properties.

Naturally, the greater number of cultivated barberry bushes and those escaped from cultivation have been found in the older settled areas where shrubbery grows readily. However, common barberry bushes have been scattered into almost every county of the 13 States. To find all of these bushes requires systematic and conscientious effort.

As the types of properties and the attending conditions vary so greatly, the State leader in each State must use careful judgment in supervising the surveys. He in turn must allow the squad leader and the field men some latitude in deciding the manner of conducting the survey of each type of area and property. This range of judgment must not be too wide.

Training a changing personnel so that all properties will be uniformly well surveyed is a large part of the task. Thorough survey and eradication depend largely upon the selection, instruction, and training of field men. Uniform thoroughness of survey must be stressed continually.

The State leaders, squad leaders, and field men may be better able to accomplish uniformly thorough surveys by answering the following questions.

GENERAL QUESTIONS

When sending men into the field, the State leader should ask himself these questions:

1. Has the squad leader been informed of all the known facts concerning the history of barberries and stem rust in an assigned area?

2. Have all the squad leaders and field men a uniform and clear idea of how given types of territory should be surveyed?

SURVEY QUESTIONS

A. As the field man enters a property and surveys it he should ask himself these questions:

1. Is each property being approached as a possible hiding place of one or several common barberry bushes?

2. Has the property owner or occupant been made familiar with the purpose of the work and the reasons for careful survey of the property? Has his support been enlisted?

3. For every farm visited has information been ascertained as to whether or not stem-rust losses ever have been experienced?

4. If rust has occurred, were the losses greater than on near-by farms?

5. Have there been common barberry bushes on this property or on neighboring properties in the past? If so, have they been fruiting bushes and were records made of their location?

6. Is this property part of or near an area of escapes?

7. Are there farm buildings or abandoned building sites on this farm near which shrubbery may have been planted?

8. Do the grasses or grains indicate early infection from stem rust?

B. Before leaving the property these questions should be answered:

1. Has every nook and corner of the yard, garden, orchard, and other parts of the farmstead been inspected for barberry bushes, cut-off crowns of old bushes, sprouts, and seedlings?

2. Has every woodlot, fence row, stream bank, pasture, etc., been as carefully inspected as the conditions warrant?

3. Has the situation been correctly summed up and the proper inspection made for that area and the property?

4. Is the property owner or occupant satisfied that a thorough survey has been made?

5. Have complete records been made, including maps?

6. Have the bushes been eradicated and how? If not killed, what arrangements have been made for eradication?

7. Can the property be certified as clear?

ERADICATION QUESTIONS

After survey and eradication the following questions are in order:

1. Has every bush been carefully treated or otherwise completely eradicated?

2. Has every seedling been found and destroyed?

3. Large seedlings may be broken off in attempts to pull them. If so, were they treated?

4. Have adequate records been made so that future resurveys and eradication of new seedlings can be easily and efficiently carried out?

5. How soon should this property be revisited?

6. Do the number of seedlings and scattered seeds indicate that this property should be inspected regularly for a long period of years?

7. Have all fruits from fruiting bushes been destroyed?

8. Have you obtained the cooperation of the occupant of the property of the end that he is interested and informed so that he can recognize barberry bushes and seedlings and will aid in resurveys by keeping constant watch for seedlings and sprouts and destroying them by recommended methods?

QUESTIONS CONCERNING SURVEY OF AREAS OF ESCAPES

Each area of escapes large or small is a special problem. Not only the questions covered in the survey and eradication should be considered but these additional ones:

1. Has complete cooperation of all interested persons in the area been obtained?

2. Have the sources of the spread of seeds been determined and eliminate

3. Has an idea been formed of the places to which birds may go for water or to roost?

4. Has an outline map of the area been prepared?

5. Have the outer limits of the spread of bushes and the possible limits of spread of seeds been determined and mapped?

6. Has the exact location of bushes and seedlings been recorded on the map as the survey of the area has progressed?

7. Has inspection been made beyond the limit of spread to insure that there is not a clear area beyond which more escapes have spread?

8. Have adequate notes been made for complete eradication and for re-inspections?

9. Have arrangements been made for chemicals, their transportation, and application?

10. Have eradication or treatment been completed?

11. Have the property owners been instructed so that they will aid in resurveys and help effect a complete clean-up of the area?

While these questions are particularly applicable to the survey, they may be used in connection with any survey or in making reinspections.

Note: The above article by Dr. Kempton, on Thoroughness of Survey for Common Barberry, has in it many good ideas which may be used in scouting for, and destroying the gooseberries and currants in the white pine blister rust control. While some phases of the barberry eradication are different from our work, yet in the main the questions which are asked are quite pertinent.

R.G.P.

NOTES FROM NEW YORK STATE

Mr. H.H. Knowles recently resigned as Blister Rust Control Agent of District 3, comprising Fulton, Montgomery, and Hamilton Counties, to accept the position as Secretary of the Vermont Forestry Association with headquarters at Northfield, Vermont. Mr. Knowles has been Agent with headquarters at Gloversville, for the past three years, and during that time accomplished wonderful results in blister rust control work in his district.

- - - - - - -

Mr. Stanley Hamilton has recently been appointed Blister Rust Control Agent of District 8, comprising Lewis, Oneida, Herkimer, Jefferson and St. Lawrence Counties, with headquarters at Lowville.

Mr. Hamilton will take over the work recently left vacant by the transfer of George E. Stevens to the Albany Office.

- - - - - - -

Mr. John W. Charlton has been appointed Blister Rust Control Agent of District 3, with headquarters at Gloversville, New York. He will take over the work made vacant by the recent resignation of H.H. Knowles.

- - - - - - -

Blank Town
May 22, 1926.

Dear Sir:

I have heard the men say something about planting trees or killing gooseberry bushes at a place they call "Blisterbust".
I would like a job at that place if you need another man.

Very truly yours,

IMPORTANCE OF THE FARM WOODLOT IN FINANCING THE FARMER

By E.H. Thomson
President, Federal Land Bank of Springfield.

(Continued from June Number)

Another factor from a credit standpoint is that wood and timber is the only crop that is held by the first mortgage. In other words, the first mortgage amounts to a crop mortgage when dealing with timber.

Still another feature is that the wood and timber gains in volume even though a farm may be abandoned otherwise. While other income may fall very low or cease altogether, the timber crop continues to gain. This feature is especially important in maintaining the value of farms in the Northeastern states where other industries tend to tempt the farmer away from agriculture and cause him to neglect the farm business.

Wood and timber on a farm is the one crop that furnishes winter work at a period when both men and teams are not otherwise employed. It thus permits a better balanced farm unit, lowering the cost of production of all the products produced on that farm.

From a credit standpoint there is also another big advantage in a stand of merchantable timber on the farm in that as long as it remains untouched it forms a liquid asset. Farms with a stand of merchantable young growing timber sell much more readily. In fact, in many districts, a farm on which the timber has been stripped is almost unsalable.

Along with its many advantages wood and timber has some disadvantages from a credit standpoint.

In some areas it is subject to damage by fire or storm. In the experience of the bank, however, with its thousands of farm loans, little or no fire damage has been encountered. Storm damage is likely to be most prevalent and that will come mainly from ice freezing on the limbs and trunks, thus breaking down young timber.

Loss of markets is an important factor to be considered. The local wood using industries may move to other districts or the products which are being manufactured from wood may be supplanted by other material.

The discontinuance of railroads is another factor to be considered.

One of the most serious drawbacks to the development of the small woodlot in some districts is the lack of markets for small lots of timber. This is particularly serious in those districts where there is not enough timber to maintain local wood using industries and where the portable sawmill furnishes the only market. Such a condition prevents a farmer from giving the woodlot the attention it should have and necessitates the marketing of timber at one time when better results might be obtained if he could use his own men and teams a certain amount of time every winter. I believe this problem of a suitable market for small and scattered lots of timber as found on the average farm is the most serious one confronting the development of this most important crop. It is worthy of much study.

Then, there is the further problem of local taxation. The tax assessed against many of the lands suitable for wood and timber, and especially against many of these marginal farms, is almost prohibitive when it comes to handling these properties from an investment standpoint. This problem of taxation, however, applies more seriously to those farms that have been entirely abandoned for agriculture than it does to the wood and timber tract on the average farm.

From Journal of Forestry, Vol. 24, No. 4, April 1926.

(Continued in next issue)

234

FORESTRY CAN RESTORE THE ECONOMIC STRENGTH

OF NEW ENGLAND.

At the recent annual meeting of the Vermont Forestry Association,
Col. W.B. Greeley, Chief Forester of the United States, stressed the importance
of forestry to New England.

Col. Greeley stated that, "The greatest period of all in forestry
history in New England is still to come. She can be just as strong socially
and economically as she has been in the past. Forestry can restore the
economic strength of New England by the use of the millions of acres of idle
and waste land."

"The present policy of the national government is to seek through
cooperation to encourage the outward spread of forestry. We must get local
agencies to work and in this way farm and industrial forestry can be as firmly
established as it is in Europe. We should not look for too much from the
central government, the effort should be localized. The need is for Vermont
to go ahead on the forestry program of her own with reference to her particular
needs."

The speaker stated that he was heartily in favor of town and municipal
forests and said that he believed that this action would tend to solve a
portion of the problems of reforestation. . . . . . .

Col. Greeley spoke of the importance of conserving the natural resources of the country by the preservation of the forests, by planting more
trees to take the place of those cut, by fighting disease and forest fires and
by educating the people to the importance of such work.

- - - - - - - - -

Extract from Green Mountain State Forest News for June 1926.
Vermont Forest Service, Montpelier, Vermont.

SOME NOTES ON ROTATION OF WESTERN WHITE PINE AND

EASTERN WHITE PINE.

By Elers Koch.

The following is taken from an article by Mr. Koch on "The Future
of Forest Lands in Montana and Idaho", Journal of Forestry, May 1926, p. 518-534.

Regardless of theoretical figures which normal yield tables may show,
no⁺ one who is really familiar with the Idaho white pine region will expect to
grow a merchantable crop of saw timber in less than a rotation of 80 years or
more on average land. We all know that in spite of a few exceptions on
specially good sites, the general run of 60-year stands is nothing more than
large poles, and it is out of the question for a sawmill industry, either
now or under conditions approaching present European practice, to be maintained on timber of such size. The usual rotation for coniferous timber in
Europe is from 80 to 120 years.

Even now in New England, where we have been hearing about fabulous
yields of white pine on extremely short rotations, they are beginning to
realize that there is not much in this small low-grade timber. They can not
even compete with West Coast lumber. As Prof. R.T. Fisher of Harvard University
has recently stated it, in a discussion of the New England timber-growing situation, there is a necessity for "cutting only larger, older timber. Low grade is
always the difficult thing to sell. Small timber means high costs and a low
yield of better grades. Too much timber is being cut that is not only hard to
market for these reasons, but would be making more money for the owner if left
standing . . . . The place to start grading is in the woods before the timber
is cut."

I would, therefore, put the minimum saw-timber rotation at 80 years for
the white pine type. - - - - - - - -
    Edit: The whole article is well worth reading by our blister rust
control men, especially those engaged in work in the West.

QUARANTINE NOTES

Results of quarantine inspection for the spring of 1926 show a slight
decrease in the total number of violations of Federal Quarantine 26 which prohibits the movement of blister rust host plants to states' west of the Mississippi Valley line. Of 44 violations of this quarantine reported during the
spring, 25, or nearly 57 percent were committed by nurserymen. This percentage
is large, but it is due to the marked falling off of the numbers of private individuals making such illegal shipments. Compared with previous spring seasons,
the figures are:

Spring	Violations by Nurserymen	Violations by Private Individuals	Total	Percent by Nurserymen.
1921	188	43	231	81
1922	60	58	118	50
1923	33	34	67	50
1924	28	41	69	40
1925	26	47	73	35
1926	25	19	44	57

In the West, 17 violations of Federal Quarantine 54 were found,
apparently all of which were shipped by private individuals not connected with
the nursery trade. The numerous shipments of red flowering currants constitute
a serious problem in the quarantine work in the State of Washington, as ten out
of the above 17 illegal shipments contained red flowering currants. In
reference to the danger involved in shipping this plant, Mr. Leslie N. Goodding,
Assistant Pathologist, Botany Department, Oregon Agricultural College, recently
stated:

R. sanguineum carted around as it is in the flowering season
certainly constitutes a menace. It is picked up any place,

possibly from beneath a diseased pine and after it has wilted it
is thrown into the back yard perhaps among currant bushes, or else
the bush is planted. R. sanguineum replaces R. aureum and R.
odoratum in western Washington and western.Oregon. It is not so
extensively raised by the nurseries because it is so frequently
obtained in the woods. It is, however, highly favored as an ornamental.

June 22, 1926.

M. Thompson.

- - - - - - - - - -

WESTERN NOTES

A NOTE ON RIBES BRACTEOSUM

At Cheekye, B.C. some bushes of Ribes bracteosum were measured.
The bushes were very large, many of them being 14 feet tall and containing 250
feet of live stem. The diameter of the crown of one of the bushes observed
was about 5 inches. Many of the roots were eight feet long.

- - - - - - - - - -

The Uredinial stage of the blister rust was found on Grossularia
divaricata at Brackendale, B.C. on April 25, and on Ribes bracteosum and R.
lacustre April 27, at Daisy Lake, B.C.

- - - - - - - - - -

Edit: They do grow bushes out there in the West, where the tall
trees grow. Putnam, did you ever try ringing or girdling some of
these sapling Ribee bushes?

Mr. F.F. Franklin, former blister rust employee in New York State was a recent Washington visitor. He is still with the Pennsylvania Railroad in woo preserving work, with headquarters at Indianapolis, care of Republic Creosotin Company.

- - - - - - - - -

Mr. S.B. Detwiler who has been on a few weeks' trip through the north-eastern states, returned to the Washington Office on July 3.

- - - - - - - - - -

Dr. J.F. Martin and G.B. Posey have taken to the woods to look over the eastern and western districts, respectively.

- - - - - - - -

A letter from R.R. Hurst, Asst. Plant Pathologist, at Charlottetown, Prince Edward Island, Canada, to Dr. J.F. Martin includes the following note: "It occurred to me that you would be interested to hear that I have collected white pine blister rust on P. strobus at the Experimental Farm at Charlottetown There are only a few trees here but these show heavy infection".

- - - - - - - - -

Agent Brockway reports blister rust in the uredinial stage, found on wil gooseberries at Hingham, Massachusetts, on May 19. He also located a new gener infection area in this town. Tarbox mentions finding extensive pine infection the towns of Kennebunk and Parsonfield, Maine.

E.C. Filler.

- - - - - - - - -

Mr. Roy G. Pierce left Washington July 7th for field duty in the Northeastern states where he will be engaged in checking state records and compiling data on early blister rust infections.

- - - - - - - - -

Mr. Dean K. Knutson was appointed as temporary agent, July 1, 1926, with headquarters at St. Paul, Minnesota. Mr. Knutson was on blister rust work last summer, working with Mr. W.F. Peel, in Minnesota.

- - - - - - - -

239

Agent Doore of Franklin County, Massachusetts, writes: "The Blister Rust
Card #29 is serving a double purpose in this district. I find the data upon them
especially convenient in clinching some of my arguments, especially at the close
of interviews. Please send me another lot of the cards.

Cooperation could harley be better than at present. Several farmers have
taken time from planting operations to assist in Ribes eradication."

E.C. Filler.

- - - - - - - - -

Mr. M.H. Wolff, of Missoula, Montana, assistant forester of District 1,
United States Forest Service, and Mr. S.B. Detwiler made a week's field inspection of rust conditions and control work in New York, Vermont,Massachusetts
and New Hampshire. While in New York, they were accompanied by Mr. Ovid M.
Butler, Secretary of the American Forestry Association. Mr. Butler has given a
statement of his experience, which appears elsewhere in the News.

One of the questions not satisfactorily answered was the extent to which
pine infections took place in 1923. At some points young cankers were appearing
quite extensively on 1923 wood, while at other points they were not abundant.
The observations of field workers generally on this point will be of interest.

What is a fair transfer value for a well stocked stand of native white
pine 20 years old, within 5 miles of railroad or mill, where both seller and
buyer are willing to trade, but where the sale is not forced? This question
was much discussed, and many inquiries made, with so much variation in the
answers as to be confusing. Any actual data on transfers of this character would
be of interest to many foresters.

PUBLICATIONS

Sugar Pine

Root, George A. - Saving the Sugar Pine.
Farm Bureau Monthly, May 1926. p. 28.

Show, S.B. - Timber Growing and Logging Practice in the California
Pine Region. Measure Necessary to Keep Forest Land Productive
and to Produce Full Timber Crops.
U.S.D.A. Bulletin 1402, May 1906.
Edit: Not only sugar pine, but other forest trees are
dealt with in this bulletin which is well illustrated.
While this bulletin seems a far cry from blister rust
control, yet an analysis of it shows that there is a
striking similarity in certain aims. On page 38 we find
"The new forest depends absolutely on the saving of young
growth and seed trees; and any method of logging which leaves
less than half of the young growth intact defeats the purpose
of keeping the land productive." One aim of blister rust
control is to keep land in such condition that young growth
will have a chance to grow up and stock the land.

Western White Pine

Brewster, D.R. and J.A. Larsen - Girdling as a means of removing
undesirable tree species in the Western pine type.
Journ. Agri. Research, 31, (1925) No. 3, p. 267-274.

Hofmann, J.V. - Laboratory tests on effect of heat on seeds of
noble and silver fir, western white pine and Douglas fir.
Journ. Agri. Research 31, (1925) No. 2. p. 197-199.

Korstian, C.F. - Forest Planting in the Intermountain Region.
U.S.D.A. Bul. 1264. February 21, 1925. Page 37.
Plantings of western white pine were made on Wasatch
National Forest as early as 1912. After 8 years there was
a survival of 53.5% but the average height was only 13.4
inches. Mr. Korstian writes: "Although this species has
shown promise for limited planting on the moister moderately
open aspen-and-brush-covered sites, it is doubtful whether
it should be used extensively on account of its relatively
slow growth. This species is therefore not recommended for
planting in this region."

White Pine

Tubeuf, C. von. - Blasenrost der Weymouthskiefer (Blister Rust of
the Weymouth or White Pine)
Zeitschrift fur Pflanzenkrankheiten 36: 143-146. 1926. no.5/6.

BLISTER RUST

NEWS

August 1926.

Volume X

Number 8

U.S. DEPARTMENT of AGRICULTURE

Office of Blister Rust Control.

C O N T E N T S - V O L. 10, No. 8.

Page

Agents' Work
    A Case of Mistaken Identity 264
    Data on Escaped R. nigrum Wanted by Washington Office 260
    Winter Scouting for Blister Rust in New Territory Suggested 256
Blister Rust Situation
    Blister Rust Found in Susquehanna County, Pennsylvania 257
    Heavily infected Pine at Hingham, Massachusetts 254
    Observations on the Blister Rust in German Forests. 258
    Random Notes from Vermont 249
    Some Notes from Franklin County 257
    The Rush Lake Infection Area in Minnesota 255
    Unusual Infection Area in the Town Park in Newburyport, Mass. . . . 244
Editorial
    Open Letter to New Agents in East 243
    Johnny Appleseed. 263
Educational
    Blister Rust Education and Summer Campers 251
    Blister Rust Float in Sesqui-centennial Celebration 245
    Exhibits, Tags, and Posters Act as Silent Salesmen. 248
    New Use for Panel Exhibit 252
    Some Notes on Color Photography 249
    Summer Campers - An Opportunity 252
Eradication Work
    Ribes Eradication Completed in Plymouth County, Massachusetts . . . 247
    Eradication Speeds up in Warren County, New York. 254
    Pines in Norfolk and Bristol Counties also being Protected. 257
Forestry
    Importance of the Farm Woodlot in Financing the Farmer. 251
Personals 266
Publications 265
    Brockway Uses New State Law to Keep the Ribes out of Plymouth
        County 247
    Planning your Family Expenditures 266
Quarantines
    New Blister Rust Quarantine 260
State and Foreign News
    Germany 258-260
    Maine .248, 249, 256, 264
    Massachusetts 244, 247, 249, 250, 252, 253, 254, 257, 265
    Minnesota 255, 256
    New Hampshire 251, 267
    New York 245, 246, 254, 262, 268
    Pennsylvania. 257, 267
    Vermont 249
    Western States. 267, 268
    Norway 265

```
        E D I T O R I A L   S T A F F
Roy G. Pierce  . . . .  Editor - Washington, D. C.
E.E. Tarbox . .     Assoc. Editor - Maine
Thos. J. King . .       "      "    - New Hampshire
S.V. Holden . . .       "      "    - Vermont
W.J. Endersbee. .       "      "    - Massachusetts
O.C. Anderson . .       "      "    - Rhode Island
J.E. Riley, Jr. .       "      "    - Connecticut
George H. Stevens       "      "    - New York
H.J. Ninman . . .       "      "    - Wisconsin
C.R. Stillinger .       "      "    - Western States
```

UNITED STATES DEPARTMENT OF AGRICULTURE
BUREAU OF PLANT INDUSTRY
WASHINGTON, D.C.

T H E   B L I S T E R   R U S T   N E W S

Issued by the Office of Blister Rust Control
and the Cooperating States,

VOL. 10, No. 8   August, 1926.

OPEN LETTER TO NEW AGENTS IN THE EAST

To Agents Hamilton, Charlton, Strait, Swain et al

That "al" tacked on the end means others, not Al Fivaz.
Welcome to the honorable ranks of blister rusters. While you may get
razzed a little about your work, don't let that worry you, for you've
joined up with a bunch of forest protectors who are putting across the
best job of disease control of a forest fungous pest that any country has
ever done. Our job is as good forestry work as forest fire fighting or
planting trees; also, it is no better.

Blister Rust Control you'll find is helping put across
lots of other good forest practices. In fact this protective work is taking
pine owners out into their timber lots where they haven't been for sometime,

In short, remember the honor of your calling and if in
need of help

Call on

Ribes Bill.

AN UNUSUAL INFECTION AREA IN THE TOWN PARK AT

NEWBURYPORT, MASSACHUSETTS

Recently, while hiking up the long steep hill to the Waterford infectio area, the remark was made that Universities and infection areas are generally located on the top of hills. Apparently, such stimulus is needed for higher education, while hill top infection areas are warnings of disaster to stimulat blister rust control workers to go "over the top" in control achievements.

However, all infection areas are not on hilltops. Can you visualize a severe infection on medium age pine located near the mainhighway, along level paths shaded by arching trees with vistas of radiant flower beds, sparkling fountains, and nurse maids airing the royal heirs? It does exist. A visit to the town park at Newburyport, Massachusetts, will show you what happens when the beautiful gets contaminated with the damned.

Several hundred white pines were planted in this park some years ago. These trees are now about 30 to 40 feet high and form one of the most attractive features of the park. Blister rust has infected at least 15 to 20 per cent of these pines; the majority of which have stem cankers. Dead branches, tops and trees are becoming increasingly conspicuous. The nearby cultivated Ribes, which caused the infection, have been destroyed, but unfortunately the need for control work was not appreciated until considerable damage had been caused.

In the June Blister Rust News, I was glad to learn that the city of Springfield, Massachusetts, has prevented such damage to the pine in their city park by the timely eradication of nearby Ribes. Similar control measures should be encouraged in all parks containing white pine.

August 3, 1926.   E. C. Filler.

BLISTER RUST FLOAT IN SESQUI-CENTENNIAL CELEBRATION

The village of Fort Ann in my district is historically important because of certain events that occurred there during the Revolutionary war and in order to secure markers and be in a class with other historical villages and cities it decided to put on a sesqui-centennial celebration July 5. This celebration was to include a number of varied events, most important among which was a parade of floats depicting historical ideas and customs. Non-historical organizations were also asked to take part in the program, such as the grange, industries, churches, fraternal organizations, etc.

The New York State Conservation Commission was asked to put on a float and the matter was referred to me. With the assistance of eradication assistant Raymond Paige we secured a state Ford truck and started working up a white pine blister rust float. Asst. state leader George E. Stevens made a timely arrival on the scene with posters and ideas for working up the float.

It required about three days of very hard work to decorate the truck according to plans and specifications. The entire truck was enclosed from the ground up so that no part of it was visible. This required $9.00 worth of light lumber, 30 yards of white muslin, 8 bolts of green crepe paper, some green mosquito netting, two gooseberry bushes, two infected pine trees, several boxes, carpet tacks, a ford-load of white pine boughs, many busted thumbs, and two sleepless nights.

A large sign, "WHITE PINE BLISTER RUST", extended from the front of the cab to the rear end of the truck and was the topmost and, perhaps the central part of the float. The two sides were arranged with shelves which carried the

gooseberry bushes, and infected pine trees together with appropriate signs and
tags. The front and rear ends carried various signs on blister rust. Small
pine twigs were used for decorations along with the green crepe paper; thus
the color scheme was green and white and it made a very pleasing appearance.
A border of small pine twigs extended completely around the float about three
feet up from the ground.

Our framework was built a little to close to the ground and we had to
be very careful about scraping the road in rough or uneven places. On the
whole the float went through the parade very nicely and I think it was well
worth while, not only for the educational part of the thing, but also for the
sentiment and good feeling that our co-operation created among the people of
the town. I do not believe that it served very much to acquaint the people
with the most simple phases of blister rust, because the thing was all the
time in motion and there was very little opportunity to examine the specimens
or read the posters, but the name, "white pine blister rust must have reached
a larger number of people than ever before.

I have been wondering whether such an outfit could be used to advantage
at fairs. Our float, however was very fragile and would not withstand any
inclement weather whatsoever. This would probably be a big drawback. Incidentally we won third prize in the non-historical class. Yes, there were more than
three floats in this class; eight in fact. The prize money, $5, was used toward
defraying expenses of the float.

J. D. Kennedy,
District 4, New York

RIBES ERADICATION WORK COMPLETED IN PLYMOUTH COUNTY, MASSACHUSETTS

Ribes eradication work in Plymouth County, Massachusetts, has been completed with the exception of four areas which will be worked by crews. These areas will probably be worked by August 15.

E. M. Brockway, Mass.

Note: Mr. Brockway is to be congratulated on getting rid of the currants and gooseberries in the blister rust control area in Plymouth County.

- - - - - - -

BROCKWAY USES NEW STATE LAW TO KEEP THE RIBES OUT OF PLYMOUTH COUNTY

The following article appeared in The Plymouth County Farmer for June, 1926. Since the law is probably a new one, its quotation in other papers in the State, or the quotation of new or old quarantine laws in other states than Massachusetts may be used with telling effect:

Order of the State Department of Agriculture Prohibiting the Further Planting of Currant and Gooseberry Bushes in Certain Cities and Towns in Massachusetts.

In order to assist in preventing the further spread of the white pine blister rust, a dangerous plant disease now prevalent throughout the Commonwealth, the following order has been issued by the State Department of Agriculture.

"In accordance with the authority provided by Section 27 of Chapter 128, General Laws, the sale, transportation, or further planting of currant and gooseberry bushes (Ribes sp.) is hereby prohibited in certain cities and towns in the Commonwealth."

This order applies to all towns in Plymouth County.

Any further information about the control of the blister rust may be obtained from E. M. Brockway, Blister Rust Control Agent, care Extension Service, 106 Main St., Brockton, Mass.

EXHIBITS, TAGS, AND POSTERS ACT AS SILENT SALESMEN

1923 Exhibit Still Bearing Fruit.

Three years ago I happened to place a large log canker in a grain store window over in Saco, Maine. We are still hearing from that log. At least three pine owners that I have interviewed for cooperation this spring have spoken of it in particular.

Home Made Posters.

Two years ago this Fall, Mr. Frost printed me some small posters in red ink, bearing the legend "There is Blister Rust in this Lot". Lambert and I used them extensively in York County during the winter wherever we found rust. Men in numbers have told me during an interview that they realized the rust was plentiful in their locality because of seeing those posters. This plan is an excellent one to try by any agent who has a difficult town. Interviews and demonstrations are best, but the little red posters work while you sleep.

Concerning Tags.

All of our men in York County are using large numbers of the various tags. We use them along the roads or miles back in the woods. It makes no difference. They serve both as an advertisement and as a guide for the foreman who goes on to a lot after the scout has located Ribes there. I have found tags in fine condition which have been on trees and Ribes for nearly a year. This means that in the Fall when the woods swarm with hunters, they are sure to find tags in remote places where we have been. They will also serve as an answer to certain individuals who claim that we never get far from the road. I always stamp my address on every tag used in the woods.

- - - - - -

I wonder if every agent realizes the number of leads and tips which he hears during the field season which can be put to valuable use after eradication work is over in the Fall. It seems as though nearly every day I get some first, second, or third hand information regarding someone who is interested in blister rust, or regarding someone who thinks he is not interested. These stray bits of information are of special value if they come from some town with whom you are seeking cooperation. To prevent these leads from slipping my mind, I am keeping a book for their entry. Next fall, I will be able to put them to good use.

E. E. Tarbox, Maine.

RANDOM NOTES FROM VERMONT

Our rainy season is on , for it rains nearly every day. Ribes eradication crews in Vermont have lost very little time on account of rain until lately. However, because of the lateness of the spring our field season in which we can eliminate currants and gooseberries will probably be a short one.

Fairs in Vermont are coming unusually early, starting about the middle of August. Blister rust exhibits are being planned for some of these fairs.

The pine infection along the Champlain Valley is at about the same point now as it was in the lower Connecticut and West River Valleys in 1920. The wild Ribes are much more abundant in the Champlain Valley and the cost of eradication is much more per acre than in the lower Connecticut River Valley district.

S. V. Holden, Vermont.

SOME NOTES ON COLOR PHOTOGRAPHY

A Perfected Color-plate Would be of Great Value
in our Blister Rust Control Work.

Color photography was introduced to this county about 1900, but during and since the war little has been heard of or been done with color plates.

One reason for this is the fact that the plates can only be obtained from Fran
or Germany. The Autochromes made by Lumiere in France and Agfa Company in Ger
many are the best known. The results obtained from either are about the same.
The plates have a regular silver coating like an ordinary plate, and also a
coating of microscopic grains of gum arabic, dyed in three colors, red, green,
and violet. It is the different combinations of these colors that give all th
colors you see. Plates of this kind must be used (exposed) within thirty days
from the date they are made. They are of lantern-slide size, therefore adapta
to our educational work. There is a distinct advantage in being able to show
upon the screen a well-blistered pine in natural colors. The only disadvantag
is that the greatest focus distance is limited to about ten feet. I have a fe
excellent slides which I have made using these color plates.

G. S. Doore, Franklin Co., Mass
Note.--Professor David Lumsden of the Federal Horticultural Board has also use
Lumiere color plates extensively. He states that he has been able to show the
color slides successfully at distances between 75 and 100 feet. This was made
possible by using more light. With this additional light, the operator should
be cautioned to leave slides in the holder but a short time.

Mr. F. M. Blake, in charge of photographic work for the Department, sta
that in using the Autochrome color plates higher power can be secured as follo
If a Mazda lamp is used, secure one with higher wattage and if a carbon-arc is
used in projecting, use higher amperage. With either it is preferable to use
a water-cell between the light and the slide to absorb the heat and prevent
cracking the slide.

R. G. P.

BLISTER RUST EDUCATION AND SUMMER CAMPERS

In most boys' and girls' summer camps nature study is one of the many interesting features. Enemies of the forest trees might well be discussed under nature study, and our greatest enemy is white pine blister rust.

Blister rust specimens, and in some localities Ribes, may be found on the camp property. Local specimens arouse most interest.

Many of the summer campers come from other states, and a talk to a group of them spreads a knowledge of blister rust much more widely than to the average group. I have talked to some boys whose fathers were lumbermen in Michigan. Many of them are familiar with the disappearing chestnut.

I have talked to no more interested group than a group of summer campers.

####

On July 15 I gave a blister rust talk at Camp Kehonka near Wolfeboro, New Hampshire, 75 being present.

I became acquainted with Camp Kehonka through a request for an examination of its white pine for blister rust in the summer of 1924. There were no Ribes that I could find. They had been removed through town appropriations. However, several old infections were located on white pine.

They value their white pines very highly as do most summer camps. Without them the camp would lose its attractiveness and they realize it. They have a natural depression in their pine grove which makes an ideal place for a meeting.

####

The State of New Hampshire publishes a small booklet giving the name, location and number of campers as well as other information regarding the summer camps. I think it is published by the Board of Health.

THE SUMMER CAMPS - AN OPPORTUNITY

Agent Boomer of New Hampshire has written a short note concerning work
he had carried/on at a summer camp in New Hampshire.

This opens up a large field for educational work which it might pay us
to look into. It is admitted that the camps are conducted in summer, which is
the busy eradication season, but some time can profitably be taken from other
work to reach these young people. These camps depend usually on two or three
main things as drawing cards, namely forests or woods, and nearby water, scener
and climate. In the northern states white pine is frequently one of the principal trees in the forest community. Its loss would be a grave one to the
camps. Hence blister rust control will always be of interest at least to the
camp management.

Have any of the Agents worked out a regular program which includes a
visit to the summer camps in their district, scouting for ribes, and instruction to the campers concerning the menace from blister rust and the means of
controlling it? Do any of the boy campers ever engage in a hunt for the stray
gooseberries and currants which might have been missed or sprung up since
eradication was carried on?

Roy G. Pierce.

- - - - - - - - -

NEW USE FOR THREE-WING PANEL

Agent W. J. Endersbee has recently made good use of the Eastman Kodak
panels which were secured some time ago. A sketch showing the use of these
panels appears on the opposite page. The panels are exhibited in some prominen
store window in a town, the central panel showing a map with the infected area
in the town, as well as parts of town already protected from the rust, the outside panels showing by thermometer-method the cumulative record of Ribes pulled
in the town and acreage protected. The use of local material in such a window
exhibit is a very excellent one.

NEW USE FOR PANEL EXHIBIT

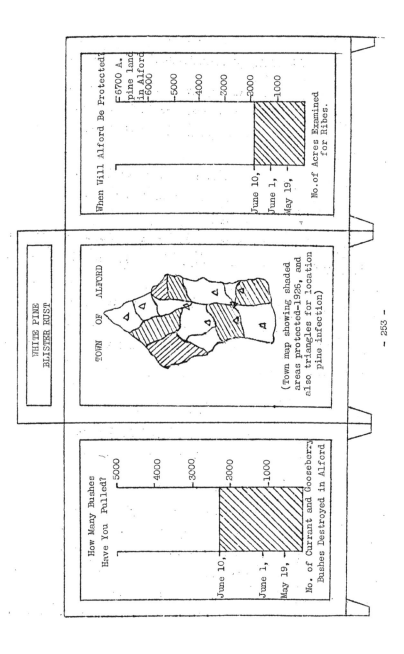

WHITE PINE
BLISTER RUST

When Will Alford Be Protected?

6700 A.
pine land
in Alford

—6000
—5000
—4000
—3000
—2000
—1000

June 10,
June 1,
May 19,

No.of Acres Examined
for Ribes.

TOWN OF ALFORD

(Town map showing shaded
areas protected—1926, and
also triangles for location
pine infection)

How Many Bushes
Have You Pulled?

5000
4000
3000
2000
1000

June 10,
June 1,
May 19,

No. of Currant and Gooseberry
Bushes Destroyed in Alford

ERADICATION SPEEDING UP IN WARREN COUNTY, NEW YORK

Ribes eradication work in Warren County, New York, is going strong. At pres
we have five foreman and a scout at work. From the present interest that is shown
by the pine owners, it appears that there will be several thousand acres protected
this year.

The interest in reforesting is increasing year by year. Several hundred tho
sand white pine were planted here in the county last spring. The prospect now for
a real good fall planting looks fine.

Folks are getting interested in the control of blister rust so much that the
stop us in the road and ask when we are coming to clean the gooseberries out of
their pine.

Between the rattlesnakes over on Tongue Mountain and some of the summer
boarders, believe me, it is getting to such a pass that it is hardly safe for a
blister rust man to drive on the main roads. Nevertheless we are still here in War
County for which we are thankful.

Noble Harpp, New York.

- - - -

HEAVILY INFECTED PINE AT HINGHAM, MASS

Over 400 blister rust cankers counted.

One large tree was recently examined by C. C. Perry and E. M. Brockway on a
new general infection area in Hingham, Massachusetts. The number of infections we
not counted, but this tree beats the tree by far that was examined by L. W. Hodgki
and E. M. Brockway at the Pembroke Arms infection area where nearly 400 infections
were found. Both trees will be "burned up" before a single infection will reach t
trunk, through death of the individual twigs and branches.

E. M. Brockway, Mass.

THE RUSH LAKE INFECTION AREA IN MINNESOTA

The history of the blister rust in Minnesota is closely connected with that of Rush Lake area. Although it was not discovered there as early as in other parts of the State the infections in some cases date back to 1908.

The Rush Lake area is a very interesting one in which to study the blister rust, because you get a variety of conditions there ranging from pure white pine stands of young growth to stands of both mature trees and reproduction. There are the mixed white pine-hardwood types on high and dry locations and in low moist situations; as well as white pine and tamarack growing in swampy areas.

It is interesting to note that in our work at Rush Lake we have found the disease to be most severe in low areas in which there is an abundance of moisture. Here you get better growing conditions for both pines and Ribes with consequent greater possibility for the infection of the pines.

At Rush Lake we have areas where eradication has been carried on as well as non-eradicated areas; in some blocks Ribes eradication alone was practiced, while in others all currants and gooseberries and infected pine were removed.

This summer we are establishing some permanent plots to study the infection that takes place on pines from year to year, and other plots to study the return of Ribes seedlings. In some instances these plots were established in close proximity to large Ribes bushes where there is a better chance of the Ribes reappearing. Other plots were established in the Ribes-cleared area. The plots are one rod square. On the first plot I established which had been eradicated in 1919, I found 37 Ribes cynosbati seedlings and bushes. Twelve were 2 inches in height, 8 were 4 inches, 7 were 6 inches, 5 were 8 inches, 2 were 10 inches, 1 was 16 inches, and 2 were over 2 feet in height. It is

possible that the last two bushes had been overlooked during eradication.
Thirty-seven bushes per square rod is at the rate of 5920 bushes per acre.
From a study of the height measurements of these gooseberry seedlings, it
would seem that in the Rush Lake area, Ribes eradication should take place
at least every seven to eight years, if not oftener.

Dean K. Knutson, Minn.

WINTER SCOUTING FOR BLISTER RUST IN NEW TERRITORY SUGGESTED

Blister rust is so very common in York County nowadays, that it is impossible almost to find Ribes on land without finding rust. Unconsciously
perhaps, we are now scouting with our heads up part of the time where formerly
it was "heads down" to find the Ribes.

Lambert has suggested the interesting idea of winter scouting for
blister rust in new territory, and lining up the owners for necessary eradication the following summer, provided the town cooperates and raises money. We
impress the owner at the time that it is for his personal interest to see that
the town does cooperate.

The idea was tried a few years ago with poor results. Blister rust
was not so common then by far as it is today. Pine owners were interviewed
in the winter at that time, and in the following season in many cases it would
be found that the man had no Ribes. The reaction would be rather unfavorable
to blister rust after so much selling talk the winter before. This now seems
impossible for our finding is "no rust, no Ribes."

E. E. Tarbox, Maine.

SOME NOTES FROM FRANKLIN COUNTY, MASSACHUSETTS.

Uredinia were found in Shelburne, Mass., June 8th, and telia were discovered in Colrain, July 8th.

During June we located infected pine in 42 privately owned lots; also
two spot infections in the Colrain State Forest and one spot in Vermont, just
over the state line bordering the forest. Arrangements have been completed for
the protection of this area, consisting of twelve hundred acres.

G. S. Doore

- - - - - -

PINES IN NORFOLK AND BRISTOL COUNTIES (MASS.) ALSO BEING PROTECTED.

Ribes eradication in the town of Cohasset, Norfolk County, has been completed this year. Only one large pine area was found; this was owned by the
Whitney Woods Association of Boston, Massachusetts. Part of this area was
worked by the Ribes eradication crew.

The towns of Taunton, Raynham, Berkley, Easton, Freetown, Acushnet, and
Fairhaven in Bristol County are now being scouted for Ribes. It is mostly a
question of cultivated bushes in these towns so far; the wild Ribes being
found only scatteringly.

E. M. Brockway.

- - - - - - -

BLISTER RUST FOUND IN SUSQUEHANNA COUNTY, PENNSYLVANIA

Dr. W. A. McCubbin of Pennsylvania Bureau of Plant Industry has just reported that Paul B. Smith, blister rust control agent in that state, has discovered a case of blister rust on wild Ribes in Susquehanna County in the
neighborhood of Brooklyn. The only other blister rust infection that has ever
been reported from Susquehanna County was found in 1921 at Montrose on black
currants. These two towns where infections have been located are seven miles
apart and are in the center of the county.

OBSERVATIONS ON THE WHITE PINE BLISTER RUST IN GERMAN FORESTS
by
C. von Tubeuf

(A Review published in "The Review of Applied Mycology" Vol. V.
Part 5, May 1926. p. 260-262.

Basing his observations on an article by Harrer in the Yearbook of the
German Dendrological Society for 1923, in which the substitution of Pinus
monticola for P. strobus in German forests is recommended, the author discusses some of the problems in connection with the cultivation of five-needled
pines in Germany.

P. monticola, together with P. strobus and P. lambertiana, was found by
Klebahn to be attacked by blister rust (Cronartium ribicola) at Bremen in
1887-8. The disease, which was introduced into Germany on the Siberian P.
cembra, was widely distributed with nursery stock not only in Europe but also
in America, where it was previously unknown. On P. monticola its ravages have
been so severe that the cultivation of this species is being abandoned in England. P. peuce, a native of the Balkan States, and P. aristata are also susceptible to the disease, while P. excelsa cannot survive the rigours of the German
winter except in the southernmost regions. In view of the great susceptibility
to blister rust of pines of the strobus group, Harrer's advocacy of P. monticola
as a suitable tree for German forests appears misplaced.

Although the whole blister rust epidemic is believed to have originated on
P. cembra from Russia, it was found that plantings of Alpine stock of this species remained healthy near diseased P. cembra at Leningrad. The single infection reported on this host from Switzerland is thought to have spread from
an imported P. strobus.

Harrer's statements that blister rust is less injurious than is commonly
represented, and that the disease was permanently eradicated from Prof. Mayr's
experimental garden at Grafrath, near Munich, are also challenged. The disease

has not only maintained its footing on P. monticola, P. peuce, and P. cembra (all of which are attacked quite as severely as P. strobus,if not more so), but it has recently appeared on P. aristata, and has spread to other gardens in the vicinity as well as to old plantings in the forest.

The disease is stated to flourish, under German conditions, in open stands, so that no protection is afforded by wide spacing. Saplings and the lower whorls of older trees are attacked with special intensity, but the uppermost branches of large trees are also affected.

In the writer's opinion, the further spread of blister rust in Germany can only be prevented by discontinuing the cultivation of P. monticola and P. peuce and restricting that of P. strobus. The importation of, and commerce in, five-needled pines should be prohibited, as in America. In cases where the retention of P. strobus is desirable on sylvicultural grounds, and where the risks of a spread of infection are too great, propagation should be effected exclusively by seed. Nurseries should be located at a distance of at least one to two hours' journey from dwellings and gardens, unless the growing of Ribes is entirely prohibited, similar restrictions applying also to forest plantings and individual trees. All infected individuals should be destroyed. Where currants are grown (and this should in no case be permitted in or near the nurseries) the immune Red Dutch variety should be distributed free from a State garden.

The organization of the Biologische Reichsanstalt fur Land- und Forstwirtschaft is described, and suggestions are made for extended co-operation, primarily between Bavarian scientists and practical forest workers, with a view to the solution of the blister rust problem.

Note: Dr. C. von Tubeuf retracted the statement that P. peuce was susceptible to the blister rust. The supposed P. peuce to be attacked in the Grafrath experimental garden was really P. monticola. See B.R.News, Vol.11, 1927, p.73.

Note: A variety of red currants growing under the name of Red Dutch was used experimentally by the Office of Forest Pathology. These were not found to be immune to the blister rust. Reference is made in this connection to Bulletin 957 of the Department of Agriculture by Dr. Perley Spaulding, in which on page 21, he discusses experiment with various species, and tests on Red Dutch and New Red Dutch showing that they became infected.

R. G. P.

- - - - - -

DATA ON ESCAPED R. NIGRUM WANTED BY WASHINGTON OFFICE

Mr. S. B. Detwiler in charge of this Office would like to receive any information available on the location of escaped cultivated black currants (R. nigrum). If any of these bushes are found growing wild, specimens should be sent in to the Washington Office for examination with a statement showing the conditions under which they were collected, (that is, in pasture or meadow or in the woods) and notes on date and place of collection and collector. Very few if any R. nigrum have been reported from the northeastern states as escaped from cultivation.

NEW BLISTER RUST QUARANTINE

On July 1 a tentative draft of the new blister rust Quarantine No. 63 was sent out by the Federal Horticultural Board for suggestions and criticisms. As a result many letters have been received by the Board and this office proposing modifications. This Quarantine has been rewritten taking into consideration the various suggestions which have been offered and has been sent to the Secretary for action.

August 21.   R. G. P.

IMPORTANCE OF THE FARM WOODLOT IN FINANCING
THE FARMER

By
E.H. Thomson, President
Federal Land Bank of Springfield.

(Continued from last month)

The Federal Land Bank of Springfield requires that its borrowers obtain permits to cut or remove wood or timber in all cases except for domestic use. Over 900 such permits have been granted and these largely in the last two years. Our experience has shown that there are many farm loans that could not be made if it were not for the woodlot on the farm being an important part of the security. For instance, I have in mind a certain farm of 300 acres in Vermont. This farm is of rather poor to average quality. There were 100 acres in the woodlot, the balance of the land being cultivated and in pasture. The buildings were fairly good. A loan of $3,400 was granted on this farm. Six years later this borrower asked for a permit to cut 80,000 feet of lumber paying one-half the proceeds on the mortgage. This payment reduced the mortgage to $1,900 thereby not only materially helping the borrower but making the loan a very safe one for the bank. This borrower used his own men and teams in this work.

Another illustration of the importance of timber from a credit standpoint is the case of a 795-acre farm in Massachusetts.

This was a good productive farm with a large and excellent barn, and a colonial type house which needed some repair. The bank had a loan of $7,500 on this property. The owner died, the property passed into other hands and rapidly depreciated in value. Frequent requests were made to the bank for the release of the timber on this property, but no permission was granted until a buyer was found who was willing to pay a reasonable price for the stumpage and who was reliable financially.

When the timber was sold $5,500 was applied on the bank mortgage, leaving a balance of $1,500, a very safe loan.

With a farm of this size, located in a somewhat marginal district as regards agriculture, no loan would have been made in the first instance if it had not been for the growing timber on this property.

The bank has found an increasing interest in this wood and timber question. There is need of more education especially in the care of the woodlot now at hand. While the bank encourages reforestation and the use of tracts of idle lands, we especially stress the care and improvement of stands of wood and timber now found on the farm. There is also the need of education of the farmers as to the value of the wood and timber which he owns. Very few farmers are able to appraise or estimate timber. Interest and greater appreciation in this crop will come as its value becomes better known.

As already mentioned probably the most outstanding need is the development of home markets. While the work of the Federal Land Bank of Springfield is to furnish credit we have been calling attention to the neglect of one of the most important farm crops in this district and it is our policy to continue to support constructive steps that will tend to make the farm woodlot better appreciated and more valuable.

(The End)

From - Journal of Forestry, Vol. 24, No. 4 - April 1926.

- - - - - -

Prof. Ralph Hosmer of the College of Forestry at Cornell University spent June 28 and 29 with Mr. A. F. Amadon in the field making a study of white pine blister rust conditions in New York.

(From The Observer, N. Y. for July 1, 1926)

JOHNNY APPLESEED

By

Glenn Frank

The story of Johnny Appleseed is an old story, but it inherits endless retelling so that generation after generation American youth may know the thrill of his romantic career and catch something of the spirit he symbolizes.

Johnny Appleseed, whose real name was John Chapman, was born in New England in 1775. He died near Fort Wayne in 1847.

He was less than 30 years of age when he began a picturesque and purposeful adventure.

In 1803, or perhaps a bit earlier, young Chapman moved westward to the neighborhood of Pittsburgh. There he began to work out the settled purpose of his life.

The plan of his life was to move ever westward, keeping always a little in advance of the peopled frontier, planting orchards as he went.

As civilization periodically caught up with him, he would dispose of his trees for a "fip-penny bit" apiece, for food or old clothes, or, more frequently, give them away.

For 46 years he walked barefoot and unarmed through the wilderness. He was often clothed only in an old coffee-sack, with holes for his head and arms, and carried a tin pan, which often served as his hat.

The Indians regarded him as a great "medicine man," doubtless because he scattered through the woods the seeds of medicinal plants, such as catnip and pennyroyal.

It is said that he was never harmed by the Indians or by the beasts. He was welcomed everywhere. He lived to see his trees bearing fruit over a territory of a hundred thousand acres.

To me, the story of this secular mendicant friar is fascinating, not on for its essential interest as a tale, but for its suggestive symbolism.

The man who discovers ways and means for making government finer and fairer, the man who invents new and better ways of doing the world's work, the man who adds even one touch of beauty to a world that is all too sordid for th many, or the man who flings a creative thought against the sky of the future i another Johnny Appleseed, rendering unselfish service on the spiritual frontie of mankind.

Washington Post, May 26, 1926.

Edit. - As workers for Blister Rust Control, we have our own section on the big frontier of forestry. With ragged breeches for Johnny Appleseed's coffee sack, an old flivver for his tin pan, as definite a purpose, as staunch a heart we too can leave fruits of progress and helpfulness along our trails.

- - - - - -

A CASE OF MISTAKEN IDENTITY

I had an interesting and amusing experience the other day. I knocked at a farmer's door to talk it over with him. There was no response, although I could see him just inside. He must have thought I was a tramp, and the belief was probably justifiable. Feeling a bit peeved, I hammered the door in good fashion. He came to the door in a sour way and snapped "Whadderyuwant". The moment I told him who and what I was his face lit up like a church. He grabbed me by the arm and we started for the woods, His woods. If there is any point to this incident, at all, it is never say die, and you can't tell which way a frog is going to jump by the way he's sitting.

E. E. Tarbox, Maine.

- 265 -

PUBLICATIONS

Blister Rust

Anon. Blanket Quarantine For Blister Rust. The National Nurseryman,
August 1926, p. 216.

Anon. Prevent spread of Blister Rust. The Plymouth County Farmer.
Order of the State Department of Agriculture prohibits the further
planting of currant and gooseberry bushes in certain cities and
towns in Massachusetts.

Jorstad (1). Norske skogsykdommer. 1. Naletre-sykdommer bevirket
av Rustsopper, Ascomyceter og Fungi Imperfecti. (Norwegian
forest diseases. 1. Diseases of conifers caused by Rusts,
Ascomycetes, and Fungi Imperfecti.)-- Reprinted from Medd. Norske
Skogforsoksvesen, 6, 186 pp., 1925. (English summary.)
(2) White pines (p. strobus)free from blister rust (Cronartium ribicola) are stated to be of rare occurrence, and the
practical extinction of this tree after nearly 100 years' cultivation in Norway must be exclusively attributed to this
disease. The uredo- and teleutospores are most commonly found
on black currants (Ribes nigrum), but occur also on other species
of Ribes.

Tubeuf (C. v.). Anbau oder Abbau von funfnadeligen Kiefern. (Cultivation
or decline of five-needled pines.)--Allg. Forst- und Jagdzeit., c,
3, pp. 89-100, 1924.

Note. A lengthy extract of this article which appeared in the Review of Applied Mycology, (Kew, England) May 1926, p. 260-261, is
given in another part of the Blister Rust News.

PLANNING YOUR FAMILY EXPENDITURES

The above is the title of a new Miscellaneous Circular No. 68-M, by
Chase G. Woodhouse, of the Bureau of Home Economics, of this Department.
This circular should be of interest to all members of the Blister Rust Control
Family. Anything which will help you lead a happy home life free from
financial worries, which is one of the aims of the family budget, will help
put across the blister rust control program.

A copy of this bulletin is therefore being sent each of the blister
rust workers. If you don't get your copy write the Office of Information,
Department of Agriculture for it.

R. G. P.

PERSONALS

Mrs. Leolia E. Halper, formerly a stenographer in the Treasury Department, has been transferred to the Washington Office.

Mr. H. P. Avery, Chief Clerk, Washington Office, has been on a vacation at Silver Creek, New York. We understand that H. P. bought a new machine
to make the trip.

- - - -

Miss Nina Schnell, stenographer at the Washington Office, has been
transferred and is now working with Mr. Allanson.

Mr. Lewis C. Swain has been appointed Agent to succeed Mr. Kenneth E. Barraclough in Rockingham county, New Hampshire. Mr. Barraclough resigned August 7th to take up his new duties as Forest Extension Specialist for New Hampshire. His headquarters will be care of the Experiment Station, Durham. We hate to see you go "Barry", but good luck to you.

- - - -

Mr. Ray R. Hirt was appointed Field Assistant at Syracuse, New York. He will assist Dr. L. H. Pennington and Mr. E. C. Filler in preparing a series of maps to show the status of blister rust spread and control work. These data are needed in connection with the study of the epidemiology of the rust which Dr. Pennington is making for the Office of Blister Rust Control.

- - - -

Mr. Paul B. Smith, who worked on blister rust control in Pennsylvania last year, has again been appointed Agent with headquarters in Harrisburg. His appointment was effective August 1.

- -

Mr. Thomas Large, who has been appointed on Blister Rust Control for the past four seasons has again been appointed Field Assistant with headquarters at Spokane. His appointment was effective July 16.

Miss Mamie L. McWold, clerk in the Washington Office, suffered from heat prostration early in August and was so seriously ill that she was taken to Emergency Hospital. She had sufficiently recovered by August 13 to proceed to her home at City Point, Wisconsin. Miss McWold is being transferred to the Spokane Office where she expects to begin her duties on September 15.

Mr. J. D. Kennedy is being brought into the Albany Office of the New York Conservation Commission as Assistant State Leader in Blister Rust Control

Mr. Dow V. Baxter of the University of Wisconsin, has been appointed Assistant Professor of Forestry at the University of Michigan. Bully for you Dow! Couldn't resist the appeal to return to your Alma Mater.

Dr. Baxter is a loyal Blister Ruster, having scouted in Wisconsin for several seasons, and later having charge of this work in Michigan. A card recently written by him from California reads: "I can certainly agree with you when you say that the sugar pines are wonders. I have been visiting the important Western National Forests this season and have examined several Ribes bushes for you. I thought of Detwiler, too, when visiting a cherry orchard out here in the west." When interviewed, Detwiler said: "I cannot tell a lie; but Baxter tempted me. No man could resist luscious Michigan cherries."

BLISTER RUST

NEWS

September 1926.

Volume X   *Number 9*

U.S. DEPARTMENT of AGRICULTURE

Office of Blister Rust Control.

Bureau of Plant Industry

C O N T E N T S - V O L. 10. No. 9.

Page

Agent's Work
    Blister Rusters in Cumberland County, Maine, Hold Field Day 276
    With the New York Agents 281
Blister Rust Situation
    Blister Rust in Pennsylvania 284
    Blister Rust Infection on Pine on Olympic Peninsula, Wash. 271
    Three Red Currants Killing Seventeen Pine In State Forest
        In Massachusetts 278
Editorial
    Weekly Itinerary Reports May be a Mine of Information 280
Educational
    Blister Rust Demonstration at Springfield, Mass. 284
    Demonstrating at Weymouth Fair 274
    Poster Used in New Hampshire 278
    This Letter to Oregon Fire Wardens Gets the Attention 277
Eradication Work
    Boy Scouts as "Ribes Hounds" on Town Forest in Mass. 282
    Brookline's Town Forest Protected 274
    Cooperation with Colleges, Clubs, and Lumber Companies 273
    Experimental Local Control in Northern Idaho 272
    Progress Report on Protection from Blister Rust in California . . . 275
    Protecting Pines the President Planted 275
    Word Pictures - Pro and Con 283
Forestry
    Adirondack Forestry Tour 279
    White Pine Weevil in the Spotlight 285
Office Comment 290
Personals 289
    White Pine Blister Rust Control Districts and Personnel in
        Northeast States 286
Publications 291
Quarantines 291
    Federal Customs Official at Spokane intercepts Shipment of
        Conifers from British Columbia 272
State News
    California 275
    Idaho 272, 273
    Maine 276
    Massachusetts 273, 274-5, 282, 283, 294
    New Hampshire 273
    New York 273, 279-280, 281
    Pennsylvania 284
    Vermont 273
    Washington 271, 272

EDITORIAL STAFF

Roy G. Pierce . . . . . Editor — Washington, D. C.
E.E. Tarbox . . . Assoc. Editor — Maine
Thos. J. King . .   "   "   — New Hampshire
S.V. Holden   . .   "   "   — Vermont
W.J. Endersbee: .   "   "   — Massachusetts
O.C. Anderson . .   "   "   — Rhode Island
J.E. Riley, Jr.   "   "   — Connecticut
George H. Stevens   "   "   — New York
H.H. Ninman . . .   "   "   — Wisconsin
C.R. Stillinger . .   "   "   — Western States

UNITED STATES DEPARTMENT OF AGRICULTURE
BUREAU OF PLANT INDUSTRY
WASHINGTON, D.C.

T H E B L I S T E R R U S T N E W S

Issued by the Office of Blister Rust Control
and the Cooperating States.

VOL. 10, No. 9.   September, 1926.

BLISTER RUST INFECTION ON PINE ON OLYMPIC PENINSULA, WASHINGTON

Recent findings of blister rust on the Olympic Peninsula have demonstrated how difficult it is to locate small local infections of this disease on pine. During 1922 the coast region of Washington was scouted quite thoroughly for blister rust, but none was found except on currants and gooseberries. As a result it was believed that this was the initial infection for this region. However, in the spring of 1924, besides incipient cankers on a few pines which were to be expected from the infection on Ribes in 1922, a canker was found which had fruited on 1918 wood indicating that this pine had become infected possibly in 1919.

Scouting during 1925 and 1926 has revealed not only incipient cankers but some cankers even older than the one found in 1924. During August of this year an infection on a cultivated pine was found near Bremerton, Washington, which was apparently on 1915 or 1916 wood, indicating that the disease was present at this early period, starting probably on the currants. Several other cankers have been found on the 1919, 1920, 1921, and 1922 wood of the tree. Thus we now know that the disease was established in the pine forests of Washington, in spotted areas on the Olympic Peninsula some time before the 1922 spread.

                                        C. R. Stillinger.

FEDERAL CUSTOMS OFFICIAL AT SPOKANE COOPERATING WITH DEPARTMENT OF AGRICULTUR
INTERCEPTS SHIPMENT OF CONIFERS FROM BRITISH COLUMBIA

A shipment of coniferous trees consisting of cedar, juniper, jack pine
and white pine from Kaslo, British Columbia, to a resident of Spokane, was
recently intercepted by the customs officials of Spokane, Washington. Kaslo
is on Kootenay Lake and in a region where blister rust has been found on both
currants and on white pine. No permit had been obtained to import this
material and no inspection had been made of the material up to the time it
reached Spokane. The individual had collected the trees from the woods near
Kaslo. Upon request by wire the Agricultural Department allowed the importation with the exception of the pine. The pine were inspected carefully by th
local state inspector and by members of the blister rust office, but no blist
rust was found on them. The two cases which had white pine were destroyed in
their entirety by the local state inspector while the other two cases were
passed. Shipments of this nature are very dangerous if not intercepted.

EXPERIMENTAL LOCAL CONTROL IN NORTHERN IDAHO

Experimental local control work in northern Idaho was started on June
15. Over 5000 acres in excellent white pine type were worked before July 12.
On this date a severe lightning storm occurred and all the eradication men as
well as the men on methods study were called for fire suppression duty. The
fire situation continued to be so serious that the men were kept employed
fighting fire continuously up to August 16. Although this long period of fi
fighting has seriously interferred with the local control experimental work,
special effort will be made to continue the eradication work and methods experiments, in an effort to derive all benefit yet possible from the season's
work.

C. R. Stillinger.

- 273 -

COOPERATION WITH COLLEGES,CLUBS,LUMBER COMPANIES, ETC.

During the past few weeks, re-eradication of Ribes has been in progress on the Harvard and Yale Forests at Petersham, Mass., and Swanzey, N.H., respectively. The New York State College of Forestry is also having its newly acquired pine forest, near Warrensburg, cleared of currants and gooseberries. In Vermont, control work has recently been cpmpleted on the U. S. Morgan Horse Farm, the Middlebury College tract, and on properties owned by the Rutland County Club, the Vermont State Hospital, Bomosum County Club, and the Vermont Sanatorium. The S. D. Warren Lumber Company of Maine has also appropriated funds for control work on their lands. Such cooperation is most encouraging.

Recently, the heads of the forestry colleges in New York visited infected areas im the Adirondacks, and were very much impressed by the damage caused to pine. The foresters in the senior class at Cornell will make a special trip this fall through the Adirondacks to study the white pine and blister rust situation.

Aug. 2, 1926.   E. C. Filler.

- - - - - - - - - -

COMMENDATION FOR OUR FIRE FIGHTERS

A recent communication has been received by Dr. W. A. Taylor, Chief of the Bureau of Plant Industry, regarding the services of the men working on blister rust control, in fire fighting which reads as follows:

- - - - - - - - - - -"The assistance given by your employees in the
extremely bad fire situation which existed in the Northern
District in July and August is very greatly appreciated.
                    Very sincerely yours,
                         (Signed) L. F. Kneipp,
                              Acting Forester.

NEWS FROM PLYMOUTH COUNTY MASSACHUSETTS

Demonstrating at Weymouth Fair

Space was promised Agent Brockway at Weymouth Fair for a blister
rust exhibit August 20-21; this also being the first time an exhibit had
been shown at the fair. On the arrival at the fair grounds in A. M. of
August 20 it was found that all space in building had been taken. It was
no use to kick and so the Superintendent of Grounds was interviewed and
was induced to give us a space by grand stand ordinarily paid for by a
fakir in the midway. We put a good specimen infected tree on each fender
of the old Ford and put the big U. S. Department of Agriculture cooperating
sign on the windshield. We then lined the hood and fenders and running board
with Riker mounts and signs and pictures and infected limbs. We talked to
375 people in two days. I left the exhibit by request to go with the fire
warden of Weymouth to an estate owned by Mrs. Edward Nobius. I found her
pine and a patch of 50 cultivated red currants both diseased. She ordered
the gardener to leave off work on the lawn and pull out the currants at once.
This one thing alone pleased me enough to pay for the whole exhibit and in
closing I will say that the old flivver paid for itself at last.

Brookline's Town Forest Protected

Brookline's town forest lies in the town of Dedham around the
reservoir and mills. Some 145,000 pine trees have been planted. It is all
sandy land. We called at 69 houses and found 49 houses had cultivated bushes
all but 15 had black currants. We found the disease was just getting started
in the pine. Many people have already removed their bushes. We will rework
the rest this fall. Question: - Does it pay to protect town forests - think
it over -

Protecting Pines the President Planted

The town of Walpole has about 165 acres of town forest land.
Much of it is natural and the rest is being planted. The first town
forest in Massachusetts is this one in Walpole and the first tree planted
was planted by Calvin Coolidge then Lieutenant Governor of Massachusetts,
now President of the United States. For cooperation we had the fire
warden and all his men go with us and scout all the land. They then went
with us checking cultivated Ribes eradication. We had previously called
at houses and asked people to remove bushes. We pulled all bushes not
pulled and they were loaded onto a truck owned by town of Walpole and
taken to town dump and burned. Blister rust is present in this town
forest but it is now thoroughly protected and many thanks are due the
fire warden and his men for splendid cooperation and support.

E. M. BROCKWAY, Mass.

- - - - - - - - -

PROGRESS REPORT ON PROTECTION OF WHITE PINE FROM BLISTER RUST IN CALIFORNIA

"Although blister rust has not yet reached California, active steps
are being taken to keep it out, as well as to determine methods to cope with
it successfully when it appears. It has been decided by the United States
Department of Agriculture, as well as the several states which have stands of
white pine of which sugar pine is the predominating member of this group in
California, that the eradication of the cultivated black currant is a very
necessary step in retarding the establishment of this disease in uninfested
territory. Extensive evidence indicates that this currant is the most important agent in the introduction of the disease for long distances."

From California Department of Agriculture News Letter
of September 4, 1926.

BLISTER RUSTERS IN CUMBERLAND COUNTY, MAINE, HOLD FIELD DAY
Second Annual Outing Held at Bridgton, Maine

The second annual outing of the Cumberland County blister rust scouts and
foremen was held Sunday, August 22, at foreman Haley's camp on Ingalls Pond, in
the town of Bridgton. The majority of the foremen brought their wives and there
was a total attendance of thirty two. In the forenoon a trip was made to the
blister rust demonstration area on Peaked Mt. in Sebago. Returning to the camp
at noon, lunch was eaten on the shore of the pond. Immediately after lunch, Mr.
and Mrs. Haley were presented with a set of andirons in order that they might
have something to remind them of the Ribes Hound's picnic.

Scout Petersen won the prize of a pipe, offered for the scout who obtained
the largest number of cooperators between May 10 and July 30. The big event of
the afternoon was the shooting contest. The first prize for the men was won by
Mr. Roberts of Gray, while Mrs. White of Baldwin won first prize for the women.
After the shooting contest, the crowd took to the water and those who did not
go in bathing enjoyed the lake in boats. The festivities of the day were brought
to a close by the group assembling on the piazza of the camp and partaking of
delicious ice cream and cake which was served by the host and hostess.

S. D. Conner, Maine.

Note.--Such a jollification as Conner and his coworkers have pulled off in
Cumberland County is a good thing. It cements friendships, gives a respite from
interviewing and Ribes pulling, and makes for increased efficiency.

- - - - - - -

PINE OWNER BELIEVES IN FREQUENT INSPECTION FOR BLISTER RUST

"My plantation has been gone over thoroughly as well as all my other
land, 3 years ago, by state and other men to remove currants and gooseberries.
I have been around occasionally since then looking for them."

August 25, 1926.   Arthur L. Hayes,
                                              Limerick, Me.

THIS LETTER TO OREGON FIRE WARDENS GETS THE ATTENTION

Mr. John Doe,
Fire Warden,
- - - - - - -

Botany Department, O. A. C.,
Corvallis, Oregon,
July 15, 1926.

Dear Mr. Doe:

The man who thought blister rust would never reach Oregon was a wild guesser. It was located last fall on Gnat Creek in Clatsop County and at Wheeler and Pacific City in Tillamook County. At Pacific City it was found on cultivated black currants and at the other points on wild black currants. If we found it in three places it doubtless occurred in others.

Scouting this spring in Washington revealed blister rust on pines in nine different localities on or near the Olympic Peninsula. There is little question that the spores from the Olympic Peninsula blew into Oregon and caused the infection found last fall.

If you are keeping two jumps ahead of this blister rust you are some jumper. It is on the way to the sugar pines and sooner or later, probably sooner, we will have to fight it by our developed local control methods.

We wish to know whether blister rust is in your section. Please hold a tight rein on your horses now. Blister rust may be in your section even if you do not have white pine within many miles. We found no white pine at Pacific City, Wheeler, or Gnat Creek but we found blister rust all the same.

Look for blister rust on the wild stink currant along the streams from August 15 until winter. If you find anything on these bushes you think may be blister rust, send a specimen to me and we will write you about it.

If you are a new man on the job and have not received publications on blister rust let us know and we will supply you. Thanking you for your cooperation, I am,

Very truly yours,

L. N. GOODDING, Assistant Pathologist

THREE RED CURRANTS KILLING SEVENTEEN PINE IN STATE FOREST IN MASSACHUSETTS

The Colerain State Forest consists of 1206 acres located in Franklin County, Massachusetts. Approximately one-third of this area is in the town of Heath and it is in this town that data for this note was gathered. The study was made in an eighty acre plantation of white pine (Pinus strobus). Three year old stock was used and the trees are now fourteen years old. The average height is fifteen feet, while the diameter is about three inches. The three bushes of cultivated red currants (Ribes vulgare) two feet tall were all that could be found in the entire plantation. The bushes were large and healthy with pine on all sides.

One lone bush had infected three trees while the other two bushes growing close together at a distance of four hundred feet from the first one had caused infection on fourteen trees. All Ribes were heavily infected this season. Pine within a radius of two to five hundred feet were found to be infected. The majority of the infected trees were found in a northwesterly direction from the Ribes. Infection ranged in origin from 1915 to 1923, but was especially heavy in 1917. A study of one tree revealed 27 cankers ranging in origin from 1915 to 1921. Stem cankers and branch infections one foot from the stem were considered to be fatal to the tree.

                                        G. S. DOORE, Franklin Co.

August 25, 1926.

POSTER USED IN NEW HAMPSHIRE

On opposite page, there will be found in copies sent to our own employees a reproduction of a large two-color poster used in New Hampshire.

TO · DAY
BLISTER RUST CREW
WORKING HERE
COME IN
AND LEARN HOW
TO CONTROL THE
DISEASE

ADIRONDACK FORESTRY TOUR

For the purpose of stimulating interest in reforestation, the New York Conservation Commission and the Extension Service of the New York Department of Agriculture, in cooperation with the Farm Bureau Organization, conducts annually a joint forestry tour which covers the Adirondack region. The tour this year takes place September 17-20, inclusive. Those who take advantage of this trip will have an opportunity to observe various state and private plantations in the Adirondacks, types of soil suitable for certain species, particular species growing in plantations renging from 1 year to 26 years old, and the effect of insect pests and fungous diseases.

The first stop will be at the State nursery at Saratoga, the largest tree nursery in the world, where there are at present being grown between 40 and 50 million young trees for distribution. A stop will be made at T. C. Luther's 50,000 acre forest preserve. Mr. Luther has plantations of various species including among others the white pine, red pine, and the Riga variety of scotch pine. These plantations are from 1 to 14 years old. After passing through the plantations on the Glen Falls city water shed various stops will be made in Warren County. At Chestertown is the Remington lot, where white pine has come in naturally since 1865 (at that time the land was in wheat) the average stand per acre on this is about 30,000 feet. A stop will be made at Horicon, where the blister rust has been present for 18 years, and at least 60 per cent of the trees have been killed or are dying from this disease.

The trip will continue to Ticonderoga, Elizabethtown and Wilmington. Passing through the famous Wilmington Notch we come to Lake Placid. There are several thousand acres of State plantations near here dating back to 1906. Plantations of 400 acres of white pine at Goldsmith

will be visited, which is without question, one of the most rapid-growing
plantations on State land. A growth of 3 feet per year can be seen throughout this plantation. Other excellent plantations of Scotch pine, red pine,
spruce, and European larch will be visited, at various places on the trip.

September 15, 1926.

R. G. P.

(Extract from five page itinerary of Forestry Tour)

WEEKLY ITINERARY REPORTS MAY BE A MINE OF INFORMATION

Several of the Agents in Blister Rust Control have had the practice of noting in their weekly itinerary reports items of interest, such
as the discovery of a new blister rust infection center, a talk at a school
house, a meeting with Boy Scouts, etc. I am not sure to what extent these
comments are made use of by the State Leaders, but the Washington Office
finds them very useful. Suggestions have been made, which when followed
up have lead to valuable contributions to our knowledge of the location
of the disease and have opened vistas for types of new educational work.

A perfunctory "two interviews and a follow-up" on the Report
Blank may record all that was done that day, but they convey little information of value to the Office.

R. G. Pierce.

OUT OF BOUNDS

More than a thousand Ribes lacustre were destroyed in the town of
Heath, Mass. during eradication work on the Colerain State Forest.

G. S. Doore.

WITH THE NEW YORK AGENTS

Mr. Harrison G. Strait a new agent with headquarters at Hudson, N. Y. is swinging into the harness in good shape according to his weekly itinerary reports.

One thing of interest was the trip over Columbia County on August 4 with the Farm Bureau Agent to meet men of influence in the county. This kind of close cooperation with the Farm Bureau is much appreciated and the cooperation is probably not all one-sided. Besides carrying on regular interview work to secure cooperative control, and overseeing the work of several foremen, Mr. Strait collected material and put on fair exhibits at Cairo in Greene County and at Rhinebeck in Dutchess County.

- - - - - - - - -

Mr. Harry A. Williams, Agent in charge of blister rust control in southeastern New York, had a busy month in August interviewing among others the Water Boards at Middletown, the Superintendent of Water Works at Port Jervis, the Superintendent of Torrehill Farms at Montgomery, the Chief Engineer of the Park at Bear Mountain, the Water Board at Liberty as well as numerous unofficial persons. Besides the interviews, he carried on scouting for infection in pine plantations and native growth, and for the presence of Ribes; putting on a blister rust demonstration at county picnic at Oneonta, and at the Norwich Fair, as well as starting the Ribes eradication crews throughout the district and inspecting their work.

The above is only a sample of the work accomplished by a blister rust control agent, all to the end of protecting our valuable white pine forests.

R. G. P.

BOY SCOUTS AS "RIBES HOUNDS" ON TOWN FOREST IN MASSACHUSETTS

Belchertown in Hampshire County, Massachusetts, has a town forest of 150 acres on the site of the Town Farm. The wooded area of the farm is coming up rapidly to white pine reproduction, which the town fathers desired to protect from the white pine blister rust. The only question was how to do it, for large numbers of Ribes had been found on a portion of this area. Why not the Boy Scouts from a Springfield troop already familiar with the control of this disease?

Arrangements were accordingly made with the Scoutmaster of the troop and with the town officials. On the morning of August 31st the Agent took three Scouts, fourteen years old, to the Belchertown Forest, where they met the two state inspectors stationed in the town, who acted as foremen for the day. A few minutes later the attack was in full swing, the gooseberry bushes rapidly succumbing. At noon, mess call sounded from the Town Farm house, and everyone sat down in a private dining room where a fair waitress supplied the ingredients of a New England boiled dinner. Stuffed to repletion at the town's expense, the boys resumed the attack. Recall sounded at 3 P. M., and fishing became the order of the day. A nearby pond supplied the sport, which met with great favor and success. That night three Scouts returned home tired but happy.

Inasmuch as the area had not been completely worked, it was necessary to take the crew back two days later. Were they willing to go? Ask them! They had no prospect of another fishing trip, but maybe it was that free feed. This trip completed the job, of the eradication of 5,000 wild gooseberry bushes, and the consequent protection of Belchertown's future forest. Incidentally we have three embryo inspectors if occasion arises.

R. E. Wheeler, Mass.

- 283 -

WORD PICTURES - PRO AND CON

In connection with the removal of cultivated Ribes in Massachusetts, a detailed card record is kept for each case. One of the entries on these cards is, "Attitude of owner." The following descriptive expressions have been taken at random from these records and are presented in the BLISTER RUST NEWS with the feeling that they are too expressive to keep in the files. To what blister ruster in New England do they not present a colorful picture?

Fine	Unwilling but reasonable
Abusive	Obstinate
O.K.	Interested
Not cordial	Very Indignant
Good	Willing
Rather reluctant	Indifferent
Very good	Splendid
Dislike losing plants	Combative but intelligent
Cheerful	Fair
Reluctant	Stubborn
Fairly agreeable	Friendly
Belligerent	Threatening bodily injury
Very courteous and	Paradoxical
helpful	Tearful
Reluctant cooperators	

A casual reading of the above list might give the impression that one half of the cases dealt with are of the unfavorable or unfriendly type, but a further analysis on the basis of number of cases involved, indicates a most favorable condition; for example, from the beginning of the Ribes eradication season of 1926 to August 31, reports actually received from the field show that 4,120 cultivated Ribes have been removed from 321 locations. Of this number of owners, 289 or 90% are classed as of a friendly type, and only 32 or 10% were in any way unfriendly. Furthermore, the cooperative owners have been willing to sacrifice 3,407 bushes or 83% of all those removed, while those who have cooperated reluctantly or not at all, possessed but 713 bushes or 17% of the total.

When it is considered that in a great number of cases, owners are
actually deriving an appreciable income from cultivated Ribes and that many
such owners possess no pine, the records are most gratifying. It is not
the easiest thing in the world to "sell" blister rust control to a none-pine
owner of cultivated Ribes, but, nevertheless, it is being done in
Massachusetts as the records show.

- - - - - - - - - - -

BLISTER RUST IN PENNSYLVANIA

Dr. W. A. McCubbin on September 10th notified the office of the
discovery of blister rust by Mr. H. W. Thurston of Pennsylvania State
College and himself at a single place in each of three counties, Pike,
Monroe, and Lackawanna. In each case the infection was found on cultivated
black currants (Ribes nigrum). This makes the fourth county in which the
blister rust has been discovered this year; an earlier infection having been
reported from Brooklyn in Susquehanna County by the Federal blister rust
agent, Mr. Paul B. Smith.

R. G. P.

BLISTER RUST DEMONSTRATION AT SPRINGFIELD, MASSACHUSETTS

Our blister rust demonstration at the Eastern States Exposition
at Springfield will be something worth while. We have the biggest space
ever, 31 ft. x 10 ft. (31 ft. frontage with an inset measuring 15 ft. front,
10 ft. deep, banked at an angle of 45 degrees.) It is hoped that some of
the blister rust agents from other states will be present.

R. E. Wheeler, Mass.

WHITE PINE WEEVIL IN THE SPOTLIGHT

Amherst, Mass. — How a drop in the eastern market for boxboards turned the spotlight of scientific investigation upon the hitherto inconspicuous but exceedingly busy white pine weevil is told by Director S. T. Dana, of the Northeastern Forest Experiment Station.

As long as there was a good market for boxboards in the Northeast, little attention was paid to the necessity of exterminating the white pine weevil if more clear white pine lumber was to be obtained. The boxboard manufacturers could utilize the limby, crooked trees which result from repeated attacks by the weevil, and what little market there was for clear lumber was dominated by western white pine, which was as cheap as good quality eastern pine. Now that the boxboard market has slumped, however, timberland owners are deeply interested in growing high grade timber and, consequently, in ways of getting rid of the weevil.

H. J. MacAloney, Assistant Entomologist at the Northeastern Forest Experiment Station, in cooperation with the Bureau of Entomology of the Department of Agriculture, State foresters, entomologists, and certain forest-land owners in Massachusetts, is accordingly seeking out practical control measures for this forest pest. Among the control measures being studied is that of "bug eat bug" or control by parasites. Another hope is that attacks may be reduced by some means of regulating the selection of trees for cutting in logging operations.

WHITE PINE BLISTER RUST CONTROL DISTRICTS
and PERSONNEL IN NORTHEASTERN STATES
September 10, 1926

STATE COOPERATORS

State	Cooperators	Address
Maine	Neil Violette, Forest Commissioner	Augusta,
New Hampshire	J. H. Foster, State Forester	Concord,
Vermont	R. M. Ross, Commissioner of Forestry	Montpelier,
Massachusetts	R. H. Allen,	Room 136 State House, Boston,
Rhode Island	J. J. Dunn, Sec'y R.I. State Board of Agriculture	State House, Providence,
Connecticut	W. O. Filley, Station Forester	Agri. Experiment Sta. New Haven,
New York	C. R. Pettis, Commissioner	Conservation Comm Albany.

FEDERAL PERSONNEL

Supervisor-in-charge	E. C. Filler	Office of Blister Rust Control, Room 403, 408 Atlantic Ave., Boston,
Assistant (Experimental Work)	A.E. Fivaz	Box 51, Warrensburg, N.
Assistant (Educational and Experimental Work)	L.W. Hodgkins	6 Anderson St., Taunto. Mass.
Assistant (Boston Office)	K.K. Stimson	Room 403, 408 Atlanti Boston, Mass.

STATE LEADERS

State	Leader in Charge	Address
Maine	W. O. Frost	State Forestry Dept. August
New Hampshire	L. E. Newman J. M. Corliss, Ass't.	State Forestry Dept. concor " " " Conco
Vermont	S. V. Holden	Box 472, Burlington,
Massachusetts	C. C. Perry	Room 136, State House, Bosto

STATE LEADERS

State	Leader in Charge	Address
Rhode Island	O. C. Anderson	c|o State Board of Agriculture Room 129, State House, Providence,
Connecticut	J. E. Riley, Jr.	State Agricultural Experiment Station, New Haven,
New York	Dr. H. H. York A. F. Amadon, G. E. Stevens, Ass't.	Conservation Commission, Albany, " " " " " "

State	District	Agent in Charge	Agent's Address
Maine	1. Cumberland County ...	S. D. Conner	904 Washington Ave., Woodford',
	2. Oxford County	D. S. Curtis	North Bridgton,
	3. York County	E. E. Tarbox	127 Main St., Sanford,
	4. Androscoggin and Sagadahoc Counties ..	G. H. Kimball	374 Court St., Auburn,
N. H.	1. Upper Grafton and lower Coos Counties ...	T. L. Kane	c/o Farm Bureau, Woodsville,
	2. Lower Grafton and part of Sullivan Counties ..	G.F. Richardson	2 Billings Block, Lebanon,
	3. Carroll County	S. H. Boomer	c/o Farm Bureau, Conway,
	4. Strafford and Belknap Counties	W. J. Cullen	c/o Farm Bureau, Rochester,
	5. Merrimack and part of Sullivan Counties ...	T. J. King	c/o Farm Bureau, Concord,
	6. Rockingham County ...	L. C. Swain	c/o Farm Bureau, Exeter,
	7. Hillsborough County ,		c/o Farm Bureau, Milford
	8. Cheshire and part of Sullivan Counties ...	F. J. Baker	c/o Farm Bureau, Keene,
Vt.	1. Central Conn. River Valley District (Composed of portions of Orange and Windsor Counties	F. E. Rose	Box 42, White River Jct.
	2. Chittenden County ...	S. V. Holden	Box 472, Burlington
	3. Addison & Rutland Counties	W. E. Bradder	33 Temple St., Rutland,
Mass.	1. Middlesex County	W. T. Roop	32 Paul Revere Road, Arlington Heights,

State	District	Agent in Charge	Agent's Address
Mass.	2. Norfolk & Plymouth Co's.	E. M. Brockway	106 Main St., Brockton,
	3. Upper Worcester County ..	William Clave	Box 173, Gardner,
	4. Lower " " ..	E. J. McNerney	19 Court St., Worcester,
	5. Franklin and part of Hampshire Counties	G. S. Doore	Extension Service, Greenfield,
	6. Hampden and part of Hampshire Counties	R. E. Wheeler	719 Bridge St. West Springfield,
	7. Berkshire County	W. J. Endersbee	81 Grove St., Great Barrington,
R. I.	District includes all of state.	O. C. Anderson	c/o State Board of Agri., Room 129, State House, Providence,
Conn.	1. Litchfield County	E. D. Clark	R. F. D. #1, Litchfield,
	2. Eastern Conn. District	H. J. Miles	Box 62, Putnam
N. Y.	1. Essex, Clinton and Franklin Counties ...... and	B. H. Nichols	Lewis,
	2. Warren County .... and	N. H. Harpp E. G. Woodward	Warrensburg,
	3. Washington and Rensselaer Counties	J. D. Kennedy	17 Pearl St., Hudson Fall
	4. Saratoga, Schenectady, and Albany Counties	C. E. Baker	Saratoga Farm Bureau, Saratoga Springs,
	5. Lower Hudson River Valley District	H. G. Strait	Farm Bureau Office, Hudson,
	6. Otsego, Schoharie, and Delaware Counties	H. A. Williams	3 Spring St., Oneonta,
	7. Fulton, Montgomery, and Hamilton Counties	J. W. Charlton	Farm Bureau Office, Gloversville,
	8. Lewis, Herkimer, Jefferson, Oneida, and St. Lawrence Counties	S. W. Hamilton	31 Waters Terrace, Lowville,

E. C. Filler.

Mr. Robert S. Caruthers and Mr. Thurston L. Corbett are now (Sept. 15) at Washington, D. C., engaged in working up field notes collected during the past summer.

Mr. Francis C. Scofield resigned as Field Assistant on September 9, 1926.

Mr. Ralph A. Sheals was appointed Agent, effective September 16, 1926. He will be in charge of field supervision of the quarantine inspection work.

Messrs. Fred R. Allen, Charles C. Baker, Cecil W. Guptill, Jos. G. McMacken and Thos. D. Mallery have recently resigned from the blister rust work.

Miss Maude A. Thompson and Miss Alma Bishop of the Washington Office have left for their vacation.

- - - - - -

Mr. S. B. Detwiler and Louis A. Barr left Washington on September 12, for a short trip through eastern Pennsylvania, where they will be engaged in scouting for the blister rust, principally on the cultivated black currant.

O F F I C E   C O M M E N T

REIMBURSEMENT VOUCHERS SHOULD BE SUBMITTED PROMPTLY

"MEMORANDUM FOR HEADS OF OFFICES.

Gentlemen:

Under date of June 26, 1924, a memorandum was sent you calling attention to delays in the submittal of reimbursement vouchers, these delays causing uncertainty in the financial standing of projects and general tending to interrupt effective administration. You were requested to see that all accounts be submitted monthly, and in no cases to be delayed beyond thirty days after the close of a quarter. Delayed reimbursement vouchers must be satisfactorily explained in order to be approved.

We are experiencing some delays in the submittal for payment of vouchers covering miscellaneous expenditures, commonly referred to as "white vouchers. It is of the greatest importance that these be submitted prompt in order that the credit of the Government may be maintained and our finan cial records kept up to date. Hereafter, all white vouchers must be submitted promptly, and not later than within sixty days after the incurring of the obligation. Delays in submitting vouchers will be considered administratively incident to the personnel record of the individual concerned.

Your hearty cooperation is requested.

Very truly yours,

Wm. A. Taylor,

Chief of Bureau."

```
┌─────────────────────────────────────┐
│                                      │
│   P U B L I C A T I O N S            │
│                                      │
└─────────────────────────────────────┘
```

Blister Rust

Allen, P. H.

Report of the Division of Plant Pest Control (Mass.)
White Pine Blister Rust. p. 15, 16. Annual Report of the
Commissioner of Agriculture for the year ending November
30, 1925.

Report of the Division of Plant Pest Control (Mass.)
White Pine Blister Rust p. 25 - 27. Annual report of
the Commissioner of Agriculture for the year ending
November 30, 1924.

Ribes

Palmer, E. F.

Currants and gooseberries. Ontario Department of
Agriculture. Horticultural Experiment Station at
Vineland. Bulletin 318, April, 1926. Gives a paragraph
on the European currant rust (Cronartium ribicola) p. 19.

```
┌─────────────────────────────────────┐
│                                      │
│   Q U A R A N T I N E S              │
│                                      │
└─────────────────────────────────────┘
```

BLISTER RUST

NEWS

October 1926.

Volume X   *Number 10*

U.S. DEPARTMENT of AGRICULTURE
Office of Blister Rust Control.

C O N T E N T S - V O L. 10. No. 10

Page

Blister Rust Situation
  Blister Rust Control in Maine moving into Lincoln County 298
  Heavy Infection in Southern Worcester County, Mass. 299
Editorial
  On the Firing Line with Ribee Bill 315
Educational
  A Blister Rust Field Trip 301
  Demonstrations at Fairs 302
  Forest Service Official Impressed by Waterford Infection Area 294
  Frost Does His Bit, Appears Before Rotary Club 303
  Lantern Slides Available 307
  New York Agents Enjoy Adirondack Forestry Tour 298
Eradication
  A Ten Year Old Boy Makes Good on Eradication Crew 305
  Massachusetts Field Work Ends for Season 303
  Owner of Cultivated Ribes Becomes Interested in Forest Protection .. 300
  Ribes Eradication Carried on in Connecticut Till September 29 303
  Ribes Eradication in Rhode Island 303
  Summary of Ribes Eradication in Northeast for July and August 300
Forestry
  Value of Forest Plantations 308
Personals 311
Poem 305
Publications 314
Quarantines 309, 313
  Oregon 309
  Rhode Island 309
  New Hampshire 310
  Federal Quarantine 63 310
State News
  California 296, 297
  Connecticut 303, 304, 305
  Idaho 311
  Maine 294,298,303,311
  Massachusetts 299, 303,307,311,312
  New Hampshire 295,310
  New York 295,298, 299,300,301,302,305,306, 311
  Oregon 309, 311
  Pennsylvania 301, 302
  Rhode Island 302,303, 309
  Vermont 294,301, 308
  Western States 296,297,309,311,312, 313
Technical Studies
  Connecticut Agent Correlates Types of Soil with Prevalence
    of Ribes 304
  Experimental Ribes Eradication in California 296
  Field Study at Wolfeboro, N. H., Demonstrates Effectiveness
    of Control 295

E D I T O R I A L   S T A F F

Roy G. Pierce . . . . Editor - Washington, D. C.
E. E. Tarbox . . . . . Assoc. "   - Maine
Thos. J. King . . . . . "   "   - Now Hampshire
S. V. Holden . . . . . . "   "   - Vermont
W. J. Enderstee . . . . "   "   - Massachusetts
O. C. Anderson . . . . "   "   - Rhode Island
J. E. Riley, Jr. . . . "   "   - Connecticut
George H. Stevens . .. "   "   - New York
H. J. Ninman . . . . . "   "   - Wisconsin
C. R. Stillinger . . . "   "   - Western States

UNITED STATES DEPARTMENT OF AGRICULTURE
BUREAU OF PLANT INDUSTRY
WASHINGTON, D. C.

T H E   B L I S T E R   R U S T   N E W S

Issued by the Office of Blister Rust Control
and the Cooperating States.

VOL. 10. No. 10.   October, 1926

FOREST SERVICE OFFICIAL IMPRESSED BY WATERFORD INFECTION AREA

A recent letter has been received from Mr. R. M. Evans, Assistant
District Forester of the Eastern District of the United States Forest
Service. Part of his letter to Mr. Detwiler is as follows:

"Incidentally, I should like to tell you that during
the last week in August I spent a very interesting and instructive couple of hours with Mr. Filler on the Waterford Blister
Rust Tract. This is certainly a horrible example of what the
disease can do when it has an opportunity and it is also mighty
disturbing to realize that timber of merchantable size is by no
means immune. I am glad to have visited the area for it has emphasized the necessity of keeping on our toes.

"Perhaps I have already told you that I have a little
patch of pine timber in Fryeburg, Maine, containing stuff all the
way from a few years old up to merchantable trees. I have been
a bit uneasy about this and took occasion this summer to scout
it rather carefully. I am glad to say that I found only a few
Ribes and no blister rust."

Note:- It is a good omen, that of another forester becoming an
honest-to-goodness timber owner. The cause of forestry and forest protection
will progress faster because technical foresters are caring for their own
timber.

R. G. P.

FIELD STUDY AT WOLFEBORO, N. Y., DEMONSTRATES EFFECTIVENESS OF CONTROL

During the past summer, special cooperative field studies have been
conducted in several of the states to determine the effectiveness of control
and Ribes regrowth. The study made at Wolfeboro, N. H., on a demonstration
control area, originally cleared of Ribes in 1919, has just been summarized
and yields some impressive data.

An analysis of this information secured on 302 acres, shows the crew
originally pulled 17.7 bushes per acre from several different forest types.
A thorough check in these plots, this summer, revealed only 0.88 of a bush
and 11.7 lineal feet of leaf bearing stem per acre, after a period of seven
years since the original control work. Excluding one large missed bush, the
LBS (leaf-bearing stem) is reduced to 10.6 feet per acre. Of the Ribes found
on the check, 84% had developed as seedlings since the initial eradication
work, 2.2% were sprouts or partly pulled bushes, and 13.8% were missed bushes

The area was very carefully type-mapped, and the original and check
data kept according to small plots and types. The original crew rated as an
average one. The Ribes were gooseberries, skunk currants, wild black currants, and escaped red currants.

E. C. Filler.

- - - - - -

The New York State College of Forestry will hold a forest protection
conference November 10th to 12th, at Syracuse. Blister rust will be given
full consideration. Dr. H. H. York will speak on "White Pine Blister Rust
in New York State" on November 12.

EXPERIMENTAL RIBES ERADICATION IN CALIFORNIA

The eradication of the wild currants and gooseberries in the sugar pine

forests of California appears to be somewhat a different problem from that en-

countered in northern Idaho in the western white pine. Due to the difference

in habit growth of the sugar pine from that of the western white pine as well

as differences in soil, the Ribes eradication types will be quite different

from those of northern Idaho. (The eradication types used in the table are

only preliminary. Further study will probably lead to new designation of types.)

There is also a great difference in the type of brush that is associated with

the Ribes.

It has also been found that hand pulling, which is successful in the

white pine region, is not practical in the sugar pine region. This is due to

different species of Ribes being present and to different soil conditions.

Since the habitat of the sugar pine is somewhat more xerophytic than that of the

western white pine, the ground is harder and the root systems of the Ribes are

better imbedded, so that hand pulling breaks off the Ribes plants and leaves

much of the root system in the ground. As a result it has been found necessary

to have some sort of a tool to excavate the Ribes. The common grub hoe or

"hazel hoe" has been found to be the most satisfactory, thus far.

The presence of seedlings, assocated with the mother plants, is also

presenting an entirely different problem from that encountered in northern Idaho.

In the western white pine region in northern Idaho, the occurrence of seedlings

in association with mother plants is not frequent. In California a great abun-

dance of seedlings is found associated with the older plants, in the case of Ribes

nevadense and Grossularia roezli. However, this condition does not exist for Rib·s

cereum, the third species which has been encountered in California. It has been

found very expensive to eradicate all of the Seedlings. From plot studies it has

also been found that a great number of these seedlings which are found around the

mother plants in the spring, die out during the hot summers. In order to determine how many of the seedlings survive and consequently their importance in
blister rust control, extensive plot studies have been started. If it is found
that most of these seedlings die out and possibly all of them, if the mother
plant is removed, it may be practical not to pay any attention to them in the early
part of the season when they are so abundant. No conclusions can be drawn at
present, but this is an important part of the eradication problem in California.
In order to give some idea of the conditions as they have been found in California
the following table of the results of the eradication work for July and August is
presented. From this table it is apparent that exposure is also a great factor
in controlling the presence or absence of seedlings. Likewise, it is interesting
to note the considerable decrease in the number of seedlings as compared with the
larger plants in August as compared with July. (In the table the upper figure for
each eradication type is for July and the lower is for August.

| Type | Acreage | Species of Ribes | | | | R. cereum | Grand Total | Ribes per Acre |
| | | G. roezli | | R. nevadense | | | | |
		Large Plants	Seed-lings	Large Plants	Seed-lings			
Mature, N. Exposure	246	5722	434	1566	458	2	8182	33.2
	665	24276	422	4022	1150	7	29877	44.9
Mature, S. Exposure	315	600	5	3	--	--	608	1.2
	55	2413	--	--	--	5	2418	44.0
Mature, Flat	225	1716	--	76	--	--	1792	8.0
Mature, Stream	86	5458	1657	2646	2319	--	12080	140.0
	180	7441	914	6387	5144	19	19905	110.6
Cutover Stream	25	7419	4419	435	--	2	12275	491.0
Brush Thicket	125	62	--	3	--	--	65	.5
20 yr.cutover,S.Exposure	102	5980	2936	93	--	2	9011	88.3
Mixed	135	1841	305	166	--	1	2313	17.1
	2159	62928	11092	15397	9071	38	98526	45.6

G. A. ROOT.

BLISTER RUST CONTROL IN MAINE MOVING INTO LINCOLN COUNTY

Mr. E. E. Tarbox writes under date of October 9 of work in his new district in Lincoln County:

"As I am to be in Lincoln County in a short time, Mr. Frost sent me down to the Lincoln County Fair at Damariscotta this week, and I was there four days. Last week we spent two or three days looking around hastily.

Blister rust and Ribes appear to be very plentiful in that region, and there is a great deal of young pine growth. The people showed much interest in the exhibit, and appeared eager to learn about the disease. During the course of the fair I got the names of forty-five interested pine owners who want their lands examined.

All the material for the exhibit save one large trunk came from right behind the Fair Grounds. This made a big talking point as the people constantly asked where the diseased trees came from. Mr. Frost and myself laid out a plot of one quarter acre (approximately) having on it 150 pines of an average height of five and one-third feet. 45% or sixty seven of these trees were infected.

The number of infected trees is listed with date of oldest infection.

1917	1918	1919	1920	1921	1922	1923	1924
3	2	2	2	4	20	23	11

We counted only the oldest canker we could find on each tree."

The date when infection occurred is assumed to be the same as the year's growth in which the blister rust is seen to have had its origin.

- - - - - -

NEW YORK AGENTS ENJOY ADIRONDACK FORESTRY TOUR

Much credit is due Mr. A. F. Amadon who was in charge of the Adirondack Forestry Tour, which began September 15 and continued through September 20. Fifty-five persons made the tour as compared with thirty-three in 1925. The blister rust agents present were Messrs. Kennedy, Woodward, Harpp, Strait, Nichols, and Stevens.

HEAVY INFECTION IN SOUTHERN WORCESTER COUNTY, MASS.

Spencer

There is a plantation of about 300 acres in Spencer about 14 years old. Infection is almost as abundant as the pine, and there are only 1000 trees to the acre. It is the most dilapidated forest a man ever looked at. Infection has been present for 10 or 12 years; the white pine weevil has also taken heavy toll. Blister rust has spread from this area throughout the township and bordering towns.

Southbridge

The Southbridge infection dates back to a plantation made in 1913, the oldest infection having occurred during that year. It is possible that this planting was of German stock. The heaviest infection is a ten acre lot, of which the planted stock covered about 5 acres. The area of pine in which this 10 acre lot is located is approximately 3 miles long and 1 mile wide. Blister rust infection can be found in all parts of this area.

Sept. 15, 1926.   E. J. McNerney, Mass.

NEW YORKER CONTEMPLATES LARGE REFORESTING JOB

The following appeared in "The Observer" for October 1, 1926, the news letter of the New York Conservation Commission.

> "We have received word in the office from a prominent man in New York City that he wishes to purchase a tract of land from 1000 to 10,000 acres, adaptable for growing white pine or spruce in New York State. He intends to plant this entire area with a forest cover."

Edit:- Boy, page the "Ribes hounds" for this job.

SUMMARY OF RIBES ERADICATION IN THE NORTHEASTERN STATES
FOR JULY AND AUGUST

Type of Cooperation	Total for All States		Average per Permanent Agent for July and August, 1926. All States
	July and August, 1926	July and August, 1925	
Individual Cooperation			
Cooperators completing work	1483	1414	26.2
eage eradicated	98,887	81,476	2717.7
t of Eradication Work	$24,878.71	$23,622.84	$627.15

Town Projects in N. H.   (Work completed for season during July and August, 1926)

No. Towns 49
Estimated Acreage eradicated 105,495

M. C. Filler

- - - - - - -

OWNER OF CULTIVATED RIBES BECOMES INTERESTED IN FOREST PROTECTION

Mr. H. G. Strait, blister rust control Agent at Hudson, N. Y., wrote Amadon of a recent experience of his which shows how a friend may be gained forest conservation. He writes:-

"I wrote you the other day that I thought I had a ticklish job on my hands, that of pulling some cultivated currants out of a garden to protect a neighbors pine that had been eradicated of Ribes. But to show you how we can fool ourselves sometimes, here is what happened. We not only dug out 50 black, red, and white currant bushes notwithstanding the fact that the owner prided herself on having enough English blood in her veins to inherit the love for currant puddings, but she signed up to have the remainder of her place scouted for wild Ribes another year. Furthermore, she promised us an order for forestry trees by next fall, probably white pine."

A BLISTER RUST-FIELD TRIP

Major Evan W. Kelley, Forester of District 7, U. S. Forest Service, and Mr. L. L. Bishop, Supervisor of the Allegheny National Forest, accompanied Mr. Detwiler on a blister rust inspection trip in New York, Vermont and Pennsylvania. While in northeastern New York the party was accompanied by Mr. H. B. Weiss, State Nursery Inspector of New Jersey, Mr. Rex, Assistant State Nursery Inspector of New Jersey, and Prof. R. C. Hawley of the Yale Forest School.

Pine infection areas at a number of points in Warren County, N. Y. were visited on September 30 and October 1, and the disease obseyed in all stages on both pines and Ribes. Also, many interesting pine plantations and native pine stands were examined. The members of the party gained a clear conception of the way in which blister rust works, the damage it does, and the effectiveness of Ribes eradication in controlling the disease. As one member of the party stated, a day spent in studying field conditions was far more enlightening than bulletins or lectures. Professor Hawley strongly urged the publication of a circular on blister rust from the standpoint of forest management, giving data by which the forester can estimate costs of control on a given area as part of his management plans.

From October 2 to 9 the trip was continued by Major Kelley, Mr. Bishop and Mr. Detwiler, the others returning to their homes. After Mr. Fivaz had conducted the party over part of the North Hudson experimental area, the infection area at Waterford, Vt., was visited. At North Hudson the party had an opportunity to observe the rust in the earliest stage on pine, as seedlings plainly show needle-spot infection and occasionally discoloration of the bark at the base of the needle clusters, from infection which took place in 1925. At Waterford the party found a startling example of the effects of the innocent-looking needle spots after a lapse of 15 of 20 years.

One of the points of interest visited in Vermont was the Scotch pine planting on sand dunes, made by State Forester Ross in 1910. Here is an excellent example of the value of beach grass in holding the sand, enabling the young pines to become established. To observe the vigorous growth of Scotch pine in this plantation and then to note the sterility of the soil makes one wonder if Scotch pine is not the Cinderella of the Pine family. However, white pines, growing here and there, have held their own with the Scotch pine.

The party visited the Pine Plains Military and Forest Reservation near Deferiet, Jefferson County, N. Y., on October 5. Part of this reservation is used for artillery practice. Shell holes, shattered and dead forest, and evidences of fires caused by shell fire make a vivid picture of the havoc of modern warfare in a peaceful country-side. The Plains were once covered with excellent white pine forest but only the oldest inhabitants saw this, although the stumps remain to attest the fact. The present forest is principally at the heads and on the slopes of ravines. White and Norway pine reproduce well on such sites, and will eventually reclaim the entire area if fires are suppressed.

No pines infected with blister rust was found, but Major Kelley found infection in the telial stage on cultivated red currants at an abandoned house site. These bushes grew practically in blow sand, fully exposed to wind and sun. While not heavily infected, the rust was well scattered over the foliage. Wild Ribes are infrequent on the reservation. Skunk currant and wild red currant (Ribes triste) occur occasionally, in small patches, in the moist soil at the bottoms of ravines. Ribes cynosbati is found in widely separated places and sparingly, (5 to 10 bushes per acre) on the heavier soils, and on pastured land is usually associated with maple. The scarcity of wild Ribes does not mean that the soil is unfavorable for Ribes. At a house site where it was evident that the land had been abandoned 25 to 30 years ago at least, cultivated red currant bushes were still in fair condition and flowering currants (Ribes aureum) grew quite vigorously, and had extended, in scattered clumps, over an area of about an acre. Two flowering currants were thriving in a small "blow-out" in pure sand.

From October 7 to 9, the party scouted for cultivated black currants and blister rust in the section lying between Jamestown and Olean, N. Y., and Warren and Bradford, Pa. Many black currants and other Ribes were examined but no blister rust was found. This indicates that the blister rust has not become established in the vicinity of the Allegany State Park, in New York, and in the Allegheny National Forest of Pennsylvania. In 1915, infected Ribes nigrum were found near Jamestown, and in 1921 pines diseased with the rust were found 22 miles northeast of Olean.

A pleasant surprise terminated the trip in the form of a campfire dinner beneath the magnificient virgin white pines at Heart's Content near Endeavor, Pa. Here is found the forest primeval; peace and a vision of the romance of white pine. Around the clear water of an icy spring the pines tower 170 feet and more. It is a fitting memorial to Mr. N. P. Wheeler, that pioneer lumberman who did so much to advance conservative cutting and utilization of our forest wealth. Due to his wise forethought a remnant of the virgin forest still remains to be cut. The adjacent land is covered with excellent second growth in pleasing contrast to the wreck left by less conservative lumbermen of the region.

RHODE ISLAND NEWS

Demonstrations at Fairs

A blister rust demonstration was staged at the Providence County Fair, Pawtuxet Valley Fair, Kingston Fair, and Newport Fair during September 7th to 18th. All these fairs occurred within two weeks and were attended by approximately 50,000 people.

RIBES ERADICATION IN RHODE ISLAND

The eradication season in Burrillville, Gloucester and Foster closed September 18th. The scouts worked over 28,226 acres of which 9,100 acres were re-eradication work. 16,430 Ribes were destroyed.

O. C. Anderson, R. I.

RIBES ERADICATION CARRIED ON IN CONNECTICUT TILL SEPTEMBER 29.

The State crew work in Connecticut was discontinued September 15; private cooperative work continued through September 29. Eradication scouting is still in progress (Oct. 14) in northeastern Connecticut. Mr. Clark reports that on September 30 in Cornwall from 50% to 75% of Ribes leaves were gone.

J. E. Riley, Jr., Conn.

MASSACHUSETTS FIELD WORK ENDS FOR SEASON

Field work in Massachusetts closed October 9 in all districts.

D. C. Perry, Mass.

FROST DOES HIS BIT, APPEARS BEFORE FARMINGTON, MAINE, ROTARY CLUB

The following appears in the Rotary Herald, Farmington, Maine, for September 21, 1926.

> "Last week was a real demonstration of the way our State officials co-operate with civic organizations like Rotary in getting the facts across about the various problems being met with in the various administrative branches. This one happened to be the Forestry Dept. and the most interesting description given by Mr. Frost, (W. O. of Augusta) of the "White Pine Blister Rust", its origin, causes of continued advancement of disease, and methods of combating it, illustrated by a number of excellent slides, was all greatly enjoyed, and thoroughly valuable, even though some of us may not know a white pine from a red pine at first glance. Mr. Frost's trip up here from Augusta in a blinding rain-storm was proof enough that he had something much worth-while to say."

CONNECTICUT AGENT CORRELATES TYPES OF SOIL WITH PREVALENCE OF RIBES

During the scouting season of 1926 the towns of Thompson and Woodstock, Connecticut, have been systematically scouted for pine and Ribes infection, and for the elimination of Ribes. Certain facts appear which may be of general interest.

In the town of Thompson where the soil is for the most part gravelly and sandy, there are few wild Ribes. The few wild Ribes which were found were along brook courses and in bog meadows. No blister rust was found in this town either on pine or on wild or cultivated Ribes.

In Woodstock the soil appears to be heavier and less gravelly, and there are more swampy and boggy areas, especially in the northern part of the town. More wild Ribes have been found in these swampy areas. No infection has been found on pine, but infections have been found on Ribes, particularly in the northern part of Woodstock, near the Massachusetts line. The infections are on cultivated and wild Ribes. As a matter of fact, there are more cultivated than wild Ribes.

It seems that white pine blister rust is fairly prevalent in Massachusetts, north of the northeastern Connecticut district, and that the disease is making its way into this part of Connecticut, on Ribes. It therefore behooves us to forestall the progress of this disease before it becomes established in the pine, and with this in mind the agent has attempted to secure removal of cultivated, as well as wild currants, and gooseberries in this section.

Herbert J. Miles, Agent,
Putnam, Conn.

A TEN YEAR OLD FARMER BOY MAKES GOOD ON ERADICATION CREW

When his older brother went with the State Foreman to pull currant and gooseberry bushes, the call of the wild came to ten year old John Starr of Cornwall, grandson of Rev. E. C. Starr, the Historian, so strongly that he insisted that he too could find and pull currant and gooseberry bushes. As the land owners were paying the labor bills, the Agent was hesitant about the employment of so young a boy, but finally agreed that he might try it at $1.00 a day with the approval of the land owners on whose land they might work. This arrangement proved satisfactory, /who loves trees as much as his father who
and John,
successfully passed all the forestry courses at Yale, worked until school bega:

When the wage bills were paid, instead of receiving the $1.00 agreed upon, John with the approval of his parents, received $1.40 per day, the older brothers making up the difference. This arrangement was purely a family one, affecting the land owners. The reports from two foremen, under whom the boys worked were altogether favorable regarding the work done by ten year old John. How many city boys 16 or 17 years of age would make as good a record for ener alertness, and responsible performance of duty?

E. D. Clark, Conn.

- - - - - - -

A PARODY

The "gem" appearing on the opposite page was the result of Mr. Amadon's taking the seniors of the College of Forestry, Cornell University into the field and explaining, teaching, and showing them blister rust.

CRONARTIUM RIBICOLA

(Tune:- "The Man Behind")

I

September eight dawned bright and clear when
      Pringle rang the gong,
We started out for Olmstedville with bursts
      of merry song,
To spend the day with Amadon on white pine
      blister rust,
Whose pathologic knowledge is well known—
      or so we trust.

CHORUS

From Olmstedville to Chestertown! Oh, we
      rambled over hills both up and down
Uredospores, teleutospores, are nothing
      much to dread,
The students gobbled blackberries instead!

II

Then on to Horicon we drove, where white
      pine died by scores,
The summer's peace was ruined by Sir Herbert
      Hatfield's snores!
At last we came to Remington that bears
      such mighty pine
And there we had to leave our host and hasten home
      to dine.

CHORUS

III

Oh, many are the Ribes plants that thrive
      near Chestertown,
And many Pinus strobus has this awful pest
      brought down;
But foresters are used to grief - we'll
      never quit the fight
Until we've licked the blister rust -
      Saved all the pine in sight!

CHORUS

The Muse of Forestry Camp
Newcomb, N. Y.
September, 1926.

LANTERN SLIDES AVAILABLE

Have you got your set of slides on the Waterford, Vt., Infection Area? The Office has six sets of these slides showing damage to large white pine ready for distribution. Additional sets of slides on the Uses of white pine are also available. A number of slides on uses have been reproduced from one of our Blister Rust films, White Pine Beautiful and Useful. There are available for making slides a collection of over 3,000 photographs in the Office of Blister Rust Control and many thousand photographs at the .   Forest Service. Should there be some phases of blister rust work or of the life history of the rust which you desire featured in slides, these can be made specially for your use.

If you have never used slides in educational work in your district, it would probably pay you to try this means of informing the public concerning our work. All of the slides are colored, except map and chart slides; all of them have short appropriate legends which, however, do not show on the screen. Mr. E. C. Filler, District Leader, Rm. 405, 408 Atlantic Avenue, Boston, Mass., has an excellent lantern slide projector which can be borrowed by any of the agents in the northeastern states.

Roy G. Pierce, Washington, D.C.

- - - - - - - - - - - - - - - - - -

Mr. John D. Scofield will be appointed as agent with headquarters at Boston, Mass., effective October 20, 1926. He will assist with the drafting work in the Boston office.

VALUE OF FOREST PLANTATIONS

The following information may be of interest to persons buying or selling forest plantations. The value of a plantation to the owner depends upon several factors other than the financial. These factors may be classed as the aesthetic, recreational or water shed protection values. It is very difficult to ascribe a definite money value to any of these factors.

The timber production value of a forest plantation may be determined by considering either the expectation, sales or cost value. The expectation value is the expected value at a future period, discounted back to the present time. The sales value is determined by comparing the value of the plantation with one of like age and character which has just been sold. The cost value is found by carrying forward at compound interest the cost of establishing a plantation together with the annual carrying charges. The example below shows how the cost value may be determined.

One dollar invested at 6% compound interest will have the following values at the end of 10 year periods.

TABLE I

Years	10	20	30	40	50	60	70
Value at end of periods	$1.79	3.21	5.74	10.28	18.42	32.98	59.09

The following table shows what an annual expenditure of one cent will amount to at 6%, compound interest at the end of ten year periods.

TABLE II

Years	10	20	30	40	50	60	70
Value at end of period	$.13	.37	.79	1.54	2.90	5.33	9.68

The Cost Value of a forest plantation 10 years old would be determined, viz:

Cost of trees	$6.50 per M. or $7.80 per acre	(1200 trees)
Express on trees	.50 per M. or .60 per acre	
Cost of planting trees	4.00 per acre	
Initial Cost	$12.40 per acre	
Annual taxes	.10 per acre	
Annual protection costs	.03 per acre	
Total Annual Costs	$ .13 per acre	

Thus by applying the values given in Tables I and II, the Cost Value of this 10 year plantation would be as follows:

Initial Cost	$12.40 X 1.79	$22.30
Annual Cost	.13 X .13	1.69
		23.99

In like manner the cost value of plantations of other ages may be determined by applying the corresponding values given in tables I and II.

Extract from "Green Mountain State Forest News".

QUARANTINES

Oregon

    Oregon issued a new Quarantine No. 18, pertaining to the white pine blister rust September 6, 1925. This quarantine supersedes Quarantine 15 issued December 26, 1925. Among the important regulations of this quarantine are the following:

> "Regulation 2. Five-leafed pines shall not be moved or allowed to move intrastate from the counties of Clatsop, Columbia, Lincoln, Polk, Tillamook, Washington and Yamhill.

> "Regulation 3. Except under certain provisions, currant and gooseberry plants, other than the European black currant, shall not be moved or allowed to move to any portion of the State of Oregon from the counties of Clatsop, Columbia, Lincoln, Polk, Tillamook, Washington and Yamhill.

> "Regulation 4. Wild currant and gooseberry plants, including the red flowering currant (R. sanguineum), shall not be moved or allowed to move from the counties of Clatsop, Columbia, Lincoln, Polk, Tillamook, Washington and Yamhill at any time."

    The quarantine provides also for the movement of five-leafed pines, currant and gooseberry plants in other parts of the State than the seven quarantined counties mentioned in previous regulations.

Rhode Island

    "In order to comply with the provisions of the new Blister Rust Quarantine #63, the State Board of Agriculture has designated the towns of Gloucester, Foster, Scituate, Coventry, West Greenwich and that part of Exeter west of Nooseneck State Road as a definite blister rust control area. The State regulations have been further amended to provide against planting transporting or importing white pine or Ribes into any other section of the state than the blister rust control area without a written permit from the Board."

O. C. Anderson, R. I.

New Hampshire

On September 30 the State Forester of New Hampshire issued a Press Notice concerning the establishment of a blister rust control area. Extracts of this Notice are here given:

"The State Forester has announced the establishment of a blister rust control area which includes the entire State south of the towns of Stratford, Odell, Millsfield and Errol, (in Coos County). Shipments of currant and gooseberry bushes into this control area are forbidden.

"In view of the widespread distribution of white pines infected by Blister Rust, and the efforts which have been made by 179 towns and cities, and more than 500 individuals, in cooperation with the State Forestry Department, in the control of this serious menace to white pine growth, it was felt necessary to extend existing control areas so as to make more effective past control measures, and to insure future success."

- - - - - - - - - - - - - - -

QUARANTINE 63.

For Control of the White Pine Blister Rust

Federal permits for interstate shipment of red and white currant, mountain or alpine currant and cultivated gooseberry plants are required from infected states and certain counties of Oregon.

Up to this time, October 18, 1926, the following number of applications for Federal permit have been approved.

New York	56	Wisconsin	1
Minnesota	11	New Jersey	1
Michigan	2	Oregon	1

P E R S O N A L S

Appointments

Mr. Irving C. Bowlby has been appointed Agent, effective October 16, in New York State with headquarters at Hudson Falls. Mr. Bowlby is a graduate of the Pennsylvania State Forest School at Mt. Alto, and the Yale Forest School. He has recently been working with Scotch pine rust under the direction of Dr. York.

Mr. Ralph O. Gould has been appointed Agent in Massachusetts, effective October 11. Mr. Gould has worked with the Office in 1924 and 1925.

Mr. Geo. C. Cowdrey has been appointed Agent effective October 11. Mr. Cowdrey has been employed on blister rust control for the Massachusetts Department of Agriculture the past summer.

Mr. Ezra Hornibrook was appointed Agent at Corvallis, Oregon, effective October 1, 1926. Mr. Hornibrook was with this office during the field season of 1924.

Dr. Ernest E. Hubert was appointed collaborator, Moscow, Idaho effective September 27, 1926. Dr. Hubert worked with this office during the past summer.

- - - - - - - -

WEDDING BELLS HAVE RUNG FOR TARBOX

This is how it happened as given to our reporter: "On Saturday July 10th worked hard getting out Ribes until 5:30 p.m. Married Miss Alice Stewart at 8:30 p.m. at St. Johns-by-the-Sea. Spent Sunday July 11th on honeymoon. Monday morning July 12th, bright and early, back on the job with Lambert and Biddeford."

Resignations

Mr. Robert Caruthers resigned as Field Assistant effective September
17, 1926, in order to accept a position with the General Electric Co., at Lynn,
Massachusetts. His address at present is 34 Baker Street, Lynn. Mr. Caruthers
is also taking special work at the Massachusetts Institute of Technology at
Boston. We'll miss Bob from our force for he has worked on blister rust
investigation for the past four summers.

The following Western agents have resigned during the past month:
Messrs. John E. Biker, John C. Baird, Wm. G. Guernsey, John E. Spurlock,
Leland O Drew, John F. Hume, Jr., Rene La Rocque, Ray A. Pendleton, Liter
E. Spence. Joseph G. McMacken, Galen W. Pike.

Mr. Thurston L. Corbett, Field Assistant, Ithaca, N. Y., resigned
on September 15. Mr. Corbett will resume his college work at Cornell University.

Mr. Alford P. Balch, Spokane, Washington, collaborator, resigned
September 16, 1926.

The following Field Assistants in the West resigned during the past
month: Messrs. Ralph T. Young, Geo. L. Luke, Carl O. Peterson, Nels G. Lindh,
Wm. C. Thompson, Carl C. Epling, Chas. C. Baker, Cecil W. Guptill, Herman E.
Swanson, Bernard A. Anderson, Thomas Large, Edward L. Joy, Percy B. Rowe,
Claude R. Fullerton, Frederick J. Simcoe, and Walter H. Lund.

Miscellaneous

Dr. J. F. Martin and Mr. Gilbert B. Posey, who have been studying blister rust conditions in the Western and Lake states for the past several months,   returned to Washington on September 19th, very well satisfied with their field trip.

Messrs. R. A. Sheals, L. W. Hodgkins, A. J. Lambert, and E. J. McNerney spent several days in the Washington Office familiarizing themselve with the provisions of the new Quarantine 63 before taking up active quaran- tine inspection work in the field.

Mr. Harold R. Offord's headquarters have been changed from Spokane, Washington, to Berkeley, California, effective October 1, 1926.

- - - -

Mr. Percy E. Melis' headquarters have been changed from Corvallis, | Oregon, to Berkeley, California.

Mr. E. J. Streator who worked on blister rust from 1920 to 1924, called at the Washington Office September 30th. Mr. Streator was very much interested in the experimental work being carried on at the Eau Galle demon- stration area in Wisconsin and the North Hudson demonstration area in New York. He laid out these demonstration areas. Mr. Streator is now Washingt representative for Congressman Martin L. Davey of Ohio.

- - - -

Mr. Amihud Grasovsky, collaborator with this office, stopped over i Washington September 23rd en route to Yale University where he holds a Fellowship.

Miss M. Thompson of the Washington Office spent part of her September
oliday at Asheville, N. Carolina. She writes: "Drove thru the Biltmore
state this p. m. and saw the wonderful stands of white pine with trunks having
the look of pillars in a temple. Made a call at the Pisgah National Forest
Office. Did not meet the supervisor, Mr. W. R. Mattoon, as he was away."
Edit:- E'en on a vacation she pines for pines, I opine.

PUBLICATIONS

Blister Rust

    Spaulding, Perley. The White Pine Blister Rust in Germany,
    Journal of Forestry, Vol. 24, No. 6, p. 645-652.

White Pine

    Brown, R. M. and H. D. Petheram. The Conversion of Jack
    Pine to Red and White Pine: (on Minnesota National
    Forest) Journal of Forestry, Vol. 24, No. 3, p. 265-271,
    March, 1926.

    Chittenden, A. R. Thinning a White Pine Plantation. Michigan
    Station Quarterly Bul. Vol. 8, No. 3, p. 142-5 Fig. 2.

    Woodward, K. W. and E. D. Fletcher. The Farm Woodlot in New
    Hampshire. Univ. of New Hampshire Extension Bul. 30,
    June, 1926.
    Note: This 58 page Bulletin is a very practical one,
    splendidly illustrated with photographs and diagrams.
    Copies can probably be obtained by writing the University
    of New Hampshire Extension Service, Durham, N. H. Among
    the enemies which are listed, a paragraph has been given
    to the white pine blister rust, page 26.

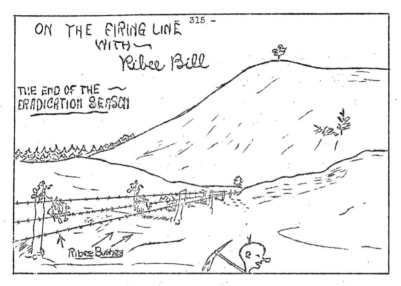

Well Agents, there's a treat in store for you in Professor Woodward's new bulletin on The Farm Woodlot in New Hampshire. Have you read it yet? A considerable portion refers to the white pine, and much of the publication is applicable to the white pine region of the Northeast. It should enable you to answer many a question that is put to you on woodlot practice.

Miles of Connecticut has hit the nail squarely. He looks at some soil in his district and says no Ribes - further on - soil changes and he hunts for skunk currants. In other words he is finding that a relation exists in his district between soil types and presence or absence of Ribes.

The story comes to me that pine owners have told the Agents that they were doing the state a favor by getting out the Ribes. How do they get that way!!

II

BLISTER RUST

NEWS

NOVEMBER 1926.

Volume X   *Number 11.*

U.S. DEPARTMENT of AGRICULTURE
BUREAU of PLANT INDUSTRY
Office of Blister Rust Control

C O N T E N T S - V O L. 10, No. 10.

Page

Agent's Work
    Fourth Annual Blister Rust Meeting of the New York Agents 331
    Western Meeting of Blister Rust Men 326
Blister Rust Situation
    Blister Rust Ruins 95 per cent in Hingham Area,Mass. 328
    Notes for 1926 on Some New Jersey Blister Rust Infections 326
Editorial
    The Welcome Man 318
Educational
    Blister Rust Control Agent Holds Instructive Meeting with scouts
        and Foremen. 319
    High School Class Becomes Interested in Blister Rust. 329
    Lantern Slides. 325
    New Use for Topographical Maps. 326
Eradication Work
    Blister Rust Control in Southeastern Massachusetts. 333
    Ribes Eradication on Templeton State Farm Worcester Co., Mass 330
    Some Eradication Figures for Massachusetts. 334
Forestry
    "Magic Garden" Forests are Planted in Memory of Gene Stratton-Porter. 336
    White Pine and Muskrats 335
    White Pine Logs Cut Century Ago Bring Good Price. 334
Personals 337
Publications. 337
Ribes
    Inspection for Ribes Plantings in Michigan. 329
    Not Ribes - Viburnum. 321
    Ribes hudsonianum Infected with Blister Rust. 329
    Ribes in Newly Cultivated Soil. 319
    Some Ecological Notes on the Local Distribution of Ribes. 322
    Some Ecological Notes on Ribes from the Eau Galle, Wisconsin
        Demonstration Area. 327
State News
    California 337
    Connecticut. 335
    Maine 325, 326
    Massachusetts. 328, 330, 333, 334
    Michigan. 329
    Minnesota. 329
    New Hampshire. 319,325,329, 336, 337
    New Jersey 326
    New York 331, 333, 336
    Pennsylvania 334
    Western States 326, 337
    Wisconsin. 327, 328

Wanted!
    Galls on Scotch and Other Pines 338,339

EDITORIAL   STAFF

Roy G. Pierce . . . . Editor - Washington, D.C.

E. E. Tarbox . . . . .Assoc. "   - Maine

Thos. J. King . . . . "   "   - New Hampshire

S. V. Holden . . . . "   "   - Vermont

W. J. Enderstee . . . . . . "   "   - Massachusetts

O. C. Anderson . . . . "   "   - Rhode Island

J. E. Riley, Jr. . . . . . . "   "   - Connecticut

George H. Stevens . . . . . ."   "   - New York

H. J. Ninman . . . . "   "   - Wisconsin

C. R. Stillinger . . . . "   "   - Western States

..
-318-

UNITED STATES DEPARTMENT OF AGRICULTURE
BUREAU OF PLANT INDUSTRY
WASHINGTON, D. C.

THE BLISTER RUST NEWS
Issued by the Office of Blister Rust Control
and the Cooperating States.

VOL. 10. No. 11.   November, 1926.

THE WELCOME MAN

There's a man in the world who is never turned down, wherever he chances to stray; he gets the glad hand in the populous
town, or out where the farmers make hay; he's greeted with
pleasure on deserts of sand, and deep in the aisles of the woods;
wherever he goes, there's the welcoming hand - he's The Man Who
Delivers the Goods.

The failures of life sit around and complain; the gods
haven't treated them white; they've lost their umbrellas whenever there's rain, and they haven't their lanterns at night;
men tire of the failures who fill with their sighs the air of
their own neighborhoods; there's one who is greeted with love-
lighted eyes - he's The Man Who Delivers the Goods.

One fellow is lazy, and watches the clock, and waits
for the whistle to blow; and one has a hammer, with which he
will knock, and one tells a story of woe; and one, if requested
to travel a mile, will measure the perches and roods; but one
does his stunt with a whistle or smile - he's The Man Who
Delivers the Goods.

One man is afraid that he'll labor too hard - the world
isn't yearning for such; and one man is always alert, on his
guard, lest he put in a minute too much; and one has a grouch
or a temper that's bad, and one is a creature of moods; so
that it's hey for the joyous and rollicking lad - for the One
Who Delivers the Goods!

                                        Walt Mason.

                - - - - - - - - - -

S P E C I A L   A T T E N T I O N

See pages 338-339.

BLISTER RUST CONTROL AGENT HOLDS INSTRUCTIVE MEETING
WITH SCOUTS AND FOREMEN IN EXETER COUNTY, N. H.

Our new agent, Mr. Lewis C. Swain, in Rockingham County staged
rather a unique meeting in his county just before the close of the field
season. He brought his foremen and scouts together at his headquarters
one Saturday afternoon for the purpose of discussing field problems.
Previous to the date of the meeting, and after ascertaining from the several
members of his field force the various points in connection with their
work that had commanded their interest, he had them prepare papers covering
these items. The State Leader, Mr. Newman, attended the meeting and from
his reports I gather it was both highly interesting, instructive and in-
spiring. The papers were read and thoroughly discussed.

T. J. King, Assoc. Editor, N. H.

- - - - - - -

RIBES IN NEWLY CULTIVATED SOIL

Early in the spring of this year Walter B. Farmer of Hampton
Falls, N. H. decided to plant about forty-six acres of potatoes. In
order to do this it became necessary for him to have additional tillage
land. He therefore decided to cut a seventeen acre woodlot, drain and
plough it for the spring planting.

This woodlot was covered with a light hardwood growth with some
white pine, the largest being perhaps ten inches in diameter breast-high.
A small brook ran through one side of the lot and for a small portion of
its length a swamp on either side was not cut.

This ground was cleared by six men and two tractors in about eight
weeks. The smaller stumps were pulled out by the tractors and the larger

ones were blown out by dynamite. Three ditches were dug lengthwise of the piece with dynamite and the whole area turned over. The entire lot was then ploughed, with a special plough, which turned a furrow twelve inches deep and twenty-four inches wide. Most of the rock were dumped in the ditch along with some of the old stumps. The potatoes were planted the 20th of June.

The surrounding swamps and wood lots were found to be full of Ribes, most of them being old bushes from six to twenty years of age. These were badly infected. Hundreds of pine infections were also found.

On the ploughed area and in the ditches Ribes were found to have made an unusual growth, many of them being two feet high. They were fully as numerous, or more so, than those in the adjacent lots. Practically all of these bushes were sprouts, and although the land had been burned over and the bushes ploughed under twelve inches, they were making better growth than any in the surrounding lots.

This was due to one or both of two causes. In the first place much of the land, which is a very hard clay soil, was broken up by the use of dynamite which loosened it and gave the roots a better chance to grow. Secondly, the ground was fertilized for the potato crop. This also served to stimulate Ribes growth.

One fact especially striking was that none of these bushes on the ploughed area were infected while practically all the bushes in the areas surrounding it and in the swamp by the brook were badly infected. This is accounted for undoubtedly by the fact that the bushes were not above the ground until after the fruiting season of rust on pine.

The result of this clearing of woodland and turning it into tillage

land would have been very bad for the nearby white pine had the bushes not
been removed. Previous to the cultivation of the land the Ribes were under
a cover the nature of which, would tend to retard the spreading of the spores
by the wind, and they were making only a normal growth, which for that
locality, judged by the bushes found, was not great. This was at once
changed. The Ribes in the open were exposed to all winds, and the lot was
bordered on two sides by white pines that were not yet infected. The bushes
were making an exceptional growth, and would soon have become dangerous had
they not been destroyed.

> Howard E. Swain, Scout
> Rockingham County, N. H.

- - - - - - - - - -

NOT RIBES - VIBURNUM

During a talk on blister rust at a Wolfeboro field meeting, Ribes
were mentioned and as there were none to be shown, the owner volunteered to
get a specimen from the surrounding woods. The Agent had just told how the
nearby woodlots had been eradicated. The situation was rather uncomfortable
until the owner appeared with a branch of maple-leaved viburnum, which he had
already decided was not Ribes.

> S. H. Boomer, N. H.

- - - - - - - - - -

Ribes eradication for the year, was finished in Maine, on September
20, the last work being done in Mr. S. D. Conner's district.

SOME ECOLOGICAL NOTES ON
The Local Distribution of Ribes
in the towns of Newmarket, Hampton and Stratham, N. H.

Foreword: In general, plants tend to group themselves in natural
societies or associations as do humans, and the old saying "a man is
known by the company he keeps" may also be applied with reservations in
the study of Ecology (the relation of plants to their environment).
However, any such blanket assertion concerning either men or plants is
liable to be false when applied to the small but ever present minority
which in spite of reliable conclusions based on majority action refuses
to be classified. In other words we may make all the rules we please,
but Nature continues to produce all manner of men and plants, in this
case Ribes, and to distribute them with apparent total lack of reason.
With this thought always in mind, the writer intends to outline a number
of sites and conditions which seem favorable to the growth of Ribes, and
also to mention a few natural groupings which are apparently at times
inimical to the continuance of the species.

Before discussing the various types with which Ribes may be
associated, it should be observed that between towns, and even between
different blocks of the same town, changes perhaps concomitant with soil
may occur which will absolutely prohibit the growth of these species on
a type usually denoted as favorable. This was illustrated in the reverse
in Newmarket where several hundred bushes were pulled from Juniper----a
type supposedly unfavorable to Ribes.

The occurrence of bushes in such inaccessible places as the forks
of trees must focus the attention as well on the agencies by which
Ribes are distributed, and these may be briefly noted as gravity, running water and birds. In the opinion of the writer, this latter agency
(birds) is responsible for the greater share of the spread of Ribes,
and must be considered both in scouting for bushes and also in planning
any scheme of semi-permanent eradication.

Ribes Types: In one or all of the towns worked, Ribes were
found in or associated with the following:- swamps, pure pine, hardwoods,
slash lots, Juniper and barberry bushes, pastures, walls and fences,
forks of large trees (mostly willows), rocky "islands" near the center
of fields, alder thickets, and finally anywhere at all!

Swamp type: The occurrence of Ribes in swamps is so obvious
to anyone who has worked at Ribes eradication, that it would receive
passing notice were it not that one or more factors may enter which
will at times totally inhibit the growth of the species in an otherwise

typical Ribes swamp. Peat moss (sphagnum) where it occurs abundantly either prevents or indicates conditions which prevent the growth of swamp Ribes.

Several swamps of this nature have been observed where very few if any bushes (Ribes) could be located. At other times, however, several of these plants might be found rooted in sphagnum. On this basis, it is likely that peat moss merely serves to indicate conditions for the most part unfavorable to Ribes' growth. It seems probable that drainage is one of the problems involved here, since the presence of sphagnum has been linked with soil acidity ("sourness") and the production of toxic bogs which seem to exclude such plants as Ribes. If these facts are at all pertinent, these Ribes depend on a certain amount of drainage and will not usually be found in stagnant poorly-drained swamps.

Pure Pine Type: It is a common occurrence to find Ribes growing under middle-aged or mature pine where a practically clear forest floor has been produced by dense shading above. The bushes found are usually only a few years old and have evidently seeded in by the agency of birds from older swamp or pasture bushes.

Hardwoods: Ribes evidently are at home on moist, rich lands which at the same time present the best site for the more valuable of the hardwoods.

Slash Lots: Pine slash lots offer a favorable site for the growth of Ribes since the customary piles of branches offer a natural roosting place for birds, and also tend to keep the soil from drying out beneath. On this site, numerous small bushes may usually be located pushing their way up from beneath the piled debris. In this situation it is necessary at times to remove a part of the pile to get at the bushes.

Pastures: Given proper soil and moisture conditions, pastures prove favorable to Ribes' growth. If the pasture be in use, spotting and eradication are made more difficult by the repeated grazing off of the tops of the bushes.

Juniper and Barberry: It has been stated frequently that "Ribes do not grow in Juniper." As noted at the start this conclusion would not hold for Newmarket where several hundred bushes (Ribes) were found intimately associated with both Juniper and Barberry bushes. The Barberry-Ribes combination might possibly be explained on the grounds that both species produce berries attractive to birds. However, this suggestion is weakened by the fact that in no other town worked was this combination noted, and also that barberries ripen a great deal later in the season than do gooseberries. In Stratham and Hampton very few Ribes were found in Juniper mats. It is likely that soil is the determining factor in this case.

Stone Walls and Fences: Being natural roosting places for birds, these barriers produce as a rule a substantial quota of Ribes.

Forks of Large Trees: Bushes growing in such places 8 or 10 feet from the ground indicate particularly well the role of birds in disseminating Ribes, since it is hardly conceivable that these plants could become established on these sites except by the agency of birds.

Rocky "Islands": Isolated islands or peninsulas jutting out into clear fields will often yield Ribes which may produce sufficient fruit to seed in nearby areas. One old bush in particular was found which bore at the time it was pulled, more than 40 ripe berries. With between 15 and 30 seeds per berry, the chances of reproduction will be obvious. At the base of this same bush 70 small seedlings were pulled.

Alder Thickets: As an indicator of Ribes they may or may not prove useful. They probably are worthless except as tell tales of abundant moisture, and since Ribes at times are favored by moist location, all Alder thickets should receive a fair amount of inspection.

Negative Indicators: A number of visible indicators may be used with caution in forecasting the absence of Ribes. As noted above, lack of drainage may account for such a dearth. Any or all of the following may also be involved: The presence of dry sandy soil, the formation of heavy moss mats with heath vegetation (Blueberries, sheep laurel, sweet fern, etc), and stocking with heavy stands of grey birch. Reasons for lack of Ribes under these conditions of soil and cover would involve considerable experimentation which, so far as the writer is aware, is yet to be undertaken.

Wm. M. Harlow, Scout
Rockingham Co. N. H.

Comment:

The conclusions of the writer that birds are a contributing factor, to a large degree, in distributing Ribes seems to be quite logically arrived at, especially that referring to the presence of Ribes in juniper and barberry sites. I recall definitely conditions in the town of Newmarket for I happened to be the foreman in charge of eradication crew which worked the areas checked there by Mr. Harlow. Both juniper and barberry appear in abundance in these sections which are for the most part, I recall pine areas. After thoroughly "stripping" large areas where both juniper and barberries abounded and failing to find any Ribes it was decided that such sections should be checked in a very general manner. When these same areas were rechecked in 1926 Ribes (gooseberries) were found quite frequently. Examinations of at least 25 bushes per day, revealed the fact that they had "come in" since the first working of the areas. The distribution of the Ribes found would seem to quite definitely indicate, from what observations I had the opportunity of making, that birds were responsible for their being there.

This paper of Mr. Harlow's should create considerable discussion on the part of the readers of the Blister Rust News. It presents an admirable opportunity for the Agents and State Leaders to present their views and reasons for same on this subject, all tending to add to the general knowled of the subject.

T. J. King.

LANTERN SLIDES

A set of 22 colored lantern slides was sent to Agent S. D. Conner, Portland, Me., on November 1. The set consisted of 9 slides on white pine uses and 13 slides on white pine silviculture, and will make a valuable addition to the slides featuring the white pine blister rust and its contro which Mr. Connor already has.

NOTES FOR 1926 ON SOME NEW JERSEY BLISTER RUST INFECTIONS

Mr. H. B. Weiss, Bureau of Statistics and Inspection at Trenton, writes in a recent letter:

> "I had a very pleasant time with Mr. Detwiler
> in the Adirondacks and was very much impressed with the
> effect that the white pine blister rust has upon stands
> of young white pines.
> "Mr. Grant, in connection with his other work
> in New Jersey, visited the places where infections were
> found on Ribes last year and found the disease still
> present at one place in Red Bank, one place in Shrewsbury,
> and one place in Greenwood Lake. At thirteen places the
> infected bushes had been destroyed.

NEW USE FOR TOPOGRAPHICAL MAPS

Mr. Tarbox of Maine has recently called on the Washington Office for 2 enlargements each of topographical maps for 14 different towns in Lincoln County, Maine. The topographical sheets will be cut so that each town will be on a separate sheet. These will then be enlarged 3 times by photographic process and mounted on cloth. Mr. Tarbox in his letter writes concerning the use of these:

> "I am going to place these maps in local post
> offices, and as scouting for blister rust proceeds in
> these towns, I am going to put in on the map in red,
> the location of infected lots. It is hoped that this
> will be one way in which interest can be aroused, as I
> know that the maps will be liberally spotted with red
> before I get through. As many of the towns are quite
> small I want them enlarged in order to make a more
> imposing map, and I will letter them with information
> as to what it is all about. A liberal margin should be
> left between the boundaries of the town and the edge of
> the paper."

Note:-If other agents desire similar photographic enlargements of topographical
sheets for their towns, they should write the Washington Office, requesting them.

R. G. Pierce

- - - - - - - - -

WESTERN MEETING OF BLISTER RUST MEN

Mr. S. N. Wyckoff has prepared an excellent program for a meeting of the western blister rust workers for December 8-11, 1926 to be held at

SOME ECOLOGICAL NOTES ON RIBES FROM THE EAU GALLE (WISC.) DEMONSTRATION AREA

An interesting feature of the work in the Eau Galle area this year was the unusual growth made by all of the different species of Ribes. This was probably due to the weather conditions.

Early in spring there was the usual amount of snow, or possibly a little less. The ground was but slightly frozen, and when the snow had melted the surface water soon disappeared. Then came a long dry spell, but there remained sufficient moisture in the ground so that plants in general did not suffer much. Cool weather prevailed.

When Mr. Thompson and I made a trip to Eau Galle on June 12, it was already apparent that the Ribes were making growth beyond the ordinary.

When measurements were made in connection with ecological studies during July and August, it was found that the average annual growth of all branches or stems frequently was six inches or more. Many bushes made an annual growth of eight to nine inches, and exceptional bushes eleven to twelve inches.

Not only was the average annual growth much greater than usual, but individual shoots made growth which was surprising. Growths of twenty-four to thirty inches were frequently found, and some new branches made a growth of thirty six inches. Crown sprouts thirty-six inches high were not uncommon, and exceptional ones were forty-eight inches in height. The live stem in case of small bushes was sometimes doubled, while that of the large bushes was usually much increased.

After June 20, the dry spell was broken, and from that time until the work at Eau Galle came to a close on September 8, there was an abundance of rain. Thunder storms occurred two or three times each week, and sometimes it rained every day for several days. The temperature was usually moderate; although there were some hot days, of which one broke the record for thirty-two years.

A photograph of a Missouri gooseberry (R. missouriense), was taken September 2, two branches of which made a growth of thirty-six inches. The bush is seventy inches high.

BLISTER RUST INFECTION RUINS NINETY-FIVE PER CENT IN HINGHAM AREA, MASS.

- - - -

Showing Necessity of Removing Currant and Gooseberry Bushes to Save Trees

During the month of June, 1926 a very bad area was found in Hingham, Mass., on Derby Street, in connection with pine blister rust. About 95 of every 100 trees are infected and many have already died and the balance of the 95 per cent will have to go eventually. There are no wild currant or gooseberry bushes around this locality and the disease came entirely from a patch of some one hundred black currants, white currants, and gooseberries some seven hundred feet away. This may prove to some who are in doubt as to the necessity and practicability of removing currant bushes.

These bushes in question were imported from England some twelve years ago and in that time 95 per cent of the pine has become infected. This proves the necessity of removing bushes now, whether infected or not, to save the pine.

For further information address E. M. Brockway, care Plymouth County Extension Service, 106 Main St., Brockton, Mass.

- - - - - - -

Extract from "The Plymouth County Farmer," October 1926.

Edit: A short article like the above, dealing with but a single infection area is very good. It gives local news and is short and snappy.

HIGH SCHOOL CLASS BECOMES INTERESTED IN BLISTER RUST

Mr. Geo. F. Richardson, Jr., Agent in southern Grafton County, New Hampsh
writes under date of October 18 concerning an interesting trip with a class from
the Lebanon Junior High School:

> Last week I took one of the High School classes to
> a white pine lot and showed them the blister rust disease.
> Had about 36 boys and girls, ages running from 14 to 17,
> and the teacher. This was not the first introduction which
> the class had to blister rust, since some time ago I spoke
> before them, at which time they took notes and later wrote
> up the talk without asking any questions. Then came this
> field trip. All kinds of questions concerning the blister
> rust and its control were asked. The class are now going
> to write up the story of blister rust and the trip, and I
> am to see some of the best write-ups. The children certainly
> showed a lot of interest.

- - - - -- -

INSPECTION FOR RIBES PLANTINGS IN MICHIGAN

"We found black currants in a number of nurseries, and this of course,
was a violation of our quarantine. Some plantings were of considerable size.
All in all, we found twenty-seven different plantings of black currants,
seventy-one plantings of red currants and twenty-nine plantings of gooseberries.
Some of these plantings are in nurseries and where this was true, a special
effort was put forth to have a closer examination made than is usually made
of nursery stock."

E. C. Mandenburg,
Nov. 9, 1926.   Bureau of Agricultural Industry,
In Chg. Orchard and Nursery Inspection.

- - - - - - -

RIBES HUDSONIANUM INFECTED WITH BLISTER RUST

Mr. Dean K. Knutson, who was engaged in blister rust control work this
summer, forwarded the Washington office on October 20, several specimens of the
Hudson Bay currant, (Ribes hudsonianum, Richards) infected with the white pine
blister rust. The same bush which was found infected in the fall of 1925 was
again found infected this fall. This is the second infection reported for this
species.

RIBES ERADICATION ON TEMPLETON STATE FARM, WORCESTER CO., MASS.

On the eradication program for the past season was the two thousand
acre farm of the Massachusetts School for the Feeble Minded.

This land when purchased by the State twenty-five years ago was largely
forest land, but before the purchase every bit of mature timber has been cut.
Today it supports some fine stands of mature pine and hardwoods. Within
the two thousand acres is found almost every forest type that occurs in
this section. A swamill has been kept in operation the past season supplying the demand for timber used for construction work on the farm. Several
plantings of white pine were made about fifteen years ago and the trees are
doing very well.

Fortunately the rust had not done much damage in these plantations.
On one of his visits to the farm, Mr. Perry found one 1916 infection on
one of the planted trees which had undoubtedly come from skunk currants
growing in an exposed place about two hundred feet away. Six years ago the
cultivated red and black currants were removed and the farm superintendent
believed the pine amply protected from blister rust. When first interviewed he doubted the fact that there were wild currants or gooseberries on
the farm. After a few Ribes had been found he agreed to cooperate and
a man was hired to go with the scouts. In this way a foreman was trained
to take charge of the crew on the work which followed.

Gooseberries, red currants and skunk currants were found in abundance
and also over one hundred infected white pine. It took an entire month
to scout the area and mark up the crew work, and another month's work with
a five-man crew to get out the Ribes.

The job was completed one week before the end of the eradication
season; 58,455 gooseberries, 86,178 skunk currants and 764 red currants,
a total of 145,395 bushes being destroyed.

FOURTH ANNUAL BLISTER RUST MEETING OF THE NEW YORK AGENTS

The fourth annual Blister Rust Agents Conference of New York State
was held this fall, October 18, 19, 20 and 21. It has been the custom of
the New York State organization to hold their annual fall conference in con-
junction with a tour, going to new territory each year. This fall it was
held in Districts 1 and 2, both in the southern and southeastern part of the
State.

The conference and trip followed very closely the itinerary, and
along with this I might further mention that New York State conferences are
characterized by instructions in disease and insect control, results of
plantings, historical features, get together meetings at night, snow, rain,
mud roads, detours, etc. But there is something about these conferences that
go to make it worth while, that add humor and jest to the occasion and make
a man forget his troubles and gives him renewed vigor to carry on for another
year. It is good to get together and learn to know those with whom we are
associated. As an organization is made up of a personnel, then such a
personnel should be a mutual one.

The first day out, Ed Littlefield proved his ability to pick the right
road out of four in following State Car 642 to Hudson City Reservoir. It
was a case of "Pick your choice" and Ed did. This trip was very interesting
all the way to Poughkeepsie, passing through the fruit district of Columbia
and Dutchess Counties. Near Hyde Park, there are many plantations of especial
interest because of the variety of trees in planting and the results.

Tuesday, the trip proceeded to Dietrick Plantations, perhaps the
feature of the whole trip. Here are shown real trees in real plantations
25 to 30 years old, and trees of various kinds such as White, Red and Scotch
Pine. Norway Spruce, European Larch, and Austrian Pine. There are several
hundred acres of these plantings, all doing nicely, and the white pine have
been protected by eradication of Ribes. Here one can see all the trees
competing for the supremacy of the land, and plantations where Scotch pines
really grow straight. It does one good to see white pines a foot or more
at the butts, 30 years old. There are Norway Spruce of like dimensions.

Mr. Gros, a German forester for Mr. Dietrick proved his title in being
so kind in showing us about the place and explaining all sorts of forestry
practices to us. He is clever, and knows his stuff. The things he taught us
and told us are too numerous to mention. However, in asking him how he controlled white pine weevil, he replied, "Whenever we find dem yellow tops mit
the holes in, we cut dem out and burn dem up."

We left the Dietrick Plantations and later crossed the famous Bear
Mountain Bridge about noon. The view from this Bridge is wonderful.
Visited West Point en route for Kingston. The Military Academy is surely
a great institution and should any Blister Rust Agent ever have a son who
does not hear the call of Ribes of the Forest, then by all means, send him
to West Point. They'll make a man of him there.

We proceeded over the Storm King Highway, reputed to be America's finest drive. At Newburgh, the boys visited Washington's Headquarters. There is still the bed that George Washington slept in during his stay here. I used to think that Washington was rather tall, but the looks of the bed don't indicate it. Nevertheless, there is something impressive about historical objects that makes one want to fight to keep the Good Old U. S. A. agoing.

There was a beautiful sunset that night and the result was that Agent Strait got lured away from the rest of the party and his Ford started tearing off the miles toward home. When Strait came to his own, he found that he was two score miles away from the rest of the party, having got started on the wrong cross road. The boys did not miss him until they returned to the hotel to change for supper. With Strait missing, the boys had to make the best of it by eating in their "Lumberjacks" and going without shaving, as Strait was carrying most of the luggage in his Ford. Strait phoned in from this distant point, sometime later and asked if he should return that night or meet the party in the morning when they came that way. "Could you beat it?" However, Strait returned several hours later with both the car and luggage. Stevens and Charlton were last seen that night heading for the boat landing 3 miles away, where they went to see the Ferry Boat come in. Bowlby and Hamilton, who disliked to see such a wonderful moon going to waste, went out and drank in some of the moonshine. The night was wonderfully clear, and as the old saying goes, the sunshine has the day, while the moonshine has the night.

The following day was wet. Several times it looked as though it might burn off, but it did not, and soon settled in for an all day rain, later snow. The plantings of the Ashokan Reservoir, the New York City water supply, were visited. These plantings are the largest municipal plantings in the country, covering several thousand acres. The plantings consist of the usual variety, all doing admirably. Even Bull pine seems to flourish on the gravel. White and Red pine do remarkably well. The worst blister rust infection in District 1, occurs in one of these plantings, and the important point to note was that several black currants growing along the fence line caused the damage.

From here, the party traveled to Walton for dinner and then went to Dumont's Plantings after which it was mud, snow, rain, detours, mountains and dangerous traveling to Oneonta. Mr. Nickols caught cold about this time and refused to emerge from the car. I don't blame him any because the mud was knee deep and it was snowing hard and the air was cold and damp.

From Oneonta we drove over to Cooperstown, thinking that we might get there before night fell in order to look over the Clark Plantations. The ride was considered the worst of the whole trip. But night fell early, and we were soon enveloped in darkness with our headlights trying to pierce a steady downpour of rain and snow. Supper was relished at Cooperstown, at which time Ed Littlefield gave an eccentric sketch, aided by Harry Williams.

The following morning, round table discussion at Hotel Oneonta at which time results of summer's work were read, with many reiterate questions to have the entire Blister Rust organization of the Northeast meet in session at Albany, sometime during December. At noon the conference closed and everyone returned happily to their respective headquarters.

Geo. D. Stevens, New York.

- - - - - - - - - - - -

BLISTER RUST CONTROL IN SOUTHEASTERN MASSACHUSETTS

Work in Plymouth County came to a close October 9, 1926, as far as field work with scouts was concerned. All records are not completed as yet but some figures are at hand such as the following: Calls were made at over 2000 houses in 13 towns in 3 counties, to locate cultivated Ribes. The Story of Blister Rust and our work of controlling it was told, a circular left, and an interview card made out for each call.

In many of the towns more cooperators pulled their own bushes than those who did not. Over 15,000 cultivated Ribes were pulled this season in this district. All town forests are protected to date in District 3. Four hundred and ninety owners had their cultivated Ribes removed. In Acushnet, two brothers had 2310 cultivated currant and gooseberry bushes removed.

Two very bad general infection areas were discovered this season. In one the percentage of infected pines will run about 35, while in the second the infection will run about 80 or 90 per cent. More crew work with men employed by owners was done this season than ever before.

E. M. Brockway, Mass.

SOME ERADICATION FIGURES FOR MASSACHUSETTS

Tentative Final Summary of Ribes Eradication - Season of 1926

	1926	1925
Area examined for Ribes	192,159 acres	194,851 acres
Area of white pine protected	80,966 acres	110,892 acres
Number of wild Ribes destroyed	953,916	706,830
Number of cult, Ribes destroyed	27,694	33,610
Number of cooperating owners	1,508	1,763
Expenditures by cooperators	$10,437.68	$5,554.15
Expenditures by State Department	17,224.21	15,625.30
Total average cost per acre	14¢	11¢
Average number wild Ribes per A. . . .- . . .	5	4

C. C. Perry, State Leader, Mass.

- - - - - - - - - -

WHITE PINE LOGS CUT CENTURY AGO BRING GOOD PRICE

In 1823 a thousand acres of fine white pine in Indiana County, Pa., at
the headwaters of the west branch of the Susquehanna, were bought by George
Smith for $83 plus taxes. Smith put up sawmills and cut some of the timber;
other owners followed and the tract finally came into the hands of the
Clearfield Bituminous Coal Corporation. Under the direction of R. D. Tonkin,
forester for the coal corporation, three white pine logs uncovered by the
high water of 1924 were taken from the bed of an old dam used in the original
Smith operation. These logs were in a splendid state of preservation and
yielded 2,000 board feet of high quality lumber worth about $240. Thus
three logs plus one century practically equalled three times the value of a
thousand acres of fine white pine. - From Service Letter of the Pennsylvania
Department of Forests and Waters.

WHITE PINES AND MUSKRATS

Do muskrats help pine trees to become established? One would say that there is no connection between this aquatic animal and pine trees which prefer dry land for their growing places. It is known that in New York State beaver often flood land and prevent pines from growing. Agent Clark at Mohawk Forest states that he can show at Upper Mohawk Lake how the muskrats are making possible additional areas on which pine may grow.

This little gem of a pond is surrounded by a rather wide marsh. White water lilies grow in great profusion in a broad belt around the margin of the lake. The lily roots are a natural food for the muskrats. Their houses, or minature island, are piled up out in two feet or more of water until the decaying roots, of which the houses are built, are level with the top of the water or somewhat higher. After a time the marsh grass seeds the little island and really begins the formation of new land. The fibrous roots of the marsh grass forms a mattress which floats, although moored to one spot. Once the new land is born it is easy for the grasses to grow season after season, and in the autumn, fall to add their little to the accumulating vegetable and mineral composition of the marsh. Already in the middle of the marsh, such water loving trees and bushes as red maple and Rhus vernix are establishing themselves.

During the centuries enough soil has been made from the grasses and weeds to furnish root and soil for the support of the trees. Further back toward the dry ground, pine trees have and are establishing themselves. On the more wet locations the pine growth is very slow and the trees are dwarf-like. On the older part of the marsh there are pines which are really veteran trees containing enough material for saw logs.

E. W. Clark, Conn.

"MAGIC GARDEN" FORESTS ARE PLANTED IN MEMORY OF GENE STRATTON-PORTER

Two living memorials of unique and permanent character have just been
established in honor of America's most popular woman novelist, the late
Gene Stratton-Porter.

On the shore of Lake George, flanked by the high Adirondacks, in upper
New York State, a forest of 10,000 white pine trees was planted last week
by authorization of Governor Alfred E. Smith and under the auspices of the
State Conservation Commission. This will be known officially as the Gene
Stratton-Porter Memorial Forest, and unofficially--to the countless
thousands of the writer's admirers--as "The Magic Garden," this being the
title of the last novel she wrote before her death in an automobile accident
in California two years ago.

At the same time, on the Barrington Highway, which skirts the shore of
Narragansett Bay, in Rhode Island, a grove of half-grown maple trees was
dedicated to the memory of the famous author, who was also a noted arbor-
iculturist and a member of the American Reforestation Association. The
dedication of this "magic garden" was by direction of Gov. A. J. Pothier.

* * * * * * * *

From Washington (D.C.) Sunday Star, Nov. 14, 1926.

Note:-If the "Ribes Hounds" have not already sought out the currants and
gooseberries in this newly planted white pine forest in New York, put them
on the trail as soon as spring opens.
R.G.P.

- - - - - - - - - -

Mr. Clarence S. Herr was appointed agent in Milford, (Hillsboro
County) N. H., effective November 1. He succeeds Mr. Henry W. Robb,
who has resigned from Blister Rust.

PERSONAL

Mr. Detwiler left on November 11 for a trip to the New England States, New York, Pennsylvania, New Jersey, Ohio, Illinois, Indiana, Michigan, Wisconsin, Minnesota, Nebraska, Kansas, and Missouri, for the purpose of investigating the operation of the new blister rust quarantine and confer with state officials and others relative to Blister Rust Control activities.

- - - - - - -

Agent and Mrs. O. H. Boomer of Conway, N. H., stopped off at the Washington Office a few weeks ago while on an automobile tour. Washington has so much to offer visitors that it was too bad they had only one day here.

Alfred H. English, Agent headquartered at Sacramento, Calif., left Blister Rust work on October 31.

PUBLICATIONS

Blister Rust

Anon. State Wide Blister Rust Control Area Established by State Forester. Merrimack County Farmers' Bul. October 1926, p. 5. (New Hampshire).

Anon. White Pine Blister Rust Quarantine in Force October 1. Agricultural Department Tells What Pine, Currant, and Gooseberry Shippers Must Do By That Date. The Florists Exchange, September 11, 1926, p. 122, 123.

Linz. Clarence L. Pine Blister Rust Quarantine Oct. 1. The Florists Exchange, Sept. 11, 1926, p. 104.

McCubbin, W. A. White Pine Blister Rust. Penn. Dept. of Agriculture General Bulletin No. 426, p. 1-25. This is a well illustrated bulletin.

York, H. H. White Pine and White pine blister rust. Tree Talk 8(1): 8-10, 1926.

W A N T E D !

GALLS ON SCOTCH AND OTHER PINES

There has been discovered in the State of New York a gall rust on Scotch pine (_Pinus sylvestris_) which has not been positively identified. As it seems to be somewhat dangerous in its possibilities, the New York State Conservation Commission and the Office of Forest Pathology have undertaken a cooperative study of it. Except at the time of fruiting of the aecia, the rust could be readily confused with _Peridermium cerebrum_, which occurs most commonly on Virginia pine.

The galls are round and conspicuous and may be very numerous on a branch or tree. Witches' brooms above the galls are common. Only one or two trees may be affected in a plantation but an affected tree may be expected to have more than one gall upon it. Cruising through a planting back and forth so as to look over several rows at a time will disclose this disease if it is present in any quantity. These galls should be looked for particularly on Scotch pine, but any galls found on any other pine should be reported. When found, collect a single specimen and leave the rest in position. Send this specimen to either Dr. Perley Spaulding, Northeastern Forest Experiment Station, Amherst, Massachusetts, or to Dr. H. H. York, Conservation Commission, Albany, N. Y. With the specimens should be a record of the locality, date of finding, and a brief statement of the number of trees having galls and the number of galls in a tree. Give your own name and address. The locality should be given in sufficient detail to enable a stranger to relocate it.

It i. not impossible that this disease is a stranger in the country and potentially dangerous to other hard pines besides Scotch, hence this request should be given as serious attention as is consistent with other duties.

Please send immediately to Dr. Spaulding or Dr. York your answers to the following questions, according to your present knowledge:

(1) When and where was the oldest forest tree plantation of Scotch pine made in your district?

(2) Of how many Scotch pine plantations in your district do you know? Total aggregate area of the same.

(3) Do you know of any plantings of Scotch pine or specimen trees for ornamental purposes in your district? If so, where located and approximate age of the trees.

(4) Do you know of any forest or ornamental plantings of Japanese Red pine (Pinus densiflora) in your district? If so, age and location.

(5) Do you know of any forest or ornamental plantings of Pinus Thunbergii in your district? If so, age and location.

Dr. Haven Metcalf

--- - - - - - - - - - - - - - - - -

Employees of the Office of Blister Rust Control are requested to furnish the information desired by Doctor Metcalf, for their respective districts. Please do this at once, while it is fresh in your mind. Further information along these lines is certain to be called for later, so keep your eyes open and be making notes.

J. F. Martin, Pathologist in Charge
13-27   Eastern District.

- -

Reference

York, H. H. - A Peridermium, New To the Northeastern United States, Science Nov. 19, 1926, pages 500-501.

12

BLISTER RUST

NEWS

DECEMBER 1926.

Volume X   *Number 12.*

U.S. DEPARTMENT of AGRICULTURE
BUREAU of PLANT INDUSTRY
Office of Blister Rust Control

CONTENTS - VOL. 10, No. 12.

Page

Agent's Work
 Experience Enables Agent to Predict Presence of Ribes 346
Blister Rust Situation
 Blister Rust Found in Pennsylvania 1925, 1926 350
 No Apparent Spread of Blister Rust this Season in the Northwest . .352
Conference
 Blister Rust Agents at Annual Conference at Albany, N. Y. 348
 Program of 12th Annual Blister Rust Conference . . . , , ...347
Editorial
 Merry Christmas! . . . . .'. 342
Educational
 Agent Richardson Gives Successful Lantern Slide Lectures 353
 Blue Print Posters 353
 High School Essays on Blister Rust . . . . , ...354
 Meeting of Northern Nurserymen's Association in Minneapolis 351
 Michigan and Minnesota Officials Visit Eastern Blister Rust Areas .351
Eradication Work
 What Price Chemical Eradication? 355
Forestry
 Large Sugar Pine Cuts Over 31,000 feet of Timber 354
 Pennsylvania Demand for Forest Trees Increasing 353
 White Pine used in Rhode Island for Christmas Trees 358
Maps
 Map of Northeastern Pennsylvania Showing White Pine Blister
  Rust Found in 1925 and 1926 350
Personals 359,360
Publications 360
Quarantine
 Quarantine Inspectors Visit Nurseries in New York State 358
Ribes
 Some Notes on Ribes Seeding and Ribes Seedlings 343
State News
 California 352,354
 Connecticut 344, 345,359
 Idaho 343, 355,358
 Maine 346
 Massachusetts 353,359
 Michigan 351
 Minnesota 351
 New Hampshire 345, 353,354
 New York 343, 347, 348,349
 Oregon 359
 Pennsylvania 350,353
 Rhode Island 358,360
 Washington 360
 Western States 352, 355-358
 Wisconsin 343,360
Stories
 Some Forward Pass - Over Ten Sets of Goal Posts 344

EDITORIAL STAFF

Roy G. Pierce . . . . Editor - Washington, D.C.

E. E. Tarbox . . . . Assoc.   "   - Maine

Thos. J. King . . . . "   "   - New Hampshire

S. V. Holden . . . . "   "   - Vermont

W. J. Endersbee . . . . "   "   - Massachusetts

O. C. Anderson . . . . "   "   - Rhode Island

J. E. Riley, Jr. . . . . "   "   - Connecticut

George H. Stevens . . . . "   "   - New York

H. J. Ninman . . . . "   "   - Wisconsin

C.R. Stillinger . . . . "   "   - Western States

UNITED STATES DEPARTMENT OF AGRICULTURE
BUREAU OF PLANT INDUSTRY
WASHINGTON, D. C.

THE BLISTER RUST NEWS
Issued by the Office of Blister Rust Control
and the Cooperating States.

VOL. 10, No. 12.   DECEMBER, 1926.

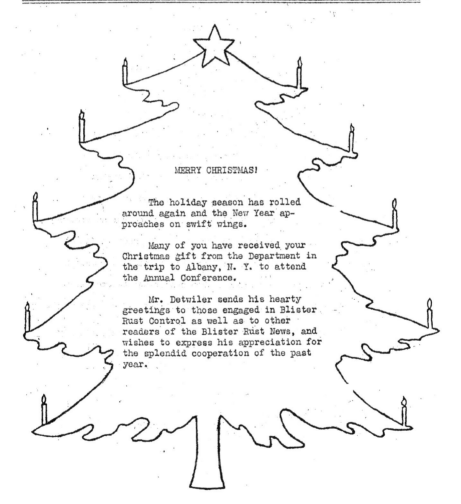

MERRY CHRISTMAS!

The holiday season has rolled
around again and the New Year ap-
proaches on swift wings.

Many of you have received your
Christmas gift from the Department in
the trip to Albany, N. Y. to attend
the Annual Conference.

Mr. Detwiler sends his hearty
greetings to those engaged in Blister
Rust Control as well as to other
readers of the Blister Rust News, and
wishes to express his appreciation for
the splendid cooperation of the past
year.

SOME NOTES ON RIBES SEEDING AND RIBES SEEDLINGS

(1) Exposed mineral soil with sufficient moisture appears to favor the establishment of Ribes seedlings (Observations in Idaho).

(2) Small plants observed in closed coniferous stands are apt to be suppressed plants nearly as old as the trees on the area rather than new seed The quick appearance of Ribes in slash is often due to the recovery of suppre plants rather than to new seedlings. Due to slow growth during the first yea or so it would require several years for seedlings to attain the size that suppressed plants attain in a single year after being released (Observations Eau Galle, Wisconsin and North Hudson, N. Y.).

(3) Birds feed upon the fruits of Ribes and if the vitality of the seed is not destroyed it must be assumed that birds are agents in the spread of th species. However, it appears that for the most part this spread is quite local and it is suggested that the protective zone used in control work is generally effective in limiting the major portion of the spread from unprotec areas to protected areas (Deductions from observations made in Idaho).

(4) The seeds of some Ribes species appear to remain dormant in the du: for a number of years and then germinate when conditions become favorable. . Light burning often produces ideal seed-bed conditions and consequently many new Ribes seedlings occur just after an area is burned (Observations in Idah

Nov. 19, 1926.   G. B. Posey.

- - - - - -

The right kind of reading will help you to rule.

SOME FORWARD PASS - OVER TEN SETS OF GOAL POSTS

The FORWARD PASS has upset a whole lot of wise dope, not only on the Football Field but also way out in the backwoods forests and thickets. It appears that before Germany started to sink our ships with her U-Boats that some of her plant nurseries shipped over many little infected pine trees which were planted here and there in New England woods and fields. After a time these little orphans began to break out with a mysterious disease new to America. The disease spread to large as well as small native white pines. It was found that it did not go directly from one pine to another. In the summer months a form of the disease was found on currant and gooseberry leaves. In the fall the new spores, or disease seeds, could survive only a short trip to some nearby healthy pine to start fresh trouble. But the disease did not progress steadily on a solid front like an old "Jim Hogan Yale Team", starting at one end of the field and rushing back all opposition until it made a touchdown at the other end. The disease appeared in spots, here and there, sometimes at very considerable distances from older known infection centers. What kind of puzzling game was Nature putting over on the Foresters and timber owners? Scientists, college graduates, who knew a little about football began to analyze the game and after a while they found that it was the new Forward Pass that was making the trouble. In football, one player must be able to make a long true throw of the ball from behind his own scrimmage line, and another player from the same team must get into position in the right place and at exactly the right instant to catch the ball and hold it far ahead in the other team's territory. The scientists found that in the spring, out from under the limbs of some diseased and battered pine tree playing substitute center, millions of little bright orange colored disease spores were snapped into play. (These were Tad Jones original "Yellow-bellies") Out over the tree tops soared many of these tiny footballs which were carried for miles down the

wind and across gridironed township and county lines. If they could just
happen to light in the arms of a currant or gooseberry bush, that was all they
asked - the ball was still in play. On no other vegetation could the spores
take root and continue the spread of the disease.

Now the football teams and the State and Government agencies are fighting
the Forward Pass in much the same way. In football they watch the man, who
tries to get into position to receive the pass, and prevent his doing so. In
the Conservation Game to save the splendid White Pines from the Blister Rust,
it is found practical and necessary to wreck the Forward Pass. This is done
by removing the dangerous bushes within a few hundred feet of the pines. With
no opposing currant and gooseberry players to catch the "yellow-bellied" footballs and nurse them through the summer and in the fall to make that sly feeble
side pass to healthy pines, the Foresters care little how many millions of forward passes may be attempted every spring from the old disease centers. The
Forward Pass is the only kind of football that Blister Rust can play and now
that his "yellow" game has been analyzed, it is only a question of bowling over
a few million of these more or less worthless bushes. They play oftentimes
behind good interference and to "get them" in their hiding places in brush and
briar thickets and from behind rocks, trees, and stone walls and even from
bal
swamps is an interesting game that is engaging many college and high school foot
enthusiasts during their vacations.

E. D. Clark (Peter Pine Planter)
Litchfield, Conn.

- - -   - -

RIBES IN NEWLY CULTIVATED SOIL

Mr. Howard E. Swain who was a scout in Rockingham County this summer, and
who wrote the interesting article on the above subject which appeared in the
November issue of the Blister Rust News, has stated that the bushes which were
found on the unclaimed soil were all gooseberries.

EXPERIENCE ENABLES AGENT TO PREDICT PRESENCE OF RIBES

Today I called to examine a man's pine lot which ran up over a very steep rocky ridge. The pine was mixed with fir. I found plenty of rust on very good pine from 12 to 30 foot in height. Just across the road from the house was a pine 9 inches in diameter and about 30 foot tall. It had a big trunk canker, which had killed the top 8 feet of the tree, and six or eight limb cankers.

Although there was snow on the ground, I was explaining that the rocky ridge and stone wall along the road at the base of the ridge looked as if they harbored wild gooseberry bushes, judging by past experience. About this time the owner's son spoke up and stated that he knew for a fact that there was a big gooseberry bush in the wall near the badly infected pine.

Incidents like the above one please an agent, for it means that he has hit the center of the target with his remarks in sizing up a situation, and it also serves as a practical example of the value of observations such as were written for the News recently by Mr. Howard E. Swain of New Hampshire.

December 14, 1926.   E. E. Tarbox, Maine.

There is no truer test of a man's qualities for permanent success than the way he takes criticism. The little-minded man can't stand it. It pricks his egotism. He "crawfishes". He makes excuses. Then, when he finds excuses won't take the place of results, he sulks and pouts. It never occurs to him that he might profit from the accident.

      Thomas A. Edison.

Program
TWELFTH ANNUAL BLISTER RUST CONTROL CONFERENCE
Room 250, State Capitol, Albany, N. Y. - December 9 and 10, 1926.

---- ---- ----

Thursday, December 9th - 9:30 a.m.

Address of welcome ....Mr. C.R. Pettis.- Supt.of Forests
N. Y. State Conservation Commission

1. Public speaking in blister rust control work.....Mr. G.E. Peabody, Instructor
in Extension, Cornell University.

2. Writing blister rust news...........Professor Bristow Adams, Editor of
Publications, Cornell University.

3. Progress of blister rust control work in the Eastern States....Mr.E.C. Filler,
Federal Supervisor.

2:00 p.m.
4. The office and field man........Mr. W. P. Cox, Assistant, in Charge of Accounts
Bureau of Plant Industry.
5. General discussion of field problems, augmented with brief, special papers
by agents Baker, Conner, Doore, King, and Holden.

6:30 p.m.
Dinner..........Grill Room, Hampton Hotel. - Dr. Haven Metcalf, toastmaster.
Talks - Motion pictures - Informal get-to-gether.

Friday, December 10th - 9:30 a.m.
6. The whys and wherefores of submarginal farm lands....Mr. L. M. Vaughn, Instruct
of Farm Management, N.Y. State College of Agri.

7. The blister rust control agent extends himself.....Mr. J. A. Cope, Extension
Forester, New York State.

8. Forest management by private owners in Adirondacks....Prof. A. B. Recknagel,
N.Y. State College of Agriculture.

9. Pests or patience ....Dr. H. H. York, Conservation Commission.

2:00 p.m.
10. Practical lessons from blister rust history...........Dr. L. H. Pennington,
New York State College of Forestry.
11. Field investigations in blister rust control........Mr. D. W. Littlefield,
and A. D. Fivaz.
12. Blister rust situation in Europe........Dr. Perley Spaulding, Northeastern
Forest Experiment Station,

13. Scientific investigations..........Dr. Haven Metcalf, Office of Forest Patholo

(Time will be allowed for thorough discussion of the subjects on
the program and such additional topics as desired.)

BLISTER RUST AGENTS AT ANNUAL CONFERENCE AT ALBANY, NEW YORK

The 12th Annual Blister Rust Conference held at Albany, N. Y., on
December 9 and 10 was of particular interest because for the first time it
was the Agents' Conference. This departure from past precedents was made
possible by Dr. W. A. Taylor, Chief of the Bureau of Plant Industry, who O.K'd
the suggestion that all Blister Rust Control agents in the northeast be authorized to attend the conference.

Was the conference a success? I'll say it was!! Look at the program
on the opposite page, and judge for yourself. New York State is to be congratulated and thanked for the excellent provision made for the conference,
as well as for providing eight of the principal speakers on the program.

Mr. W. O. Filley of Connecticut opened the conference Thursday morning,
recalling the first conference to consider the blister rust which was held in
New York State. Mr. Pettis welcomed the conferees in the name of the Governor
and the Conservation Commission.

There was much solid meat in the advice of Messrs. Peabody and Adams
of Cornell University who spoke respectively on Public Speaking and News
Writing. The individual addresses and papers given will appear later in the
Proceedings of the Conference, so the details of the conference will be omitted
here.

The conference was marked by a great freedom of discussion, very few
addresses being given which did not bring numerous comments from the floor.
Of particular interest were the discussions by Dr. Perley Spaulding on Blister
Rust Situation in Europe, by Dr. L. H. Pennington on Practical Lessons from
Blister Rust History, by Dr. H. H. York on some pests of our plantations. An
excellent collection of specimens of Scotch Pine were on exhibit, showing the
new Peridermium collected in New York called the Woodgate Rust; as well as

injuries to the pines from the Shoestring fungus (Armillaria mellea), from the sweet fern rust (Cronartium comptoniae) from ants and porcupines.

Mr. W. P. Cox of the Office of Accounts gave an excellent talk on fiscal matters, especially those pertaining to expense accounts. The Agents gained a much better idea of the whys and wherefores of certain fiscal regulations than they have ever had before. This meeting of Mr. Cox and Agents was mutually beneficial.

Agents Baker of New York, Connor of Maine, Doore of Massachusetts, King of New Hampshire and Holden of Vermont handled their subject like old timers.

Mr. Detwiler closed the conference with reference to the fact that we had passed the middle of our 8 year program and that probably the hardest work lay ahead of us. He said he felt confident that the men would buckle down to the work as they had in the past.

It was with regret that we noted the absence from the conference of three of our Maine agents. Practically all of the Blister Rust Control men from the other northeastern states were present, and their discussion of various papers presented helped make the conference a success.

We were particularly sorry that Mr. Harris A. Reynolds, Secretary of the Massachusetts Forestry Association and Secretary of the American Plant Pest Committee, could not be present. In the early days he was responsible for much of the success of getting the blister rust control program under way.

Mr. O. C. Anderson, State Leader of Rhode Island, laid up at present with sickness at his home, 506 Comstock Avenue, Syracuse, N. Y., was especial remembered by the conference with a telegram of sympathy and a gift of fruit.

There is no need to mention the banquet, every one enjoyed it.

R. G. Pierce.

MAP OF NORTHEASTERN PENNSYLVANIA SHOWING WHITE PINE BLISTER RUST FOUND
In 1925 and 1926

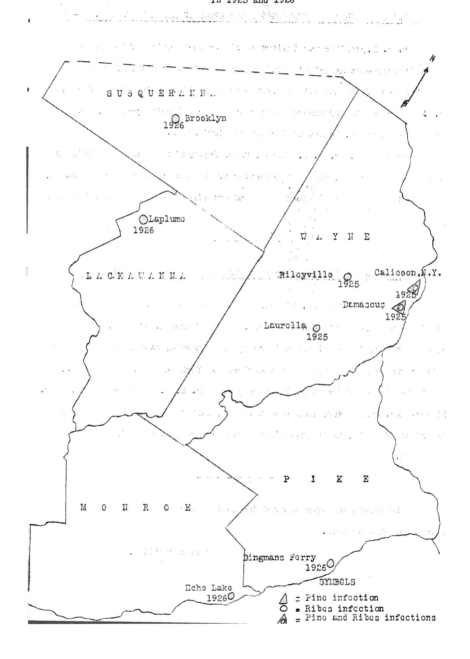

SYMBOLS

△ = Pine infection
○ = Ribes infection
◢ = Pine and Ribes infections

MEETING OF NORTHERN NURSERYMEN'S ASSOCIATION IN MINNEAPOLIS DEC. 14-16

Mr. S. B. Detwiler was invited to attend the meeting of the Northern Retail Nurserymen's Association and to give a talk before this Association on some features of the new blister rust Quarantine #63. Owing to the fact that Mr. Detwiler was in Massachusetts at that time considering proposed black currant legislation, he had to decline the invitation.

Fortunately, Mr. J. D. Winter, Chief Deputy of the Minnesota Division of Nursery Inspection, and a collaborator of the Federal Horticultural Board, arranged to be present at the meeting and explained the provisions of the new quarantine.

- - - - - - - -

MICHIGAN AND MINNESOTA OFFICIALS VISIT EASTERN BLISTER RUST AREAS

Mr. E. C. Mandenberg, in Charge of Orchard and Nursery Inspection of the Michigan Department of Agriculture, and Professor H. Schmitz, in Charge of the Forestry School of the University of Minnesota, made a tour of several blister rust control areas in northeastern New York and at Waterford, Vt., about the middle of November, in company with Mr. S. B. Detwiler and Mr. E. C. Filler. Mr. Mandenberg, in a recent letter, states the trip was a wonderful experience for him, as it gave him a better comprehension of the blister rust situation.

- - - - - - - -

No person was ever honored for what he received. Honor has been the reward for what he gave.

Calvin Coolidge.

NO APPARENT SPREAD OF BLISTER RUST THIS SEASON IN THE NORTHWEST

A final survey by the Blister Rust Control Office of the U. S. Department of Agriculture for 1926 shows no further spread of the disease into northwest timber lands. The survey of the blister rust officials included northwestern Montana, northern Idaho, northern Washington and northwestern Oregon where a slight infestation was found in 1925.

George A. Root, in charge of blister rust control in California, in cooperation with the California Department of Agriculture, announced recently that an agreement had been drawn up for work during the 1927 season which includes several states. California now has the State Department of Agriculture, the State Board of Forestry and the University of California cooperating with the Federal Government in control work.

"While blister rust does not occur in California," says Root, "control work is being conducted as a protective measure, through the eradication of wild currants and gooseberries, which are alternate hosts of the blister rust disease. The University of California will have charge of studies in the chemical eradication of these plants. Arrangements have been made whereby a program of research can be carried out during the winter season. This work will also have some bearing upon the control of noxious weeds and is therefore of interest not only from the standpoint of blister rust control but from the farmer's viewpoint as well. * * * * * * * * * * *

Extract from Calif. State Dept. of Agriculture
News for November 27, 1926.

- C-4- 353 -

AGENT RICHARDSON GIVES SUCCESSFUL LANTERN SLIDE LECTURES

Under date of November 26, Mr. G. F. Richardson of Grafton County,
New Hampshire writes:

> "I have just returned from holding meetings in
> Ashland, Bridgewater, and Alexandria. The meetings were
> all with the lantern slides. The one in Alexandria was
> held the night before Thanksgiving, which proved to be the
> best time for we had 52 out to the meeting. Alexandria is
> a very small town and only had 74 out for t own meeting.

In other words, the Blister Rust meeting pulled an audience two-
thirds the size of the annual town meeting.

- - - - - - - - - - - - - - - -

PENNSYLVANIA'S DEMAND FOR FOREST TREES INCREASING

Believing that the demand for forest trees will reach 20,000,000
annually by 1930, the Pennsylvania Department of Forests and Waters is
preparing to plant hundreds of pounds of seed in state nurseries. It is
proposed to make the plantings about 90 per cent coniferous trees, the
remainder to be hardwoods.

Under the program mapped out the department hopes to have the
following production by 1930: White pine and red pine 4,500,000 each;
pitch pine 2,700,000, Norway spruce and Japanese larch, 1,800,000 each;
other conifers 2,700,000, red oak 700,000, white ash 600,000 black walnut
100,000, black locust 300,000, and other hardwoods 300,000.

Extract from American Nurseryman. Sept. 1926.

- - - - - - - - - - - - -

BLUE PRINT POSTERS

On the copies of this News Letter which are being sent to Blister
Rust Control workers appears a photograph of some blue prints. These are
being used with success by Mr. C. C. Perry, State Leader, and the Massachusetts
agents.

WHITE PINE
THE FRIEND OF
FORESTRY IN NEW ENGLAND

BLISTER RUST
AN ENEMY OF WHITE PINE
WHERE CURRANT AND GOOSEBERRY
BUSHES ARE NOT REMOVED

EVERY WHITE PINE TREE
IN THIS EXHIBIT
IS DISEASED WITH THE

BLISTER RUST
THESE PINES COULD HAVE
BEEN PROTECTED BY THE
REMOVAL OF THE NEARBY

CURRANT & GOOSEBERRY
BUSHES SUCH AS ARE
SHOWN HERE.
HAVE YOU PROTECTED
YOUR PINES ?
DO NOT DELAY!

BLISTER RUST LIFE CYCLE CARDS

IN THE SPRING
BLISTER RUST SPREADS
FROM
DISEASED WHITE PINES
TO
CURRANT OR GOOSEBERRY LEAVES

DURING THE SUMMER
THE DISEASE SPREADS
ON
CURRANT AND GOOSEBERRY LEAVES

IN THE LATE SUMMER
BLISTER RUST SPREADS
FROM
CURRANT OR GOOSEBERRY LEAVES
TO
WHITE PINES

This is one of the best reasons for eastern pine owners to raise
quality timber rather than boxboard stuff.

HIGH SCHOOL ESSAYS ON BLISTER RUST

The November News Letter reported Mr. Richardson's educational
work with a high school class in Lebanon. A number of the essays written
by the pupils after a field trip, conducted by Mr. Richardson, have been
seen by the editor. They were read with interest.

The essays were a credit, not only to the pupils who wrote them,
but also to Agent Richardson who gave the talk before the high school class
and later a field demonstration. The essays showed that the pupils grasped
not only the essential parts of the life history of the rust and how it is
spread from one host to another, but also methods of controlling it. They
also learned the meaning of white pine in the community and its value to
the state.

Such a combination of lecture followed by a demonstration and closing
with essays on the subject have probably made a deep impress upon the minds
of the students and should be of value in the general educational work of
the community.

- - - - - - - - - - - - - - - -

LARGE SUGAR PINE CUTS OVER 31,000 FEET OF FIRST GRADE TIMBER.

The following is an item taken from the Sacramento Bee, October 2,
Tuolumne, California.

"Estimated to contain 31,080 feet of first grade lumber, one of the
most perfect sugar pine trees yet cut rolled into the local mill of the
Pickering Lumber Company on nine flat cars. Measuring nine feet in diameter
at the butt, the tree was 226 feet tall. The first limb branched out 102
feet from the ground. The tree was cut into twenty foot lengths for hauling
in from Camp 34."

G. A. Root.

Edit: Note the quality timber which is raised in the West. Some of this
comes into eastern markets and competes with eastern white pine.
This is one of the best reasons for eastern pine owners to raise
quality timber rather than boxboard stuff.

WHAT PRICE CHEMICAL ERADICATION?

H. R. Offord.

A great philosopher once said that "truth is on a curve whose asymptote our spirit follows eternally." Translated into the language of Blister Rust this means that we should never sit down, fold our hands, and tell ourselves in a self-complacent tone that we now have the best possible working method for the control of _Cronartium ribicola_. The reason is obvious--we don't know it all! Further study of some particular angle of our problem would tell us how to improve our "best plan" and how to better equip ourselves to meet the constantly changing forces of nature.

This working and re-working of material is in progress in every phase of our project. Crew work in Idaho necessitated a modification of those methods used in the East. It is not surprising then, that the difficulties involved in hand-eradicating certain species of Ribes should turn our attention to a scheme that has already proven itself successful in the control of other weeds and plants. The "raison d'etre" of this paper is an offensive, not a defensive one and so we shall discuss "the chemical eradication of Ribes by means of spraying" under the following heads:

(1) Difficulty factors involved in the eradication of certain types.

(2) A brief review of chemical methods effectively used in the control of some important weeds.

(3) The scope of chemical eradication.

(1) In the Idaho white pine region a type commonly occurs which we refer to as "flat-bottom-stream." In these areas R. petiolare and G. inermis grow in very heavy concentration, intermixed with Salix, Alnus, Crataegus and other brush. White pine stands ranging from 25% to 80% are within easy striking distance on the adjacent hillsides, and the nature of the type is such that the damp moist conditions under which the R. petiolare and G. inermis grow would lend themselves to an optimum production and spread of

sporidia. Experimental tests show that R. petiolare, possibly next to R. nigrum, is most prolific in the spread of these sporidia. Consequently, from the standpoint of local control it is most desirable to eradicate these areas and to eradicate them by the most effective and cheapest method.

Comparative experiments conducted by the chemical eradication crew last summer indicate that these highly concentrated areas can be more cheaply eradicated by means of chemicals. No figures are available on the efficiency of hand pulling this type, but the writer speaks from actual experience when he says that the roots and crowns of large clumps of R. petiolare are extremely difficult, if not impossible, to eradicate by hand. When we find R. petiolare in soft marshy locations, with its roots in many cases under water, and G. inermis intermingled with extremely thick brush, it is easy to appreciate the difficulties involved in hand pulling these bushes. The use of an effective sprayer makes it possible to stand near the edge of the stream or at the edge of an extremely dense clump of brush and spray the offending Ribes. The actual physical labor involved in the use of chemical equipment is also considerably less than that of hand eradication. This is a very important factor when one takes into consideration the morale of a crew that is bound to suffer when working over an area of this kind, presenting as it does such adverse working conditions.

(2) Relative to the eradication of Ribes it might be of interest to briefly note a few of the more important weeds that have been effectively controlled by chemical methods.

Wild Morning Glory (Convolvulus spp.) - This weed has been eradicated by means of a dilute solution of sodium arsenite sprayed on the aerial parts of the plant.

Barberry - Successfully eradicated by means of common salt applied about the crown of the plant. This method is the basis of the control work on wheat rust.

Garlic and Wild Onion - Oil sprays have been used with good results.

Charlock (Brassica sinapsis) - Controlled in United States and
England by use of copper sulphate spray. Iron sulphate has also been used
with success.

Wild Radish (Raphonus raphonistrum) - Killed by copper sulphate spra

Hoary Cress (Lepidium draba) - A troublesome weed in England and
Russia. Copper sulphate is quite efficacious as a killing agent.

Thistle (Bracken) - Destroyed in France by sulphuric acid spray.
Mustard, wallflower, vetch and various grasses can also be controlled by
this treatment.

Puncture Vine - Some success has been obtained with all sprays.
Slop distillate and an emulsion of Diesel oil in caustic soda were the
most effective.

Bindweed (Convolvulus arvensis) - Has been eradicated in England
by Kainit. Iron sulphate is also effective.

Cacti - Have been effectively destroyed in Australia by means of
arsenical sprays.

(3) The practicability of chemical methods has been convincingly
illustrated by the large number of weeds, both on agricultural and non-
agricultural land, that are now being controlled by wet or dry spraying.
Experiments with Ribes have shown that they can be killed by a single
application of spray to the aerial parts of the plant. There is, however,
a great variation in susceptibility on the part of the different species
of Ribes to any one chemical, and we are convinced that climatic conditions and the physiological state of the individual bushes are important
governing factors. The enlargement of the scope of our experiments to
include work under all conditions in various parts of the country should
throw considerable light on these problems.

In California, Oregon and the eastern states, as well as in Idaho, we have areas that are easily accessible, where a high concentration of Ribes and their growing conditions render hand pulling difficult and costly. Chemical eradication will not be highly localized in its application. Wherever local control is in progress chemical methods should work in the areas of high concentration. It is only by practical tests of this nature that we can arrive at a true conception of the possibilities of chemical eradication and its relation to the control of white pine blister rust.

- - - - - -

QUARANTINE INSPECTORS VISIT NURSERIES IN NEW YORK STATE

Mr. R. A. Sheals and Mr. L. W. Hodgkins have been engaged during part of the month of December in visiting nurseries in Rochester, N. Y., and vicinity. This is one of the larger centers of the Ribes growing industry in the east. The inspectors find that some nurserymen still believe that they may not ship currant and gooseberry plants to points west of the "Mississippi Valley Line", as established by Quarantine #63. The new Quarantine #63 did away with this line, in respect to the shipment of currant and gooseberry plants, allowing more latitude in their movement.

R. G. Pierce.

- - - - - - -

WHITE PINE USED IN RHODE ISLAND FOR CHRISTMAS TREES

I wonder how many young white pine are destroyed or mutilated for decorative purposes at this season of the year? Vendors on the streets of Providence are selling bunches of native holly berries and in nearly every case white pine twigs are added to furnish the needed green foliage. While white pine does not make a very good Christmas tree, I remember counting the number of cars, on a 21 mile trip last Christmas season, that were carrying white pine supposedly to be used for Christmas trees. I counted 56. All along our roadsides young pine are mutilated. The side branches are used in making Christmas wreaths and for porch decorations.

I think that it is safe to say that in Rhode Island alone, at Christmas time, 10,000 healthy white pine are destroyed.

R. A. Sheals, Agent.

PERSONALS

Mr. Frank P. Sipe was appointed collaborator at Corvallis, Oregon, effective December 16.

- - - - - - - - -

Mr. J. B. Detwiler, of the Washington Office, left on December 4 for a trip through Maryland, Pennsylvania, New York and New England States to confer with state cooperators and inspect nurseries for compliance with the Federal Blister Rust Quarantine. He also attended the Annual Blister Rust Conference at Albany, N. Y., on December 9 and 10.

- - - - - - - -

Mr. Wyckoff, Mr. Chas. R. Stillinger, and Mr. Ernest E. Hubert of the Spokane Office attended the Western White Pine Blister Rust Conference held at Portland, Oregon, December 4. They spoke on blister rust control work in the western states.

- - - - - - - -

Mr. Milton R. Edmunds, Agent, with headquarters at Corvallis, Oregon, resigned from blister rust control work on November 16.

- - - - - - - -

Mr. R. O. Gould, who has been engaged in blister rust control work with headquarters at Tyngsboro, Mass., resigned November 20, 1926.

- - - - - - - -

Effective November 1, 1926, Mr. E. D. Clark's headquarters was changed from Torrington, Connecticut, to East Cornwall, Conn.

Mr. H. J. Minman, in charge of blister rust control in Wisconsin, attended the annual conference at Albany on December 9 and 10, and then proceeded to the Washington Office where he is now (December 15) engaged in working up data secured on the demonstration area at Eau Galle, Wisconsin.

Mr. O. C. Anderson, State Leader in Rhode Island, has had to relinquish his work, for the present, on account of severe illness. We all missed Andy at the annual conference.

Mr. Roy Calhoun of the Western Office has recently had a run of bad luck, being hit over the eye by a hand ball, later in another hand ball scrimmage, he injured his ankle necessitating several days layout in a hospital.

Note:-Ye editor recommends Ribes pulling instead of hand ball, being less strenuous, but giving plenty of wholesome exercise.

- - - - - - - - - - - - -

PUBLICATIONS

Blister Rust

Boyce, J. S. Observations on White Pine Blister Rust in Great Britain and Denmark. Journal of Forestry, Vol. 24 #8, pp. 893-896 inc. Dec. 1926.

Lachmund, H. G. Studies in White Pine Blister Rust in the West. Journal of Forestry, Vol.24 #8,pp.874-884. Dec. 1926.

Spaulding, Perley and Annie Rathbun-Gravatt. The Influence of Physical Factors on the Variability of Sporidia of Cronartium Ribicola Fischer. Reprint from Journal of Agricultural Research. Vol. 33, No. 5. Washington, D.C. September 1, 1926.

Wyckoff, Stephen N. The Problem of Blister Rust Control in California. Journal of Forestry, Vol.24, #8, pp. 885-892. Dec. 1926.

Lightning Source UK Ltd.
Milton Keynes UK
UKHW011456160119
335572UK00011B/962/P